NIS EVANGELISTÆ.

A. Capella
B. Bibliotheca
C. Refectorium
D. Magistri Hospi
E. Culina
F. Area vetus
G. Ædificium No
H. Piscina
I. Sphæristerium

K.K. pedes 462

Tertiam jam tandem et undiq eruditissimâ Aream constituit ampla Bibliotheca, atq ædificium illud Novum, quod fluvio alluitur, et inde usque ad Aream Mediam. procurrit. Hæc quidem structura ipsius Collegii sumptibus maximâ ex parte ædificata fuit. Accessit tamen plurimorum Benefactorum munificentia. In his maxime insignes fuerunt Reverendi admodum in Christo Patres ac Dñi Petrus Gunning Cicestrensis priùs dein Eliensis Episcopus, Collegii olim Præfectus Franciscus Turner Collegii tunc temporis Magistr nuper Epise Roffensis Eliensis hodie. Reverendus etiam Pr D. Iohannes Barwick S.T.P. Ecil Paulinæ Decanus, quorū popportunis et amplissimæ liberalitate freti et aluti tantū opus aggressi sumus. Fuit hæc Collationem â jactis fundamentis ad hodiernū usq diem numerū virorū admodū fores, Ecel Patres quâ Episcop quâ Archiepisc circiter 30 facilè nume ramus. Eorū verò é viventes, qui seu Natalui et dignitatis splendore, seu literis et libris alias è Ecci meliorum è nulla nomina hic angustiis coerceri non possunt.

Benefactorum verò Albo Illustre nomen haud ita pridem accessit, Sara Somersetensis Ducissa Dotaria, benig nissima Literarum Fautrix et Patrona, quæ pluris tam apud nos quam Oxonienses, suos habet Litera rum alumnos, quos liberalibus admodum stipendiis in perpetuum sustentandos pientissimè curavit.

St John's College

CAMBRIDGE

EXCELLENCE AND DIVERSITY

St John's College

CAMBRIDGE

EXCELLENCE AND DIVERSITY

Edited by David Morphet

THIRD MILLENNIUM
PUBLISHING, LONDON

Copyright © St John's College, Cambridge
and Third Millennium Publishing Limited

First published in 2007 by Third Millennium
Publishing Limited, a subsidiary of Third
Millennium Information Limited.

2–5 Benjamin Street
London
United Kingdom
ECIM 5QL
www.tmiltd.com

ISBN : 1 903942 56 X
ISBN : 978 1 903942 56 7

British Library Cataloguing in Publication Data

A CIP catalogue record for this book is available
from the British Library.

Edited by David Morphet
Designed by Helen Swansbourne
Production by Bonnie Murray

Reprographics by Asia Graphic Printing Ltd
Printed by MKT, Slovenia

Front jacket: A view from the Chapel tower
towards the countryside which lies beyond the
College playing fields
Back jacket: The Old Library
Frontispiece: A classic view of the Bridge of Sighs
This page: Courts in sunlight (courtesy of
Alistair Crosby)

CONTENTS

ACKNOWLEDGEMENTS 6

EDITOR'S FOREWORD 9
DAVID MORPHET

1   FOUNDATION AND BENEFACTORS 10

2   EYES, ICONS, PLANTS
AND WILDERNESS 18

3   GOVERNANCE, FINANCE AND ESTATES . 30

4   THE COLLEGE AS COMMUNITY 40

5   CHAPEL AND CHOIR 46

6   THE LIBRARY AND ITS TREASURES 58

7   ST JOHN'S AND SLAVERY 68

8   SCIENCE AND DISCOVERY 70

9   INNOVATION, BUSINESS AND FINANCE . 90

10   THE HUMANITIES 94

11   POLITICS AND PUBLIC SERVICE 102

12   ECONOMICS 107

13   ENGINEERING 110

14   LAW AND MEDICINE 112

15   LITERARY ST JOHN'S 120

16   ART IN ST JOHN'S 129

17   MUSIC IN ST JOHN'S 133

18   THEATRICAL ST JOHN'S 135

19   TIES WITH THE WIDER WORLD 139

20   WOMEN AT ST JOHN'S 146

21   MASTERS AND SOME
MEMORABLE FELLOWS 153

22   COLLEGE STAFF 162

23   WAR AND POST-WAR 164

24   A GREAT SPORTING TRADITION 172

25   'DEANING' 182

26   THE LIGHTER SIDE OF LIFE 184

27   THE JOHNIAN SOCIETY AND
JOHNIAN SOCIETY OF THE USA 190

28   TODAY'S COLLEGE 192

LOOKING TO THE FUTURE 196
PROFESSOR RICHARD PERHAM FRS FMedSci, MASTER

SUBSCRIBERS 198

INDEX OF NAMES 205

ACKNOWLEDGEMENTS

6

Grateful thanks are due to the following for their contributions of text or advice:

Michael Andrews
Jeremy Ball
Professor Graeme Barker
Dr Tim Bayliss-Smith
Dr Richard Beadle
Professor John Beer
Tami Biddle
Frank Bowles
Michael Brander
Professor Patrick Boyde
Stephen Boys Smith
John Burren
Henrietta Butler
Gardner Cadwalader
Dr A J P Campbell
Dr Jim Charles
Dr David Chillingworth
Professor Malcolm Clarke
Professor Peter Clarke
Fiona Colbert
Jeremy Collis
Dr Sue Colwell
Professor Simon Conway-Morris
Sharon Chen Cooper
Madeleine Crisp
Sir Nigel (now Lord) Crisp
Ted Crisp
Tony Croft
Professor John Crook
Tom Curtis

Dr Denys Cussins
Professor Sir Partha Dasgupta
Dr Jeevan Deol
Rev. Duncan Dormor
Dr Matthias Dörrzapf
Dr Clifford Evans
Robert Evans
Chris Ewbank
Mark Feigen
Professor Sir Richard Friend
Jonathan Gilmour
Dr Robin Glasscock
Professor Peter Goddard
Professor Sir Jack Goody
Paul Gottlieb
Colin Greenhalgh
Tony Greeves
Professor Roger Griffin
John Hall-Craggs
Commodore John Harris
Jonathan Harrison
Michael Haughton
Professor Jane Heal
Dr Susan Heenan
Professor Peter Hennessy
Dr David Hill
Rev. Clive Hillman
Professor Robert Hinde
Rt Hon. Lord (David) Hope of
   Craighead
Sir Bryan Hopkin
Professor Sir John Horlock
Dr Sarah Houghton Walker
Professor Deborah Howard

Gabrielle Howatson
Professor Ian Hutchings
Hon Frank Iacobucci
Professor John Iliffe
Kay Jackson
Sir Derek Jacobi
Ray Jobling
Professor Peter Johnstone
Professor Mervyn King
Professor Ann-Louise Kinmonth
Clare Laight
Dr John Leake
Dr Mary Leng
Dr Gilbert Lewis
Dr Peter Linehan
T R W Longmore
Fiona McAnena
Professor Nick McCave
Professor John McCutcheon
Rev. Dr Andrew Macintosh
Professor David McMullen
Sean Magee
Professor Nicholas Manton
Caroline Marks
Professor Harry Marsh
Dr David Midgley
Dr Preston Miracle
Roger Morgan
Dr Mark Nicholls
Adrian Padfield
Adrian Parker
Benjamin Parker
Professor Roger Parker
Professor Richard Perham

Ken Post
Nancy Priston
Frederic Raphael
Dr George Reid
Lord (Colin) Renfrew of
   Kaimsthorne
Professor Jonathan Rhodes
Dr Peter Roe
Christopher Rundle
Mark Rushbrooke
Alison Samuels
Frank Scheibe
Professor Malcolm Schofield
Judith Slater
Dr Alan Smith
Sheila Smith
Hugh Stewart
Rev. John Tarrant
Sylvana Tomaselli
Dr Robert Tombs
Anna Turk
Malcolm Underwood
George Watson
Philip White
Dr Derek Wight
Professor Sir Maurice Wilkes
Owen Williams
Rev. David Wills
Peter Wordie

Grateful thanks are also due to the many old Johnians who sent letters, photographs and mementos which we were regretfully unable to use.

NOTE In the text, names of College members are followed by the date of their admission to the College, where this is known

*The College from the
Backs, showing New
Court to the left and
Third Court to the
right, with St John's
Chapel Tower rising in
the background*

EDITOR'S FOREWORD

David Morphet (1958)

Soon after accepting the Master's invitation to help with this book, I asked a number of Fellows for their overall perception of St John's. There was marked convergence on 'confidence' and 'size': the College, they believe, is big enough to achieve its aims, and it aims at excellence. Moreover, its size allows for wide diversity of academic and other activity – almost that of a 'university within a university'. Junior members to whom I spoke took the same broad view. Readers will find the notions of 'excellence' and 'diversity' well supported in this volume.

Beginning with an account of origins and architecture, the book shows how the College community of over a thousand people is actually run. It looks at daily life, now and within living memory, and at the dedicated work of the Chapel, Choir and Library.

It details the College's impressive achievements in science, humanities, economics, engineering, law and medicine. Chapters follow on links with the wider world, the advent of women as members, some memorable figures from the past half-century, and on St John's in wartime. Next come pages on the College's celebrated excellence in rowing and sport of all kinds, and a look at the lighter side of life, including May Balls and some notable escapades. Admission policy is always topical – never more so than today – and the College's approach is described in the penultimate chapter, which also looks at the important role which postgraduates now play in College life. In conclusion, the Master gives his views on the College's future direction.

At an early stage came the idea of recording the achievement of the world-famous Choir of St John's under successive Directors of Music. The accompanying CD, of considerable historic as well as musical interest, is the result.

The book has been a pleasure to edit. The only real difficulties have been those of selection. Many and diverse letters have been received from former members of the College, and it has been simply impossible to quote every one of them. Nevertheless, all letters have contributed valuably to building an overall picture, and warm thanks are due to those who took the trouble to provide reminiscences, photographs and evocative souvenirs of their time at St John's. Correspondence will be archived in the College Library so that nothing is lost.

The publication of this book could not have been achieved without the help of many hands. Acknowledgement is made to all who have contributed to its drafting, but special thanks are due to the Master, Richard Perham, the President, John Leake, and the Librarian, Mark Nicholls, for their help and guidance. Warm thanks also to my fellow Johnian Sean Magee for his assistance; to Mary Leng and Sarah Houghton Walker for their help in collating the science and humanities chapters; and to Malcolm Underwood, the College Archivist, Jonathan Harrison, the Special Collections Librarian (who maintained an excellent electronic log of illustrations) and Clare Laight and her colleagues in the Johnian Office, for their prompt and always helpful responses to numerous requests for information. I also pay tribute to all at Third Millennium Publishing who have helped to bring this portrait of St John's to completion with such success.

I FOUNDATION AND BENEFACTORS

FOUNDATION AND THEREAFTER

On the site of today's College, before its foundation, was the Augustinian Hospital of St John, dating from the early thirteenth century. Around 1280, the Bishop of Ely, Hugh of Balsham, introduced a number of Scholars into the Hospital, but for whatever reason the monks and academics found it difficult to live together, and the latter moved out to become Cambridge's first true college, Peterhouse.

In the early sixteenth century, the Hospital, by then badly run-down, attracted the attention of John Fisher, Bishop of Rochester (see panel). Fisher, confessor to Lady Margaret Beaufort, the mother of King Henry VII, persuaded her to build a college in place of the old Hospital: she had already refounded a similar decayed establishment as Christ's College. Regrettably, she died in 1509 before progress had been made, and it took Fisher two years to obtain approval from King Henry VIII, the Pope and the Bishop of Ely to use the funds she had in mind. Finally, however, on 9 April 1511, the Charter of the College of St John the Evangelist was granted, and the three remaining brethren of the decayed Hospital left 'for Ely … at four of the clokke at afternoon by water'.

Although the old thirteenth-century Hospital building was abandoned, the Chapel built in 1280 was incorporated into the new College, which had all its accommodation around a single court (First Court, built between 1511 and 1520): Hall and Kitchen, Chapel, Library to the south of the Great Gate, and rooms for Fellows and students. On its second floor, the ornamented gate-tower housed the Treasury, where documents and silver plate were kept. Security was important. The Great Gate was locked at night. Outside ground-floor windows were small and heavily barred: many are still there.

St John's was founded with a Renaissance, not a medieval, character. Greek, mathematics and medicine were taught from the outset in addition to the staple diet of theology. Typically, students came at the age of about thirteen, to study logic, philosophy and mathematics for three years, to become Bachelor of Arts. Thereafter, they might study philosophy and theology for three more years, to become Master of Arts. Some might then remain as Fellows of the College, teaching while studying for a further degree in Divinity. All, except two medical Fellows, had to be ordained priests. Some, like the Cecils (see Chapter 11) left the College for employment in State affairs, but for most St John's provided training for the Church.

Accommodation was crowded: only Doctors of Divinity had rooms to themselves. Everyone else had to share. Each Fellow had his pupils studying and sleeping in his room: the Statutes prescribed 'not more than two to a bed, unless they be under fourteen'. The older were to 'advise their younger chambermates, show them good example, and instruct them in discipline'. The morning bell was rung at 4 am. Private prayers and Mass were said before 6 am, and the junior members then gathered in the Hall for two hours of lectures before breakfast. For the rest of the morning there was further instruction until a well-earned break in the early afternoon, when those who wished were free to develop their skill at archery (see panel on Ascham) on the land between the College and the river. More lectures followed at 3 pm before an early

Opposite: Lady Margaret Beaufort, 1443–1509, Countess of Richmond and Derby, descendant of John of Gaunt, mother of King Henry VII, and Foundress of St John's College, Cambridge

supper at 5 pm. On feast days members of the College might stay in Hall to sing, talk or play cards. Otherwise it was back to the crowded rooms for yet more study, and devotions.

No one could leave the College without permission from the Master, to whom the key was taken after the gate was locked at 8 pm. Under the Statutes, expulsion was the penalty for an assortment of 'serious crimes': heresy, treason, usury, perjury, theft, murder, incest, notorious adultery or fornication, scaling the walls or opening the gate at night.

The Statutes also stipulated that at least half the Fellows and half the Scholars were to come from the 'nine northern counties': this strongly suggests the influence of Lady Margaret herself, who was Countess of Richmond and Derby. The Statutes have of course

been rewritten periodically as the character of the College and of society has changed. It was, however, only in 1882 that Fellows were no longer required to be ordained and unmarried.

Although, with pressure on space, the College had put up buildings behind First Court, these were pulled down in 1598 to make room for the construction of a large new Second Court with the Shrewsbury Tower in the centre of the west range. This features a statue (of 1671) of Mary, Countess of Shrewsbury, to whom the Court's construction was due (see *Benefactors* below). Although mostly providing rooms for Fellows and students, the north side formed an extension to the Master's Lodge: the whole length on the first floor was a Long Gallery with a superb plaster ceiling and wood panelling. Over time, this became today's Combination

Above left: According to tradition, this chair was used at the signature in December 1624 of the marriage contract between Prince Charles (later Charles I) and Henrietta Maria

Above: Glass roundel of Queen Henrietta Maria in the Combination Room

BISHOP JOHN FISHER (1469–1535)

It was Fisher's tenacity which brought St John's into being in 1511: a lesser man might well have found the obstacles too great. Loyalty to the memory of his patroness, Lady Margaret Beaufort, was of course a strong motivation: he had been her spiritual adviser. But he was also a Cambridge grandee. Chancellor of the University from 1504, and President of Queens' College from 1505 to 1508, he had brought about the foundation of the Lady Margaret Chair of Divinity and, in 1505, the foundation of Christ's, the sister college of St John's. He continued to exercise wide influence in Cambridge. He brought Erasmus to the University, encouraged the Cambridge tradition of Greek learning, and patronized the beginnings of the study of Hebrew.

In the 1520s he wrote treatises against Luther in support of Henry VIII. But he consistently opposed Henry's divorce of Queen Catherine and was beheaded for treason in 1535, having refused to swear to the Act of Succession, with its implicit denial of papal authority. The Pope had created him cardinal a few weeks earlier: he was canonized in 1935.

The College remained loyal to him, sending deputations to attend on him in prison. In today's College, he is not forgotten. His portrait hangs in the Hall. The figures on either side of the Chapel door represent Lady Margaret and Fisher. The arches set into the Antechapel wall come from his memorial chantry in the old Chapel. The panelling and oriel window in the Fisher Room of the Master's Lodge are thought to come from the room which in his lifetime was kept for him in St John's.

He is also commemorated in the name of Fisher House, the Roman Catholic chaplaincy to the University.

Drawing c.1532 of John Fisher, Bishop of Rochester 1504–35, by Hans Holbein the Younger (The Royal Collection © 2006 Her Majesty Queen Elizabeth II)

13

Room. In the central bay window is a small glass roundel with a portrait of Queen Henrietta Maria, the tradition being that this commemorates the signing here in 1624 of the contract for her marriage to Prince Charles (later Charles I). Another memorable, and much later, episode in the Combination Room's history is to be found in Chapter 23.

The ranges of Third Court belong to different periods. The first is formed by the Library of 1624 (see Chapter 6), the gift of John Williams, Bishop of Lincoln. The remaining two sides, one of them abutting the river, were added in 1669–72, after the College had

recovered from the traumas of the Civil War. (St John's had been staunchly Royalist in a mainly Parliamentary city and shire, and suffered the consequences when Cromwell's troops occupied Cambridge in 1643: many Fellows were expelled and First Court was used as a prison.) A Dutch gable facing the river shows the date of completion, 1671.

Social changes which followed the end of the Napoleonic wars increased the demand for university education. Between 1790 and 1850 the College grew from 120 to 370 students, and by the 1820s the lack of space was becoming acute. The architects of New

ROGER ASCHAM (1515–1568)

An inscription, dated 1555, in the beautiful italic hand of Roger Ascham

Like many Johnians, then and now, Roger Ascham was a northerner, from Yorkshire. An outstanding classical scholar, he was elected to a Fellowship almost immediately upon graduating in 1534. Dogged by chronic illness (probably malaria), distracted by College politics and always short of money, he felt obliged to seek patronage in the outside world. This came in the shape of an annuity from Henry VIII, a keen bowman, who was pleased by Ascham's dedication to him of *Toxophilus* (1545), an engagingly written treatise on archery, which argued that scholarly endeavour was more apt to be promoted than dissipated by regular physical exercise.

Court connections saw Ascham appointed tutor to Princess (later Queen) Elizabeth, to whom he daily taught both classical and New Testament Greek, Latin and calligraphy. Another no less brilliant female pupil was the doomed Lady Jane Grey, the 'Queen of nine days' after the death of Edward VI, their relationship becoming the stuff of Victorian romantic legend in paintings and plays. Though a Protestant, Ascham became Latin Secretary (principal diplomatic correspondent) to the Crown under Queen Mary, continuing in the post under Elizabeth. His warm testimony to the latter's intellectual powers, linguistic aptitudes and political acumen is amongst the most reliable that has come down to us.

Ascham's last and most influential book, *The Scholemaster*, was published posthumously in 1570, and has ever since been admired as much for the purity of its English prose style as for the civilized and humane character of its educational ideals. These included a distinct aversion to the corporal punishment of the young. Ascham left one lasting mark upon the College: a signature in his beautiful italic handwriting amongst the graffiti incised by many sixteenth-century Fellows on the fireplace in the Old Treasury above the Great Gate.

Court, Rickman and Hutchinson, built the largest single building so far erected by any college and did so in the face of considerable physical difficulties. Massive cellars were built to support the four storeys above. A further river crossing – the Bridge of Sighs – joined the existing Kitchen Bridge of 1708–12.

From the 1820s the College began to purchase adjoining properties to the north, making space for the Master's Lodge of 1865 and the Chapel by Sir Giles Gilbert Scott, built in 1866–9 to replace the chapel of the thirteenth-century Hospital. Scott's original plans included only a small *flèche*, not the 163ft-high tower which is such a feature of the Cambridge landscape. But a former member of the College offered to finance its construction. Unhappily, the College failed to insure his life, and he died two years later as a result of a railway accident, leaving the College with a large debt. This did not however stop the College proceeding in 1885 with the Penrose Building, opposite the Chapel, to provide living accommodation and lecture rooms.

At the end of the First World War, a further expansion of student numbers led to the construction in the 1930s of Chapel and North Courts, designed by Edward Maufe, architect of Guildford Cathedral. When,

by the late 1950s, it became clear that yet more student accommodation was required, the generosity of the Cripps Foundation, whose founder's son, Humphrey Cripps, was a Johnian, enabled the construction, using land purchased from Merton College, Oxford, of Powell and Moya's Cripps Building, the largest in any college

Above: John Williams, 1582–1650, Bishop of Lincoln and later Archbishop of York, who substantially financed the building of the Old Library

Right: Mary, Countess of Shrewsbury, 1557–1632, to whom the College is largely indebted for Second Court

Sir Humphrey Cripps
by John Ward CBE RA

of Oxford or Cambridge, consisting of two courts at an angle to each other.

The Fisher Building, designed by Peter Boston, followed in 1987 to serve some of the College's public activities, with a multi-purpose hall for concerts, lectures and sports, seminar rooms, art and music rooms and some administrative offices. The most recent building, the Working Library designed by Edward Cullinan, with its entrance in Chapel Court, was completed in 1994. Nor does the story end there. Across St John's Street from the Great Gate, a further development is even now taking place, on what is known as the Triangle Site (see Chapter 3), which will effectively create a ninth court.

BENEFACTORS OF THE COLLEGE

It was the wish of Lady Margaret that preference be given in the choice of Fellows and Scholars to the less well-endowed northern counties of England, and most of the early gifts of money and land to the young foundation were in fact made by northern men. Thus began a cycle of generosity in which the beneficiaries of scholarships and exhibitions contributed in turn to the College's financial needs.

To Mary, Countess of Shrewsbury (1557–1632), St John's is indebted for much of the money needed to build Second Court. Mary Cavendish was the daughter of the famous Bess of Hardwick, who after the death of

Sir William Cavendish married George, sixth Earl of Shrewsbury. A colourful character like her mother, she was in and out of the Tower of London on at least two occasions. At the age of twelve, Mary was married off to Gilbert Talbot, the son of her new stepfather. Her great benefaction to St John's came in the years 1599–1603, by which time her husband was the seventh Earl. The way to the benefaction appears to have been paved by their steward, Robert Booth, a former Fellow and Bursar of St John's. In a letter of February 1599 to the then Master, he writes that 'the new building should not be mentioned to the Earl, who has not yet been prepared for his contribution'. One wonders what the Earl and Countess talked about over breakfast.

Sarah, Duchess of Somerset (1632–92), gave extensive property in Wiltshire and Cambridgeshire to support exhibitions from Manchester, Hereford and Marlborough schools. Her father, Sir Edward Alston, President of the Royal College of Physicians, had been a student at St John's. The bequests of Thomas Baker (1656–1740), historian of the College and donor of some two thousand books to the Library, were made in a spirit of respect for the man who had provided funds for his Fellowship – Hugh Ashton, Archdeacon of York, who had died two hundred years previously. John Williams (1582–1650), having joined the College as a sizar, rose to be Bishop of Lincoln and Lord Chancellor to James I and Charles I. To him the College owes its fine seventeenth-century Library (with his name and office initialled on the superb oriel window), and the endowment of various scholarships and fellowships. As a student, James Wood (1760–1839), son of Lancashire weavers, had saved the cost of heat and light by studying with his feet wrapped in straw beneath a rushlight burning on a public staircase. He went on to become Master of the College. His legacy was valuable estates in Cambridge and Kent, large contributions towards the cost of New Court and the building of the

TRINITY COLLEGE DUBLIN AND BALLIOL COLLEGE OXFORD

In the early days of Trinity College Dublin (TCD), there were strong links with St John's. William Cecil was TCD's first Chancellor (1592–8), and Robert Cecil was also Chancellor, from 1601 to 1612. Another Johnian, Henry Alvey, was TCD's third Provost, and then Vice-Chancellor 1609–12. These links were much in mind when an alliance was established between St John's and TCD in the 1930s, including reciprocal attendance by one or two Fellows at the commemoration celebrations of the two colleges. In the early 1930s St John's also paired with Balliol as its 'sister' college in Oxford, again with reciprocal attendance at the respective commemoration celebrations. Both alliances are valued, and there is an expectation that students from both institutions coming to Cambridge will most likely apply to St John's as 'their' College.

new Chapel, and exhibitions to assist poor students such as he had been.

In recent times, generous benefactions have come from Sir Cyril Cripps (1892–1979) and his son Sir Humphrey Cripps (1915–2000). Their Foundation provided the capital endowment for the Cripps Building, which has helped to enable most undergraduates to enjoy a full three years of residence in College. Yet more recently, Nicholas Corfield, who graduated in 1981, has provided outstanding support to assist in funding student bursaries at a time of steeply rising costs in university education.

With the help of these, and hundreds like them, the College has been able over the centuries to grow and achieve great things. The long roll of benefactors is commemorated each May in a service in the College Chapel, at which their names, beginning with those of Lady Margaret and then John Fisher, are solemnly recited antiphonally by the Deans and a commemoration sermon is preached.

2 EYES, ICONS, PLANTS AND WILDERNESS

The architecture and setting of St John's are spectacular. No one forgets the long walk from the Great Gate in St John's Street through First, Second and Third Courts, over the Bridge of Sighs, through the cloister of New Court, out into the Backs, past the Fellows' and Scholars' Gardens to the Queens' Road Gate – nor, looking back, the skyline of the 'Wedding Cake' and the Chapel Tower. But detail is often forgotten. This chapter is devoted to telling details, starting with the College's 'eyes' and moving on to its icons and some curiosities in its spacious grounds.

THE EYES OF ST JOHN'S

Patrick Boyde, Emeritus Professor of Italian, now has the leisure to look harder at the buildings of St John's and to focus on features which are easily overlooked by the casual viewer. Here, he provides an unusual tour of the College, through a close scrutiny of its fenestration.

From a builder's point of view, a window is just a framed aperture intended to admit natural light and, typically, to regulate ventilation. It is usually glazed and can be opened to varying degrees. Beyond this, the variables are in-numerable. The apertures differ in size, shape and mouldings; they may project or be recessed. The window frame may swing on hinges or slide. The glass may be transparent, coloured or frosted; it may be set in big panes or held in lattice patterns of many kinds. Curtains may soften the outlines from inside the room or the windows may be flanked by shutters externally.

But from the point of view of those who live behind the walls or pass in front of them, the windows are like the *eyes* of a building. And, as Dante remarked,

the eyes are 'the windows of the *soul*'. Hence this selective survey of the windows in St John's is offered as a not wholly fanciful attempt to identify the vivifying spirit of the College over the centuries by looking hard into its eyes at various moments in its existence.

Dante went on to say that a smile in the eyes is a 'coruscation of the soul's delight'. The windows in Cripps may seem to refute this poetic conceit (Figure 1). Huge blank panes stare out from a grid of verticals and horizontals, as in a painting by Ben Nicholson, against a background limited to shades of grey and white (like the face of a *Vogue* model from the 1960s) in panels of lead, exposed concrete and Portland stone, which never change their hue as the sun changes its angle or when it disappears behind clouds. Powell and Moya chose to renounce colour, curves, diagonals and

Figure 1. Windows in the Cripps Building

Figure 2. Although this image, based on the Loggan print of c.1690, does not show the College exactly as it was when it opened for business in 1516 (there was then no statue of Lady Margaret over the screens for example), the effect of seeing First Court isolated, with its brickwork glowing in the warm colour added by Eileen Burke (1912–2006) is to return in essence to the College of St John the Evangelist 'In the Beginning'

ornaments to express their vision of a brave new world of functionality and freedom from the dead weight of the past. But perhaps Dante did have a point even here. Perhaps these unsmiling, lid-less, lash-less windows in a monochrome face are to be interpreted as the eyes of a building where soul is difficult to divine.

Figures 2 and 2A represent St John's as it was in the beginning, a newly founded religious community for the education of young male teenagers who would become priests in the Catholic Church. It was built on the site of an earlier religious community and retained the red-brick Infirmary of the medieval Hospital of St John (A) and the original Chapel (B) whose foundations are still visible on the lawn of First Court. The three broad, pointed windows between buttresses on the south wall of this chapel – three lights in a stone frame with simple stone tracery – must have been very like their thirteenth-century originals. In scale and style they exemplify what everyone then knew to be appropriate to a place of worship; and their design is adapted, unself-consciously, in the buttressed windows of the new Hall (C), where the young received food for the mind as well as the body, and in the seven two-lighted windows on either side of the original Library (one is bricked in),

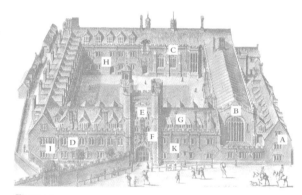

Figure 2A

another sacred space in any college, as well as those in the chambers above the Great Gate (E). Not that there was any hard-and-fast division between the style appropriate to the House of the Lord and the style of a fortified manor house appropriate to a secular lord or gentleman. The stonework surrounding the windows in the Great Gate blends with the use of the same stone to emphasize its turrets and battlements, just as the statue of St John (F) sits comfortably above the armorial bearings of our royal foundress.

To all this the dormer windows (G) of the tiny attic rooms in the south and east ranges offer a striking

Above left: Figure 3. Tudor window under relieving arch in First Court

Above: Figure 4. Dummy dormer windows in Second Court

Left: Figure 5. The Combination Room windows in Second Court

contrast, reminding us of the social mix in a college which offered scholarships to boys of poor parents, especially those coming from the north of England (the sixteenth-century equivalent of our inner cities).

In between these extremes come the windows in the Kitchens (H) and in the rooms occupied by Fellows (I), the design of which was to become the norm. Underneath the 'eyebrow' formed by the curve of the bricks in the relieving arch (Figure 3) comes the 'eyelid' of the dripstone, a bold, projecting horizontal with little flaps like a deerstalker. The 'eye' of the glass is set in small leaded panes in groups of two or three lights, framed by the same warm-coloured stone, each topped by a typically Perpendicular arch (two-centred but relatively flat). This is the typically Tudor window which the builders of Second Court and of New Court were to be specifically instructed to copy and which was reverently adopted by many nineteenth-century architects in new college buildings such as our Penrose Building. It could be called the 'Cambridge Window'.

A glance at the windows to the right of the Gate (Figure 2, K) shows how relatively unconcerned the builders were with exact symmetry in the fenestration. This was to be one of the biggest differences in the new

Right: Figure 6. Oriel window in Second Court

Below right: Figure 7. The 'old fashion of church window' in the Library of 1624

River Court (Second Court) of 1599 built in order to increase accommodation in a college which was thriving after the rupture with the Church of Rome and which had close links with Queen Elizabeth through the Cecils, father and son. St John's was now a place where the sons of gentlemen might be prepared for service of the monarch (the visual similarities between our Second Court and Hampton Court Palace are not coincidental). It came into being by the addition of three new ranges and a second gatehouse which are deliberately similar to First Court in scale, materials and many details, such as the windows and relieving arches. But symmetry is important. Dummy dormer windows (Figure 4) are placed against the west roof of the Hall to balance those of the Kitchens (they have no gleam). The 'Cambridge Windows' of the fashionably aristocratic Combination Room (new quarters for the Master) run the whole length of Second Court on the first floor (Figure 5). A very grand oriel window, with carved panels below and stone strapwork above, faces another in the centre of the south range (Figure 6).

Second Court is the last building in St John's to be unselfconscious in the design of its windows. Those in the Library (Figure 7) of 1624 constitute a deliberate return to the past, and were chosen against the first wishes of the benefactor, John Williams, a powerful man at the court of King James I, who had to be persuaded that 'men of judgement like the best the old fashion of church window, holding it the most meet for such a building' (a college library being a sacred place). The two-light pointed windows, with simple tracery, are slimmer than anything yet seen, and are especially lovely in the richly decorated bay facing the river. This bay is partly the apse of a chapel, partly the oriel of a secular mansion, as befits a patron who, as the Latin initials of the inscription tell us – I L C S – was John (Bishop) of Lincoln and Keeper of the Seal.

On the side elevation of the Library, the effect of these deliberately 'Gothick' windows is strangely altered by their rectangular stone frames which are linked above and below in continuous horizontal stone courses

22

which begin to impose something resembling the rhythms of a classical building. However, the first attempts at classicism in the College come in the two wings that were added in 1671 to provide still more accommodation. The scale remains the same and the materials are still red brick with stone facings, but the rounded arches of the colonnade in what we now call Third Court, together with the jumble of classicizing details in the central frontispiece, are a homage by an anonymous architect to the work of Sir Christopher Wren. It is in this slightly pretentious context that we experience the effect of a new fashion in windows for domestic architecture. Pointed arches have been banished even within the rectangles of stone that frame the windows. On the first floor, the windows now consist of a simple stone cross (mullion and transom) (Figure 8), while on the second floor there is only a stone vertical (mullion). St John's is on its way to becoming a secular college.

A hundred years went by with no changes to the fenestration, but in the 1770s James Essex the younger was hired to carry out the kind of modifications which he and his father had already undertaken at Emmanuel and Christ's. He transformed the appearance of the south range of First Court (Figure 9). First, he faced it with ashlared stone, so that there is no colour contrast between

Above left: Figure 8.
A window in Third
Court

Above: Figure 9.
Part of the south range
of First Court

Left: Figure 10.
A window at the rear
of New Court

Right: Figure 11.
A domestic window
in New Court

Far right: Figure 12.
A post-modern
window in the
Working Library

23

the wall and the surrounds of the windows. Next, he removed the dormers. Most important, he installed the newfangled 'sash' windows, where the panes slide up and down within slender rectangular frames, which are in perfect harmony with the elegant doorways under their classical pediments. These windows are the dominant element in the new façade, which, considered in isolation, is a paradigm of the virtues of the English Enlightenment: rational, secular, plain, relying on the geometrical proportions of an idealized version of the Roman past.

Fifty years later, in the mid-1820s, the mood of the College had changed in keeping with that of the whole nation. England was becoming proud of its native traditions and its Christian heritage. St John's gave the commission of New Court (which would more than double the existing accommodation) to Thomas Rickman, the man who, in a seminal essay of 1817, had launched the scholarly study of medieval architecture and who had coined the terms Norman, Early English, Decorated and Perpendicular as the vernacular equivalents to the Four Orders of classical architecture. Mercifully, his vision was as inventive and free-ranging as it was scholarly. On the splendidly open site across the river he erected an enormous palace which has the proportions of a French Renaissance chateau coupled with detailing which faithfully imitates the tracery and ornaments of late medieval English architecture.

Rickman's windows are wonderfully eclectic. Those on the yellow-brick rear of the building (Figure 10) are single, pointed Early English arches, with typical mouldings, whose proportions and style are repeated on a grander scale in the barred apertures of the buttressed and pinnacled arcade facing the backs. Large Perpendicular oriels adorn the centre of the three stone-clad ranges (with some very fancy Decorated tracery). The domestic windows (Figure 11) are in principle 'Cambridge Windows', as his brief required of him. But the effect they make is very different from the prototypes in Second Court. There is no contrast between stone and brick. The arch of each light has three crisply carved cusps (making them more 'Gothick'). Above all, the glass is set in a lovely wooden lattice with lozenge shapes in the centre.

Other buildings have gone up since New Court, some of them running the risk of subordinating the complexities of soul to a single idea. In the 1860s Gilbert Scott would design and execute pleasing imitations of the style of the first three courts in the Music Rooms, the Master's Lodge, and the extension to Hall (all with some splendid windows). Penrose (1885) worked in the same spirit. In his new Chapel, however, Scott built in an unrelentingly Early English style, in the conviction that this was 'the highest perfection of pointed architecture'. Powell and Moya, as we have

THE SCHOOL OF PYTHAGORAS

In 1271 Walter of Merton's property in Cambridge passed to the Oxford college which bears his name. In 1804 St John's acquired the Orchard – later to become the Scholars' Garden – but the medieval stone house now known as the School of Pythagoras remained in Merton's hands. Except in terms of its property value Merton took little interest in the building; early drawings show it much dilapidated. From the 1930s St John's and Magdalene, both looking for building land, were keen to purchase but it was not until 1959 after protracted negotiations by the then Senior Bursar, John Boys Smith, that the School, along with other Merton property, was secured for St John's. Within ten years, the new Cripps Building was to reach within a few yards of the stone house.

Thus it was that the house of the Dunnings, a prominent Cambridge family of the thirteenth century, came into the College's possession. With a first-floor hall supported by a vaulted undercroft, it is the oldest surviving medieval house in Cambridge. Credit for its restoration in the 1960s is due to the then Junior Bursar, Alec Crook, who appreciated its historical importance and saw its potential for College use. Following restoration which preserved as much of the medieval fabric as possible, the upper floor became the home of the Lady Margaret Players and the undercroft a venue for social events and, more recently, for conferences. Meanwhile, the adjacent late medieval, timber-framed Merton Hall is used for graduate accommodation.

The School of Pythagoras

Merton Hall

seen, insisted on being Modern. Edward Cullinan in the 1990s simply had to be *post*-modern (hence the tiny portcullises on the windows in the latest Library with their jokey homage to the iron bars over the windows of the sixteenth-century citadel and to the portcullis in the Beaufort coat of arms (Figure 12; cf. Figure 1). But there has been little in the past 180 years to equal the charm of Rickman's inventions.

ICONS

Icons can be seen in every part of the College and are prominent on the Great Gate, which is adorned with the arms of Lady Margaret Beaufort and a statue of the College's patron saint, St John the Evangelist.

Lady Margaret's royal arms have strange beasts rearing up on either side. These are yales, heraldic creatures with elephants' tails, antelopes' bodies and goats' heads with multi-directional horns. Mentioned in Pliny, they appealed to the medieval mind as symbols of defence *à tous azimuts*. Flanking these are the Beaufort family motifs of the Red Rose of Lancaster (recalling Lady Margaret's ancestor, John of Gaunt) and the Portcullis, popular with the Tudors, which is now the emblem of Parliament. At the feet of St John is an eagle, his traditional Gospel symbol, much in evidence throughout the College. Perhaps the fiercest eagle watches over the Cloister Gate in New Court, though the pair on the posts of the Queens' Road Gate and at the western end of the Buttery Dining Room run it close. St John, by the way, was, according to tradition, immune to a dose of poison, which showed itself as a snake escaping from his chalice.

The canopied tomb in the Antechapel is that of Hugh Ashton, one of Lady Margaret's household officers who assisted Bishop Fisher in founding the College. On its railings is his rebus, an ash tree growing out of a tun (barrel), also to be seen for instance in a group of heraldic badges above the entrance to E staircase in New Court. Another rebus is to be found on the tops of the lead rainwater pipes on the east side of the Fisher Building, where a fish and a wheatear denote the Bishop's name.

The coat of arms of Mary Cavendish, later Countess of Shrewsbury, on the tower of Second Court, includes the mottos of both Mary and her husband, Lord Talbot: the dog for the Talbots and the stag's head for the Cavendish family.

The sculptor Eric Gill designed and carved the arms of Bishop Fisher over the archway from Chapel Court into North Court, as well as the symbol of St John on the keystone of the central arch of the Chapel Court cloister, and the eagle and the marguerite on the keystone of the centre arch leading from the Forecourt. Which brings us to the yale-flanked iron gates from St John's Street into the Forecourt with their elegant superscription, 'Souvent me Souvient'. This, the Beaufort motto, explains why blue forget-me-nots appear with Lady Margaret's white daisy – the marguerite – in the decoration surrounding the College arms on the Great Gate.

The Great Gate with the arms of Lady Margaret Beaufort and the statue of St John the Evangelist, as repainted in 1982

25

PLANTS AND WILDERNESS

St John's is supremely fortunate among 'Cambridge colleges in having extensive gardens, literally at its back door. The spacious lawns and trees that stretch from the Kitchen Bridge westward to the playing fields beyond Queens' Road provide a superb natural setting for the neo-Gothic buildings of New Court and the Dutch gables of Third Court, and a fine formal approach to the College from the west.

What seems effortlessly to convey a sense of tradition, order and, on late summer evenings, tranquillity, is the result of a long history and of much care and planning. The College Gardens Committee meets regularly to discuss matters raised by Fellows or the gardening staff and to decide on planting and design.

Its most radical decisions concern trees. It fell to the Committee, for example, to decide to replace the avenue of elms in the Wilderness (see below) with oaks following the ravages of Dutch elm disease. It was the Gardens Committee, too, which resolved to take out every second lime tree in the approach avenue from Queens' Road, where Trinity, faced with a similar issue, opted to retain theirs. Visitors may judge which was the better decision.

There are many individual plantings of beauty and interest. The forbidding northern brick face of New Court has been softened by a line of four *Metasequoia*

28

Above: Ralph Thoday MVO, Head Gardener 1928–60 (© Edward Leigh)

Above right: Arabis turrita *from the 1636 edition of Gerard's* Herbal

glyptostroboides, the ancient tree known from the fossil record and discovered in Hunan, south-central China, in the course of the Second World War. The herbaceous border along the southern side of the New Court cloisters is justly famous for its sustained display of colourful perennials. The Scholars' Garden is bordered by fine shrubs and plants. In this vicinity a *Cryptomeria japonica*, brought many years ago from Kyoto, is doing well. The Master's Garden has fine tree peonies, wisteria, roses and irises. But it is perhaps the Fellows' Garden, the Wilderness, that provides the greatest interest.

The very name of the Wilderness causes amusement to those used to a wholly different scale where untamed nature is concerned. In fact the Wilderness was laid out to a design by the famous landscape gardener 'Capability' Brown in the eighteenth century and is subject to a very precise code of management. In botanical terms it is a carefully monitored free-for-all, in which species plants are allowed to compete and multiply, with only minimal supervision of its canopy of trees. The result is a superb sequence of naturalized flowers that manage to hold their own against fierce competition, and to carpet the wild areas of the garden, starting with aconites in late December, through snowdrops, the beautiful Wordsworth daffodil (*Narcissus pseudonarcissus*), *Anemone blanda*, *Scilla sibirica*, *Chionodoxa caerulea*, and culminating, in late June, with *Lilium martagon*, the 'Turk's cap lily', indigenous in

southern and eastern Europe. This rare lily was introduced in the eighteenth century, and forms one of the oldest colonies in the United Kingdom. Regrettably, the introduction of *Lilium martagon album* in the pre-war period, in an attempt to diversify the colour range, has meant that the genetic isolation of the colony was destroyed, reducing its potential interest to science.

Two other rarities are associated with the Wilderness. One is *Arabis turrita*, the great tower mustard, an inconspicuous member of the Brassicaceae family, at home in the Mediterranean region. Illustrated in Thomas Johnson's 1636 edition of Gerard's *Herbal*, it grew in the decayed mortar of ancient walls in Trinity, St John's and Magdalen College, Oxford. The only colony to survive has been on a wall at the back of the Wilderness. The second, *Epimedium cantabrigiense*, another self-effacing plant, has as its parent species *E. alpinum* and *E. pubigerum*. The natural habitats of the one, the European Alps, and the other, the southern coast of the Black Sea, meant that these two species never lived close to one another. But during the Second World War, they were planted in adjacent beds in the Wilderness. *Epimedium x cantabrigiense*, a pleasant and interesting though unspectacular plant, was the result.

The College has benefited from Head Gardeners who have been both plantsmen and managers, and from a gardening staff of rare dedication. One Head Gardener who lives on in the memory of the community was Ralph Thoday MVO, a prominent figure in the Royal Horticultural Society who in a single year won eleven RHS Gold Medals for fruit and flowers grown in the College gardens. Congratulated on his success, he replied gloomily, 'It's an awfully high standard to keep up.' He prided himself every May at the time of the Commemoration of Benefactors in decorating the staircase to the Upper Library, where a reception was held, with potted laburnum trees in full flower, and in providing new potatoes that he had grown himself for the College's Port Latin Feast. In his later years he was a towering presence as President of the College Pig Club (see Chapter 23).

Above: The Bridge of Sighs in winter, seen from the Master's Garden

The decisions of the Gardens Committee have not always been without controversy, and there was a period in the 1970s when debates on major issues were carried on in verse in the Fellows' Suggestions Book. In the 1960s and 1970s, the Committee did its work by taking walks around the College grounds, and it traditionally kept no minutes. It remains one of the most pleasant of all College committees on which to serve, and, though it does now keep minutes, it still makes its decisions while walking round the gardens.

A final word about the great lawn outside New Court, one of the glories of the College. In earlier days a place of archery butts, and more recently the scene of tennis courts and croquet (it was not uncommon for a set to be taken out there after Hall in summer), the lawn is now as often as not alive with frisbees.

3 GOVERNANCE, FINANCE AND ESTATES

COLLEGE GOVERNANCE
by the Master

St John's College is, in constitutional terms, an eleemosynary (i.e. dependent on charity) corporation established by the Charter dated 9 April 1511. The Foundation of the College is defined in the Statutes as consisting of the Master, Fellows and Scholars. The Master, in accepting election, declares that he or she will '… in all things endeavour to the utmost of my power to promote the peace, honour and well being of the College as a place of education, religion, learning and research.' A solemn undertaking indeed, and shared by us all. Over the years the College has grown substantially: fifty years ago, there were about seventy Fellows, 500 undergraduates and seventy or so graduate (mostly PhD) students; today we have nearly 140 Fellows, a little over 500 undergraduates and around 300 graduate students. All this takes a bit of managing.

Current procedures are a far cry from earlier centuries when the Master alone was allowed to marry and live in lodgings within the College; the Fellows (with the exception of a few medical men) were required to be celibate and in Holy Orders, vacating their Fellowships on marriage; in some instances they might proceed to a College living and preferment in the Church; and the College was governed by the Master and Seniors (the eight most senior Fellows).

Much of this was swept away in the mid-nineteenth century. A group of Johnian Fellows led by the Rev. William Bateson (Senior Bursar 1846–57; Master 1857–81) joined others in the University and pressed for change. In due course the Oxford and Cambridge Act of 1877 was passed and new Statutes for the College,

The Master, Professor Richard Perham FRS FMedSci, and his wife Dr Nancy Lane Perham OBE

recognizably similar to those we have today, were introduced in 1882. The Statutes, substantially revised again in 1925 and amended from time to time since then by the votes of the Fellows but subject to the approval of the Queen in Council, dictate how we run the College. Under them the College can and does make standing orders to govern its day-to-day life.

The ultimate authority is the Governing Body, i.e. the Master and Fellows collectively. But, since 1882 the

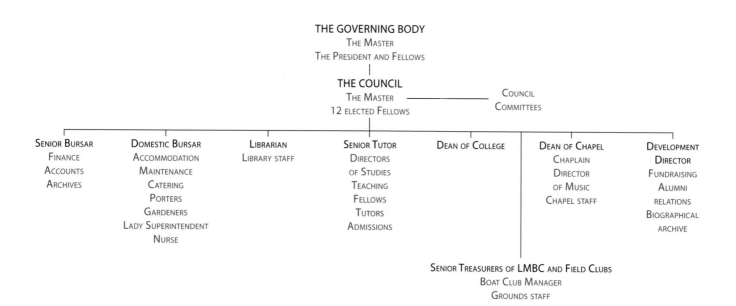

affairs of the College have been administered by the Council, a body of twelve Fellows elected by the Governing Body and chaired by the Master *ex officio*. Three Fellows are elected annually, to hold office for four years, thereby ensuring a regular turnover. The Council normally meets every other Thursday afternoon in term time (fifteen to twenty meetings a year). College Officers attend for items of business to do with them if they happen not to be members of the Council. Elected representatives of the undergraduate and postgraduate members of the College also attend for the discussion of matters directly affecting them, a dialogue bolstered through regular meetings of the Senior and Junior Members Committee. The Governing Body normally meets once per term, again with the Master presiding, but may meet more frequently if required.

Meetings of the Governing Body and Council are still rather formal affairs. Those attending wear gowns, and may address each other by College title, though a Council meeting is naturally more intimate and, without loss of its serious sense of purpose, will sometimes give way to use of first names (far removed from the memory of some of us when even close friends in the Fellowship used only surnames!)

The job of the Master, though statutorily defined, is so wide-ranging as to defy detailed description. By and large the Master is expected to foresee difficulties (a crystal ball helps), to deal with challenges as they emerge, and to win the approval of the Fellows in the decisions required to carry the College forward. A sense of fairness is everything. Much of the burden is shared with the President, a Fellow elected for a four-year term of office, to be the head of the Fellowship. And of course there are senior College Officers, notably the Senior Bursar, the Senior Tutor, the Domestic Bursar and the Deans, who have charge of great swathes of College business allotted to their respective offices. They in turn have dedicated staffs to help them. Regular and cohesive discussion is essential.

Numerous committees have come into existence to deal with specific aspects of College life, all reporting to the Council, with one exception. That exception is the Audit Committee, which has the power to examine the College accounts and to report annually to the Governing Body on such matters as it sees fit. There were some fifty standing committees at the last count; some meet often (such as the Education Forum, Finance Committee, the Investments Committee, the Buildings Committee), some may meet as little as once a year, if that. Ad hoc committees or working groups may be formed to deal with specific problems, and then discharged when the issue has been resolved. A welcome development of recent years has been the appointment of members of the College from the wider world to the Finance Committee and Investments

Committee, to broaden the mix of experience and offer expert advice on important decisions.

Another development of the past decade has been the creation of the Johnian Office, charged with the task of improving and maintaining relations with the alumni, now more than 10,000 in number and spread far and wide across the world. With the launch of the University's 800th Anniversary Campaign, and with the College's own 500th anniversary in sight, the Johnian Office is being given new tasks in fund-raising, an increasingly essential part of the changing horizons in higher education in the UK and overseas. Close liaison with the Master's Office, the Bursary and with the Fellows generally is essential here too.

Lunching and dining is an integral part of things, much business being done over meals taken together. It is not only College business that is transacted; many an academic collaboration has sprung from sitting beside a neighbour with whom one finds one has more in common than either first supposed. And it is rare to leave the dining table without having learned something of value from another Fellow or guest.

St John's is one of the most prominent colleges in the University and it plays a full part in University affairs. The Master attends regular meetings of the Colleges' Committee, at which the Heads of all Cambridge colleges and senior University Officers, including the Vice-Chancellor, meet to do business. The Master conveys the views of the College on important issues, and returns to advise the Council and Governing Body on matters of substance and to relate the views of other colleges. The Bursars likewise attend meetings of the Bursars' Committee, and the Senior Tutor meetings of the Senior Tutors' Committee. It is noteworthy that the Clerk to the Bursars' Committee and the Secretary of the Senior Tutors' Committee in recent years have both been Fellows of St John's. And, as the opportunity and need arises, the Master and Fellows will take their place on University committees, again contributing to the two-way traffic between College and University.

A word about the Fellows. The Fellows of St John's

represent an exceptionally distinguished cross-section of the senior members of the University. They come in various categories, from Research Fellows, elected more or less as they finish their PhD degrees, to Professorial Fellows, elected because of their widely acknowledged distinction, and retired Fellows, many of whom continue to pursue their academic work in College into their seventies or eighties though no longer required to undertake administrative duties. The largest category is that of the Teaching Fellows, most of whom hold prime posts in the University. In a small number of areas, additional needs are met by Fellows who are appointed as full-time College Teaching Officers. High standards in research and teaching matter and election to a Fellowship, which is in the hands of the College Council, is not offered without much prior thought. In St John's a Fellow is a Fellow, and all Fellows have equal rights in votes at the Governing Body, irrespective of

St John's College Council in session, discussing business with the Senior and Domestic Bursars, July 2006

their standing, long or short, on the roll of Fellows. It is traditionally a good-natured community, free of factions, and ready to fall in behind the majority decision after a serious debate.

It would be impossible to conclude this brief survey of College governance without a more personal word. As Master I am called upon to represent St John's at numerous functions, formal and informal, in Cambridge and elsewhere. It is an essential part of the job which my wife and I greatly enjoy. It is a pleasure to meet Johnians all over the world, whether just by chance or at events organized by the Johnian Office, and to welcome them on the occasions of the Johnian reunion dinners or open weekends in College. Some of our most agreeable times are spent with the College staff at their annual Christmas party or celebrating long-service awards – without the College staff where would we be? – and with junior members of the College at society dinners, with the Eagles and Flamingos entertaining the freshers to lunch in the Lodge, being unexpectedly invited to tea by a group of undergraduates, admitting the Scholars, awarding the Larmor Prizes. One of my most welcome tasks is to act as Deputy Vice-Chancellor at General Admission in June, conferring their degrees on graduating Johnians and then returning to the splendid celebratory lunch in College to meet them again in the company of their proud parents and friends. It is the fitting end by which one marks each passing academic year.

Richard Perham

FINANCE

The public perception of Cambridge colleges is that they are wealthy, a perception fuelled by scale and beauty. The true picture is somewhat different. St John's certainly benefits from a larger endowment than many higher education institutions in the UK. But once the many pressures on income are taken into account, it is far from a picture of wealth that emerges.

The following table shows a breakeven position for the College in its latest financial results:

	2005/06 £ million
Income	25.5
Expenditure	24.6
Operating surplus	0.9
University contribution	0.5
Accumulated restricted income	0.4
Retained deficit	0.0

Less than ten per cent of income comes from tuition fees. The College consequently suffers a substantial deficit on its core educational activities and must look to other sources of revenue to cover that shortfall. Income from endowment plays a major role, representing almost half the total. There is also revenue from charges to Fellows, students and staff for accommodation and catering (though this is far less than the true annual running costs of buildings, kitchens and so forth). The College also seeks to develop revenue from other sources wherever possible, including out-of-term conference and private catering activities. Crucially, it also benefits significantly from the help of others, both alumni and friends, in the form of donations.

With a large Fellowship and the second largest student body in the University, a significant building stock (much of it listed), and the largest grounds of any Cambridge college, the demands on income are commensurately heavy. First and foremost comes expenditure in support of the College's educational activities – teaching (including the small group supervision system for which Cambridge is renowned); student welfare, through the tutorial system; research, including a highly successful Research Fellowship programme for outstanding academics at the start of their careers; scholarships and bursaries, to ensure access for all regardless of financial means; student facilities and clubs; the Library; and the Chapel and Choir. A further significant item is maintenance and refurbishment of the College buildings and grounds; and the accounts include a charge for depreciation of buildings of some £3m per year. The College is

33

currently facing the challenge of a major building refurbishment and repair programme over the next eight years costing some tens of millions of pounds. This includes major refurbishments of the Triangle Site opposite the Great Gate, North Court and the northern side of Chapel Court, Merton Hall, and the Cripps Building.

As will be seen from the table, in addition to its domestic commitments the College makes an annual 'University Contribution', currently £0.5m, to a fund from which grants are made to poorer colleges.

Some income earned on College funds with restricted purposes is from time to time accumulated rather than spent in a particular year. This may be because the fund is being built up until it reaches a size sufficient to fund a specific project or because its purposes were not capable of fulfilment in a given year. This accumulation amounted to £0.4m in 2005/6.

The College's endowment, with a current value of some £290m, is central to its finances. The endowment assets have a substantial property component with investments ranging from agricultural holdings acquired in the first years of the College's existence to modern office buildings in the St John's Innovation Park. In addition, the College has a significant portfolio of equities and bonds. Asset allocation is being reviewed with the objective of moving into a number of new areas such as private equity (including a new pooled investment vehicle launched with the University and a number of other colleges) so as better to diversify the portfolio and enhance returns. Optimization of asset allocation will be assisted by the move, in common with many charities, to adopt a 'total return' investment policy (where the investment objective is to maximize overall return regardless of whether it comes in the form of income or capital gain). As ever, the key task is to balance the current requirements of the College with the need to preserve the real value of the endowment. In consequence, the College exercises prudence in income withdrawal which, in recent years, has been in the order of £10m annually. Four external members, all Johnians, sit on the College Investments Committee and offer valuable advice.

The Senior Bursar, Chris Ewbank, writes:

'Why is it that St John's, in common with other Cambridge colleges, now finds itself in a challenging financial situation? There is no one simple answer. A number of factors have combined and coincided to create the current environment – a significant real decline in tuition fees and charges over the last decade; a diminution in our endowment income through the loss of Advance Corporation Tax (ACT) relief (affecting pension funds and endowed charities alike); the need substantially to increase bursaries to prevent the government move to student loans and tuition fees from damaging our traditional policy of open access; the need to compete in what is now a global market for higher education; substantial increases in pension contributions which hit us hard given that half our costs are payroll; the need to carry out major refurbishment and repairs to many of our buildings; the costs of implementing the requirements of ever-increasing regulation; educational inflation continuing to far outstrip consumer inflation; and likely lower investment market returns in the future than historically.

'We are moving forward to meet these challenges. We are continually seeking to enhance our financial management through improved budgeting and management accounting so that we can better analyse our operations, allocate resources efficiently, and identify economies and value-for-money initiatives where we can. We have recently introduced new statutory accounts which conform to modern accounting standards and include, for the first time, standard financial statements – these are published in the University *Reporter* and are available on request from the College. We are placing great emphasis on optimizing the growth and management of our existing endowment. In addition, we are seeking to enhance our income from conferences and private catering to support our other activities. However, even with all these changes and efforts, it is clear that we need to increase the size of our endowment and so it is to the generosity of alumni and other friends that we must also look, as we face the future.'

34

ESTATES

One of the great advantages of Cambridge colleges over the halls and hostels of the medieval University was their solid landed endowment. This began with land inherited at their foundation from previous institutions such as dissolved hospitals, monasteries and nunneries, or through the grant of estates and manors by royal and noble founders.

The estates of the former St John's Hospital covered large tracts in the fields to the west of Cambridge as well as scattered urban property. To fulfil Lady Margaret's design, however, more income was required – not least as the revenues of her estates in Devon, Somerset and Northamptonshire, devoted to the College's initial needs, were resumed by her grandson and heir, Henry VIII, in 1515. Over the following four years, the energy of John

Fisher and her other executors, negotiating with Cardinal Wolsey and a host of royal bureaucrats, gained the sites and lands of three decayed foundations – Higham Priory in Kent, Broomhall Priory in Berkshire, and the royal hospital at Ospringe near Dover (see panel). This was followed by larger endowments, including land at Holbeach in Lincolnshire. The manor of Holbeach was one of the properties bought by John Fisher and given in 1520–1 to support his own Foundation of Fellows and Scholars, a benefaction incorporated in the main Foundation of the College following his execution. That acquisition forms the nucleus of the College's present Lincolnshire holdings, which include farms at Moulton, Whaplode and Crowland – a total of approximately 3,400 acres in the County, out of a total College landholding of 17,400 acres.

35

Atlas of Holbeach 1792. Part of a map of land at Moulton and Whaplode, Lincolnshire, with a cartouche showing a ruined church in the Fens, and fishing rods, net and eel spear

OSPRINGE

St John's acquired the site and estates of the Hospital of St Mary at Ospringe, known as the Maison Dieu, from the Crown, through a long legal process from 1516 to 1519. The Hospital itself, including the main site north of Watling Street and two properties on the south side of the street, was founded in the early thirteenth century and used as a halt by pilgrims travelling to the shrine of St Thomas Becket at Canterbury. On occasion it was also used by kings to entertain guests – the marriage suite of Edward II and Isabella stayed there in 1308, as did the captive King John of France in 1360 as he journeyed to Dover on his way home. Ospringe, with Faversham, was also famous for its gunpowder mills, parts of which were held under lease from the College in the seventeenth and eighteenth centuries until the site was sold to the Government in 1814.

The College lands and buildings are depicted in several picturesque eighteenth- and nineteenth-century maps in its archives. Old buildings, most of which have now been sold, line Ospringe Street, notably the Saracen's Head, later the Crown Inn, on a site which can be identified from at least 1255. The College still owns no. 11, which is known as 'College House'. Oast houses associated with the estate have also been sold for conversion into residential premises. Besides forty-nine acres of Parsonage Farm, the College holds ancient fields in the neighbourhood: Millfield, Lion Field, Joyce Field, and eight acres at Summerfield in Woodnesborough, for which the deeds can be traced back to the thirteenth century.

In the seventeenth century, a great many scholarships and exhibitions were founded. A notable benefactor was William Platt (1592–1637). William's grandfather, Richard, was a prosperous brewer who founded Aldenham School in Hertfordshire, to which the College still appoints a governor. William left pastures in the parish of St Pancras, Middlesex, to the College, as well as houses in the neighbourhood of Smithfield in London. From the 1860s, under powers in the Universities and Colleges Estates Act 1858, the College undertook an extensive housing development on the land left by Platt. This was the Kentish Town estate, criss-crossed by roads bearing names such as Lady Margaret, Burghley, Lady Somerset and Ospringe. The sale of the estate between 1953 and 1980 realized over £2m.

More land for building was seen to be available in the 566 acres of the old Broomhall Priory. Agricultural depression bit deep here on land which was already unpromising for farming. After one abortive scheme in 1865 in an area always subject to heath fires, roads were eventually laid and systematic development took place from 1899. The first course of the Sunningdale Golf Club was completed in 1901, with high-class residences surrounding it, and commercial premises along the London Road.

Cambridge itself offered similar potential. The West Cambridge farmland which had originally formed part of the ancient St John's Hospital property was developed from 1885 as the Grange Road and Madingley Road residential estates. Pressure to build resulted from a fall in agricultural rents during the 1880s and from the interest of Fellows in domestic housing once they became free to marry in 1882.

In 1534 a gift by a Lincolnshire rector, Thomas Thimbleby, had enabled the purchase of the area in Cambridge west of Jesus Green later known as Dovehouse Close. In 1887–8, this was leased for building the present terraces in Park Street and the neighbouring roads. The Park Street area contains both private residences and residences for College students. Landholdings in nearby Chesterton, including an enclosure of fifty-seven acres and the Chesterton Hall estate of almost 400 acres left to the College in 1922 by Mrs Johanna Gurney, have also served a dual purpose. The Hall estate has been progressively sold for local housing needs, and part of the old enclosure has been used for the St John's Innovation Centre development (see Chapter 9).

In the city itself, opposite the Great Gate, is an area now known as the Triangle Site, bounded by Bridge Street, St John's Street and All Saints Passage. It included the University Divinity School, built on land that until the 1870s housed the Pensionary, a complex of bakehouse, stables and accommodation for College staff. Before that it may well have been the burial ground of the old Hospital of St John. The rest of the site came into College ownership over the past two hundred years through bequests (such as those of Sir Isaac Pennington and James Wood) or by purchase. Older alumni will remember the Taj Mahal restaurant, the Cambridge

The Triangle Site 2006, showing the former Divinity School and work in progress

Music shop, Buttress the tailor, and Gallyon the gunmaker. A great redevelopment programme is now under way there, a combination of new student accommodation and commercial letting that will in effect create a new court. It is due for completion in 2008.

ASSISTANCE TO OTHERS

St John's has benefited greatly over the centuries from the generosity of many people. More recently the College has itself given much back to the development of the collegiate University.

In 1953 it resolved to make gifts totalling well over £1,000 to the Association to Promote a Third Foundation for Women in Cambridge, and provided accommodation in the Hermitage in Silver Street to New Hall, as the new foundation was called, for its initial years while it awaited its intended home on the Huntingdon Road. Those first gifts came with the personal commitment of Rev. J S Boys Smith on the New Hall Council from incorporation in 1954 until the

achievement of college status in 1972, and they were followed by many others (including one in 1969 to help establish that desideratum of any college – a wine cellar).

Then, in 1964, St John's, together with Trinity and Caius, founded Darwin College as a new Graduate College in Cambridge, reflecting the increasing prominence of graduate studies. Other Colleges assisted by St John's over the years include Downing, Girton, Fitzwilliam, Hughes Hall, Lucy Cavendish, Newnham, St Catharine's, St Edmund's, Selwyn and University (now Wolfson) College. The list is long; the total sum given, large.

In 1989 the College decided to build a research institute on its land at Clarkson Road for lease to the University, and to grant annually £150,000 for five years towards its running costs. The Isaac Newton Institute for Mathematical Sciences was born, and flourishes now without further College aid. Furthermore it was the catalyst for the Mathematics buildings on the remainder of the Clarkson Road site – a development marked by

Left: The Isaac Newton Institute for Mathematical Sciences (courtesy of Sara Wilkinson)

Below: The Schools Project in action – bridging Bin Brook 2005 (courtesy of Prof. Harry Marsh)

38

the College's largest ever single gift, of £1.02m to the University over seventeen years, accompanying the leading role of Peter Goddard, then Master, in founding the Institute and fund-raising for Mathematics.

And there is a whole catalogue of departments which St John's has assisted: Archaeology and Anthropology, Biochemistry, Biotechnology, Classics, Divinity, English, Law, Modern Languages, Philosophy. Not least, in the year 2000 an annual grant of £100,000 for five years was made to support the establishment of the Cambridge Centre for Research in the Arts, Social Sciences and Humanities.

THE SCHOOLS PROJECT

Together with the Gatsby Charitable Foundation, the College has also taken an initiative to help all schools in the East Anglia and East Midlands region to improve the teaching of mathematics, science and technology. Launched in July 2000, and directed by Professor Harry Marsh, former Fellow, the Schools Project identifies 'teacher associates' in the various schools and makes grants to support local schemes. In this way, no less than a hundred individual teachers in relevant subjects have been awarded funding; and grants have been made towards local initiatives, reaching some 10,000 young people each year, with the aim of attracting them to careers in mathematics, science or technology, and encouraging innovation, creativity, self-confidence, knowledge, communication and problem-solving skills, and team work.

THE EAGLE PROJECT

Since 1998 the College has participated with Lambeth Local Education Authority in a scheme designed to raise the aspiration of able secondary school pupils and encourage them to aim for university entrance. Fellows and undergraduates work directly with schools to provide workshops and seminars. Talks in schools by the Admissions Tutor and visits to Cambridge, including an insight into life at St John's, build up an awareness of what makes a successful university applicant. Since the Eagle Project began, many hundreds of pupils have been able to participate in it, and six have joined the College, while many have gone on to higher education elsewhere.

Right: New Court seen across Bin Brook, with a glimpse of the Fisher Building

Below: The Cripps Building

4 THE COLLEGE AS COMMUNITY

Above all, the College is a community. From the first moment of arrival, networks of friendship and common interest are established. Paths cross every day as people come and go through the Courts, eat together in Hall or Buttery, and drink together in one or other of the local pubs. Social bonds are reinforced through a wide range of College activities. Constant interchange promotes and strengthens the sense of a common life; the experience of living in College is never forgotten. That 'belonging' is a lifetime experience is well demonstrated by the many letters received from alumni in preparation for this book. The College never really lets go. On the contrary, it reinforces the bonds with members by inviting them back to periodic reunion dinners, and the Johnian Society (see Chapter 27) does work of its own to maintain and strengthen contact between alumni and the College. *The Eagle* and *Johnian News* keep alumni well informed about College life.

St John's also prides itself on being hospitable to all from the outset – a hospitality that is long remembered and appreciated. Sir Bryan Hopkin (1933: Hon. Fellow 1982) recalls from his own day 'a rather tolerant and "democratic" atmosphere, friendly to a young person without social advantages, a grammar school, lower middle-class country boy such as I was'. That has been the experience of many. That St John's is not a place for airs and graces may have something to do with its size, and also perhaps to its long association with the 'nine northern counties'.

More recently, the College has paid close attention to facilities for the disabled including the needs of wheelchair users. Jonathan Gilmour (2005) writes of his 'wheelchair-friendly rooms in New Court as well as copious ramps allowing good wheelchair access to most areas of the College site' and believes that the College's 'very modern and contemporary outlook' should be celebrated.

AMENITIES (OR LACK OF THEM)

In their letters alumni say next to nothing about academic work. Chris Rundle (1959) mentions 'the Chaplain arguing that intellectual excitement should now for us (ex-National Servicemen) take priority over other forms and wondering if that could really be'. In fact, the letters address themselves to nothing so refined as 'intellectual excitement'. On the contrary, many dwell

Tea party for alumni in the garden of the Master's Lodge July 2006

GROWING UP IN THE MASTER'S LODGE: A REMINISCENCE BY STEPHEN BOYS SMITH

We moved into the Master's Lodge when I was thirteen. It was the office and so never fully private. Porters left letters on the hall table throughout the day and Fellows came and went on tiptoe in the equivalent of the cathedral whisper.

It was a place of entertainment, though not for my brother and me. Food arrived by trolley from the College Kitchens. Dirty dishes went back the same way. Shy teenager that I was, official duties only fell my way in a crisis. Once I had to entertain Gilbert Ryle. He talked to me about gliding and took me round the garden to tell me the names of plants.

Yet the Lodge was also the family home, as my parents were determined it should be. I spent my teenage years with the luxury of

spaces into which to disappear at just the age when it was most valuable. The most precious were the outbuildings, which housed an ancient and leaky canoe.

One day, the architects short-listed for the Cripps Building – Powell and Moya, who won; and Lasdun – made presentations. All came to lunch in the Lodge. When they heard of the canoe they jointly bent their minds to the problem, perhaps for light relief, and recalled some plastic substance which would do the trick. Shortly afterwards, a watertight canoe, which my brother and I painted LMBC scarlet on the outside and Cambridge blue within, appeared in the river at the foot of the steps in the Master's Garden – thanks to the advice of three of the finest architects of their generation.

41

Skaters on the Cam 1963 (courtesy of Nick Timmins)

on physical discomfort, recalling with masochistic satisfaction the years of austerity before sets were centrally heated and toilets provided *en suite*. Indeed, older alumni returning to College after a long absence have been disconcerted at the transformation of their fondly remembered spartan accommodation into sybaritic, modern living quarters.

A favourite theme is the winter dash down staircases and across freezing courts to the nearest bathroom, and the memory of waking to find the bedside jug of water frozen in several degrees of frost. Denys Cussins (1944) recalls that 'most winter mornings your top blanket would be thick with the morning dew'. Ken Post (1953) remembers 'sleeping with every piece of fabric I could piled over me, including any movable carpet'. The first purchase made by Mike Andrews (1957), who found himself located in a Third Court room with 'ill-fitting iron windows on three sides and no form of heating', was a hot-water bottle, and he slept in socks, sweater and a woolly hat. In the coldest winters, everything froze. John Burren (1953) recalls six Johnians skating on the Cam all the way from the Mill to Grantchester and back.

No one thought of global warming in wartime and post-war days when one weekly scuttle of coal, collected from a bunker in Chapel Court, was the sole means of heating a room. Michael Haughton (1944) found life in those days 'monastic – probably below current living standards in an average Trappist monastery'. Like many others, however, he appreciated the old College baths

behind New Court (removed when Cripps Court was built) – 'enormous sarcophagi made of yellowish ceramic like old-fashioned sinks, in which you could float'. Roger Griffin (1954; Fellow 1962–5 and 1972–) tried valiantly to preserve these tubs for posterity, but failed to persuade the College Council of their heritage value. The last to use them was David Chillingworth (1961) who by mischance was locked in by the Porters on the very last night of term, with demolition imminent. After flashing the bathhouse lights in Morse code for some considerable time to no avail, he finally managed to wriggle out of a small window.

EATING AND DRINKING

Food and drink feature prominently in alumni letters. From the 1940s, Michael Haughton described 'the dismal procession across the Courts to Hall to collect breakfast … haggard unshaven undergraduates in ex-Army greatcoats and dirty duffel coats, a ghastly sight'. Some reminisce about dining in Hall, where the Latin grace ('Oculi omnium in Te sperant, Domine…') was not always delivered with the required dignity and where spoons would be banged appreciatively by the whole Hall below High Table when some bold, or foolhardy, Scholar delivered an original or over-rapid reading – later to be rebuked by the Dean. When Roger Morgan came up to St John's in 1947, undergraduates were still required to dine in Hall on five evenings in the week: their presence was checked by the Head Porter against a printed list and names were marked in medieval fashion with a prick by a steel stylus.

Over the years, the experience of Hall has changed considerably. Many recall clambering over the tables to get to the benches against the wall. Undergraduate dining

MATRICULATION AND ADMISSION OF SCHOLARS

Inscription on the *matricula* (College list) is the point at which undergraduates are formally received into the College. The ceremony (and subsequently treasured group photograph) is followed by a widely attended Matriculation Service in the Chapel, and by a Matriculation Dinner in Hall at which the Master addresses words of welcome and encouragement to the freshers.

Some will remember the solemn ritual of the Admission of Scholars which takes place in the Combination Room. One by one, the Scholars-elect, wearing gowns, are called to stand before the Master, who is seated, gowned and sporting his academic square. The Scholar first promises 'cheerful submission to the discipline of the College' and goes on to state: 'So far as in me lies, I will endeavour, by diligence and innocency of life, to promote the

peace, honour and well-being of the College as a place of education, religion and learning.'

Following this sobering pledge (though 'innocency of life' is tempered by 'so far as in me lies'), the Scholar-elect kneels on a stool before the Master, who takes the Scholar-elect's hands in his and recites the formula: 'Auctoritate mihi commissa, admitto te in scholarem huius Collegii. In nomine Patris, et Filii et Spiritus Sancti.' The Scholar rises, bows, and the Master doffs his cap in return. One rite is left to perform. The Scholar repairs to a side-table to sign his or her name in the register with a fine silver pen donated by a former Fellow to avoid the use of scratch pens which might shower blots on the sacred paper to the consternation of all: not least that of Professor John Crook, who has devotedly presided over this part of the ceremony for decades – and bought the ink.

THE POOR'S SOUP

The ancient College tradition of 'The Poor's Soup' can be traced back to the former Hospital of St John, which distributed 'bred to por folk on Saynt Jhon day'. In 1768 the College Baker was instructed to apply 'for directions what sum shall be given in doles and to what parishes, and that bread given to the prisoners in the two gaols be brown'. At some point soup was added to the bread, and the College Bread and Broth Charity took on full form, with a distribution of a four-pound loaf and a gallon of soup to each of fifty people on thirteen successive Thursdays over the winter months. The soup was prepared in a fifty-gallon boiler with split peas, carrots, onions, celeriac and swedes, to which two pounds of meat were added for each recipient, and distributed under the supervision of a Fellow. Peter Wordie (1952), son of former Master Sir James Wordie, recalls being taken in 1940 to witness the distribution, and seeing 'a column of recipients, all of them carrying the most wonderful collection of jugs and pails'. He tells how his father obtained (unrationed) venison from Scotland for the soup in 1946. Peter Linehan recalls attending in the 1960s in cap and gown in the kitchens to taste and give the required approval. By then, Meals on Wheels was rendering the ceremony obsolete. For a time, the Red Cross and the Salvation Army acted as distribution agents till, in 1990, a money grant for the homeless was substituted. But the Soup continues to be served to the Fellows at High Table!

This painting by Agatha Shore in the Parsons Room illustrates the distribution of the Poor's Soup in days gone by

Opposite: A view from High Table down the Hall in the late 1960s (courtesy of John A Rose)

Right: The Cripps Building at night

has since become a great deal more sophisticated, with waiter service and certainly no climbing over tables. For Madeleine Crisp (2001), 'Hall was definitely an event, not compulsory as in my grandfather's day, but not shunned as in my father's. Tickets would always sell out, and the race to make sure you got there on time to sit together was always a worry.' This will puzzle those generations of Johnians who would skip Hall any day in favour of the Taj Mahal.

Lack of variety on the menu in days of austerity led Tom Curtis (1952) to drive an old taxi he had bought into the wilds of Cambridgeshire to bag roadside pheasants with a (licensed) 12-bore shotgun. When not foraging for food he would use the cab to transport 'half a cricket or rugger team' to away matches.

Nostalgia is the mood when it comes to the Blue Boar, the Mitre, the Baron of Beef, the Little Rose and the old Buttery, where several alumni seem to have spent the best evenings of their lives. Jeremy Collis (1969) believes the College Bar in the late 1960s was 'the best in Cambridge – packed every night, students sitting on the floor, singing songs, playing drinking games etc'. Etc?

43

PORT LATIN FEAST

Although the major festival of St John the Evangelist (duly celebrated by the College) falls on 27 December, the medieval calendar found room for a further celebration of St John on 6 May, the day of St John ad portam Latinam, commemorating the saint's miraculous escape from harm when cast into a vat of boiling oil by the Emperor Domitian at Rome's Latin Gate. The early College did not let this pass unnoticed. The accounts for 1558 refer to the purchase of 'two gallons of clared and white wine upon Sanct John Port Latyn's Day'. In 1597 the wine bill came to some £250 in today's money. The diary of Simonds d'Ewes in 1618 describes how 'after the feast in hall was ended, all the fellow-commoners and bachelors of the house, according to their annuary custom, went down the river to a pretty green near Chesterton, accompanied by a band of loud music.' There is evidence that the festival was still going strong in the eighteenth century. Eventually, the annual service to commemorate benefactors settled on the Sunday nearest to 6 May, and the Port Latin Feast is now closely associated with that commemoration. There is also an association with the Linacre Lecture (see Chapter 14), which the College Council determined a century ago should be delivered 'on or near St John Port Latin Day'.

44

Aspirations to *haute cuisine* have been cultivated over the years by various College dining societies, including 'The Committee' which is still going strong at well over sixty years old. When the first thirty-nine women arrived in 1982, Gabrielle Howatson (née Hodgetts) recalls that 'there were many male societies, mostly named after birds, and a group of us decided to form a women's dining society called the Robins' – see Chapter 20.

A poignant recollection of the domestic care with which young gentlemen were at one time attended is provided by John McCutcheon (1959):

'Each morning (except Sunday) I would be awakened by a knock on my bedroom door. "Quarter to eight, Sir", were the words which invariably aroused me from my slumbers. I would lie in bed for five to ten minutes, gradually "coming to" to the sound of the clinking of cutlery and crockery as Mrs Levens, having first lit the gas fire in the sitting-room and moved the small table in front of the fire, put a cloth on the table and laid things out for my breakfast. She then withdrew and left me to my own devices.'

Décor, noise and distractions

Few photographs of individual rooms were received by the editor. Such evidence as there is suggests that interior décor was never a high priority, though an exception must be made in the case of A J P Campbell (1952) and Bill Grice (1952), who adorned their set with, amongst other things, ninety-six lavatory chains collected from all around Cambridge – with unthinkable consequences. In the 1950s and 1960s, more discerning students made their way to Kettle's Yard, where Jim Ede might loan a modern painting or two if you were lucky – see Chapter 16.

Wordsworth notoriously suffered from noise from the kitchen below his rooms 'with shrill notes/ Of sharp command and scolding intermix'd'; and from Trinity's nearby

> … loquacious Clock,
> Who never let the Quarters, night or day,
> Slip by him unproclaimed, and told the hours
> Twice over with a male and female voice.
> Her pealing organ was my neighbour too …

Nowadays the Kitchens are more muted, and the Trinity bell is silent at night. Instead, birds have been a problem. Long-standing resentments have emerged not

Interior décor 1952 (courtesy of Dr A J P Campbell)

Above: Punts at the Kitchen Bridge

Right: A College Bill of 1956 and Lodgings Bill of 1959

only about owls in Third Court, but about nocturnal ducks, and the noise made by lascivious pigeons in the eaves. And as for Canada geese…

It seems there has never been a shortage of means of distraction, particularly in summer, when punts have for generations offered relief from the dull throb of Tripos and, instead of returning from Hall to some weekly essay or desultory revision, there was the pleasure of dropping breadcrumbs, or water, or worse, from the Kitchen Bridge onto unsuspecting punters.

LIVING OUT

Before the construction of the Cripps Building in the 1960s, undergraduates had to live in lodgings for at least one of their three years. Students in lodgings were 'subject to the same regulations as residents in College', but most seem to have enjoyed the greater liberty, with warm-hearted landladies providing 'gargantuan cooked breakfasts' (Jeremy Ball: 1962) or turning a blind eye to eccentricities like 'keeping a .303 service rifle propped up in the corner' (T R W Longmore: 1943). It could still be spartan. Adrian Parker (1965) recalls an eight-roomed terrace house containing five undergraduates and the 'lodging house keeper' and her husband. 'It dawned on me that the keeper was living in one bed-sitting room and a scullery with outside toilet for the thirty weeks of term, but no one thought this was overcrowding at that time.'

BILLS

At the end come the bills. It is intriguing how many have hung on to their termly College accounts. Some of the sums from pre-inflationary days are astonishingly small. In 1948 the rent of rooms varied from £15 to £39 per year, with an annual charge for hire of furniture of £9, or less. The yearly service charge was £44.10s (£44.50) for bedmaker, shoe and window cleaning, decoration, washing of bed linen, electricity, gas, water and cleaning materials. In Chapel Court and North Court an additional charge of £6 was made 'in the case of rooms where hot water is laid on'. Caution money was £30 in those days, or £50 if your parents lived abroad. No one has said whether it was ever retained.

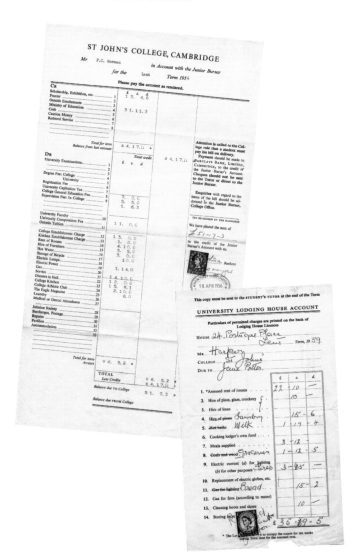

5 CHAPEL AND CHOIR

Opposite: The nave, choir stalls, apse and altar of the College Chapel

Below right: Photograph c.1869 of the old and new Chapels, before the former was demolished

THE COLLEGE CHAPEL

Historically, the Chapel has played a central part in the life of the College, which still to a degree reflects the original notion of community exemplified in the monastic model on which colleges such as St John's were founded. All Fellows with the exception of one or two doctors of physic were required to be in Holy Orders, a stipulation which continued until late in the nineteenth century. Divine services were and are regulated by statute and attendance at Chapel services was compulsory or expected until comparatively recently. Anecdotal evidence suggests that junior members were required to attend Chapel twice a week until early into the twentieth century, their names being 'pricked off' by a porter at the door.

Since the Reformation, a Dean was responsible for conducting divine service according to the rites and ceremonies of the Church of England and might be assisted by a chaplain. These roles have continued down the years. Until the mid-1960s, the Dean was responsible for College discipline as well as for the Chapel. The pastoral commitment of College clergy has long been an outstanding contribution to the College as a whole, and a succession of chaplains has done much to enhance the general welfare of junior members.

The College Prayer, which will be familiar to many and sounds as if it might date back to Tudor times, was in fact composed by H F Stewart, Dean from 1908 to 1918:

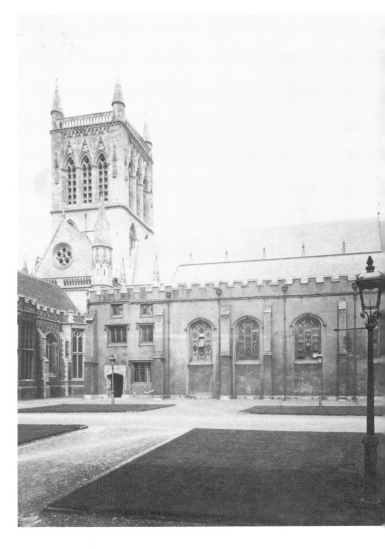

Bless, O Lord, the work of this College which is called by the name of Thy beloved disciple and grant that love of the brethren and all sound learning may ever grow and prosper here, to Thy honour and glory, and to the good of Thy people, Who with the Father and the Holy Spirit, livest and reignest one God, World without end. Amen.

BISHOP MORGAN AND THE BIBLE IN WELSH

Doctor Wiliam Morgan a gyfieithodd y Beibl drwyddi yn hwyr o amser; gwaith angenrheidiol, gorchestol, duwiol, dysgedig; am yr hwn ni ddichon Cymry fyth dalu a diolch iddo gymaint ag a haeddodd ef.

Doctor William Morgan translated the Bible throughout, in recent years; an essential, remarkable, godly and learned work; for which we Welsh will never be able to give sufficient thanks as much as he deserved.

Maurice Kyffin,
Deffyniad Ffydd Eglwys Loegr, 1595

In 1588 a complete translation of the Bible with Apocrypha, in Welsh, was printed and distributed to all the parishes of Wales, in accordance with an Act of Parliament. This was almost entirely the work of one man, William Morgan. A copy is held in the College Library.

Morgan, a child of North Wales, attended the College from 1565 to 1571 as a sizar. He began his translation of the Pentateuch voluntarily. Later, as Chaplain to Archbishop Whitgift, he was encouraged to complete his translation of the Old Testament and to revise an earlier poor translation of the New Testament by William Salesbury. Although his translation was revised in 1620 by Richard Parry, Bishop of Saint Asaph, it is mainly the work of Morgan that was read, studied and preached from within Welsh-speaking churches and chapels until the middle of the twentieth century, and indeed it still survives in many places.

Today, it is hard to appreciate the importance of such a text. It ensured that the literary culture of Wales was preserved, and gave Welsh a significant text, analogous in importance to the King James Version for the development of English. In fact it can be seen to be more important, for it was only as a liturgical language that Welsh had any official recognition. Welsh may well have survived without it, but it would never have flourished in the way it has.

The Bible in Welsh (1588) translated by Bishop William Morgan

48

Right: George Augustus Selwyn, 1809–78, Bishop of New Zealand and Melanesia 1841–67. Selwyn College was founded in his memory

Below: Henry Martyn, 1781–1812. Influenced by Charles Simeon, he turned from legal studies to missionary work in India

EMINENT CLERGYMEN

In former days, many graduates of the College entered Holy Orders, and a number attained considerable eminence. William Morgan (see panel) translated the Bible into Welsh. John Williams (1601), Archbishop of York during the Civil War, funded the building of the Old Library. John Cradock (BA 1728) became Archbishop of Dublin. In the nineteenth century, George Selwyn (MA 1834), Bishop of New Zealand, greatly influenced the development of the colonial church. John Colenso (1833: Fellow 1837), achieved notoriety as Bishop of Natal through opposing, in his *Commentary on the Epistle to the Romans* (1861), the doctrine of eternal punishment; and through questioning the historical accuracy and traditional authorship of the Pentateuch. Formally deposed by the Bishop of Cape Town, he was confirmed in possession of his see following an appeal to the Privy Council. One verse from the hymn 'The Church's One Foundation' contains the line 'by schisms rent asunder, by heresies distressed'. This was written against Colenso and is traditionally not sung at St John's.

In recent times, Donald Coggan (BA 1931 – see panel) became Archbishop of York (1961–74) and of Canterbury (1974–80). Three College chaplains have become bishops – Edward Knapp-Fisher (Pretoria); Philip Goodrich (Worcester) and Keith Sutton (Lichfield). Stephen Sykes (1958), Dean of St John's 1964–74 and Regius Professor of Divinity 1985–90, was Bishop of Ely from 1990 to 1999. Peter Carnley, a PhD graduate and Honorary Fellow of the College, became Archbishop of Western Australia in 1981 and subsequently Primate of Australia.

Notable Johnian missionaries include Henry Martyn (Fellow 1802), who served in India and translated the New Testament into Hindustani and Persian; and David Watson (1954), Vicar of St Michael-le-Belfry, York, who attained a national reputation for evangelism before his early death.

49

THE RT REV. AND RT HON. LORD COGGAN (1909–2000)

Donald Coggan (1928), the College's first Archbishop of Canterbury, served in that position for six years from 1974 to 1980, having previously been Archbishop of York from 1961.

Archbishop Coggan

At St John's he read oriental languages, gaining a Double First in Hebrew and Aramaic. Ordained to a flagship evangelical parish – throughout his career he showed a strong evangelical conviction – he went on to teach at Wycliffe College Toronto from 1937, returning in 1944 to head the London College of Divinity for eleven years. He was appointed Bishop of Bradford in 1955.

With his knowledge of the languages of Scripture, he was a natural choice to be Chairman of the joint sponsoring committee of the New English Bible in 1970. At Canterbury he sought, unsuccessfully, to promote reunion with the Methodists, and won considerable public approval for attending Pope John Paul II's enthronement in 1978 – the first Archbishop of Canterbury to attend a papal enthronement since the Reformation. Having served as Chairman of the Liturgical Commission from 1960 to 1964, it was appropriate that at Canterbury he oversaw the introduction of the Alternative Service Book which gave coherence to many years of liturgical experimentation.

In retirement he was a frequent visitor to St John's, and indeed helped out for a period during the Dean of Chapel's leave of absence in 1983 by acting as temporary Assistant Chaplain. The Chapel list read:

Dean: The Rev. A A Macintosh (on leave)
Chaplain: The Rev. and Hon. P M Templeman
Asst Chaplain: The Rt Rev. and Rt Hon. the Lord Coggan

Amongst his many honours, Lord Coggan was elected Honorary Fellow of the College in 1961.

PATRONAGE

By long-standing practice, the College has the right to present clergy to around forty parishes, often connected to places and areas where it owns or owned land, such as Staplehurst and Higham in Kent. They are to be found from Heanton Punchardon with Marwood, Devon, to Holt in north Norfolk; and from Great with Little Ouseburn in north Yorkshire to Freshwater, Isle of Wight. Such 'patronage of livings' goes back to the very beginning of the College and to the monastic establishments preceding it which – concerned as they were with the training of clergy – were well placed to make church appointments.

In the seventeenth and eighteenth centuries, the College purchased a number of rights ('advowsons') to appoint clergy to livings. At that time, all Fellows were celibate and in Holy Orders, and obtaining a living through the good offices of the College could be a very material advantage for any Fellow wishing, through marriage or for any other reason, to leave the relative austerity of College life for a comfortable rectory. Vacancies in livings were apparently announced by the Butler at Dinner in Hall, and no doubt gave rise to animated discussion. Apart from easing an individual's way from a career of academic study to one of pastoral care, the system had the potential to disseminate a

*The Chapel seen
through the Forecourt
gates bearing the
Beaufort motto –*
Souvent me souvient

modicum of learning to parts of the country which may have had very little.

Of the forty livings to which the College retains the advowson, many are deeply rural and have had to merge with others, with a consequent attenuation in the College's influence. In the past, when it came to making appointments, the views of the College on the require-ments of a particular parish have not always coincided with those of the local bishop. One well-known letter from Dean J S Bezzant ran: 'Dear Bishop, The College is glad to know that whenever it desires your advice, it has only to ask for it.'

RELIGIOUS LIFE IN THE COLLEGE TODAY

Named after the disciple 'beloved' of Christ, the College has been nurtured and shaped by the Christian tradition over the last 500 years in the belief that scholarship and the formation of moral character within the life of a community go hand in hand. Open to all, regular worship in the form of choral evensong at 6.30 pm remains an important part of the daily rhythm of the College, and many students and members of the University attend with some regularity. A much larger number, including many who would not see themselves standing clearly within the Christian tradition, attend on occasion and draw great benefit from the opportunity it provides for quiet and reflection in the maelstrom of contemporary Cambridge life.

There are a number of celebrations and commemo-rations within Chapel that form significant moments for today's students. In particular, the majority of each year group attend the Matriculation and Graduation Services which help to mark their entry into College and their imminent departure into the world beyond. The Advent Carol Service at the end of the Michaelmas Term, broadcast by the BBC, prepares the community for the season of Christmas and indeed, due to its popularity, has to be repeated to allow for all those who wish to attend. In addition, the Chapel marks a number of high points in the year with well-attended services, including: Remembrance Sunday, when the choir usually sing either the Fauré or the Duruflé Requiem; Ash Wednesday on which it has been traditional for Allegri's *Miserere* to be sung; the Meditation on the Passion of Christ at the end of the Lent Term looking to the events of the last week in Christ's life; the service for the Commemoration of Benefactors in May; and Ascension Day, when following a communion service attended by the members of St John's College School, the Choir climb the stairs to sing from the top of the tower.

The services in Chapel are those of the Church of England, but Christians of all traditions and denomi-nations – Catholic, Protestant and Orthodox – are actively involved in its worshipping life, sharing bread and wine at one of the two communion services every Sunday during term: the simple, short service at 8.30 am followed by breakfast in Hall and the Sung Eucharist at 10.30 am. College members and others also benefit from a wide range of visiting preachers on Sunday evenings including in recent years both the current Archbishops of Canterbury and York. In addition, there are a number of more informal services including sung compline on Tuesday evenings as well as an annual Confirmation service that takes place each Easter term.

Since the nineteenth century, the Chapel has had an association with the Parish of St John's Walworth in South London, through a parish mission, the Lady Margaret Church. This link has been greatly strengthened over the last twenty years and each year in December the Chaplain takes a party of students down for the weekend to help the parish put on an annual children's party for the community and to join in with worship on the Sunday morning. Many of the friendships established through this association have continued long after individuals have ceased to be students at the College. Associated with the Chapel community is the Lady Margaret Pilgrimage Society, which arranges outings to places of spiritual and historic interest. In recent years this has taken junior members and others from the tomb of Lady Margaret herself in Westminster Abbey to the mosaics of Ravenna and the pilgrim road to Santiago de Compostela.

Chapel House Party at Wydale Hall, North Yorkshire, 2004 (courtesy of the Rev. Clive Hillman)

In addition to organizing regular discussion groups on a wide range of subjects, successive chaplains have, since the 1960s, taken a party of students away during the Easter break. For many years the destination was Rydal Hall in the Lake District for a week of reading, relaxing and walking. In more recent years the venue has varied, though many former students will recall painting, digging and building as part of one of the work parties at Kepplewray, an outdoor activity centre catering for the disabled, also in the Lake District.

Whilst the Chapel welcomes all, irrespective of their faith tradition or none, it also strives to support those who wish to practise their faith – there is of course a great deal of religious life beyond the Chapel. Many Christians choose to worship in the central churches of Cambridge, are involved with the Roman Catholic Chaplaincy at Fisher House or within a number of other student groups including CICCU, the Cambridge Inter-Collegiate Christian Union.

Whilst Christians continue to make up the largest faith constituency within the College, Johnian students also play a significant part in the University-wide faith-based societies, especially the Islamic Society, the Jewish Society and the Hindu Cultural Society. In addition to their regular meetings and activities, each seeks to bring opportunities for others to learn and share something of their tradition. In recent years, there has been a strongly supported 'Islamic Awareness Week' at the beginning of the Lent Term and an increasingly successful and unique variety show – *Mastana* – held at the Cambridge Arts Theatre hosted by the CU Hindu Cultural Society to celebrate the rich cultural heritage of the Indian subcontinent.

Both the Dean (Duncan Dormor) and Chaplain (Clive Hillman) are fully involved in the liturgical life of the Chapel. Apart from regular services they conduct weddings for current residential members and recent graduates, and memorial services for Fellows who have died. They also frequently travel in support of the Choir on tour. In addition to the duties (lecturing, supervising, directing studies) which the Dean shares with other Teaching Fellows, he is also a governor at the College School, Secretary to the Livings Committee and bears overall responsibility for all the activities of the Chapel and Choir. The Chaplain's primary duties include the pastoral care of College members and staff, but especially of the students. He makes himself available to all members of the College community whatever their faith tradition or none, who may wish to consult him about their personal problems and anxieties. He is therefore thoroughly involved in all aspects of College life, is the Senior Treasurer for a number of student societies and can be found on the river, in the bar and at parties!

THE CHOIR AND CHORAL TRADITION

The history of the College Choir is a remarkable story of singers and organists building on the foundations made by their predecessors as far back as the seventeenth century. Throughout this time, the musical aspect of the Chapel has been central to, and yet distinct from, the rest of College life. The interplay between Choir and College, and, more recently, the wider musical world, has resulted in a choir with an international reputation and the widely acclaimed 'St John's sound'.

It is possible that a choir existed to support the life of the College as far back as 1623, but the primary endowment from which the present Choir stems was the Gunning Benefaction, made in the 1670s. The then

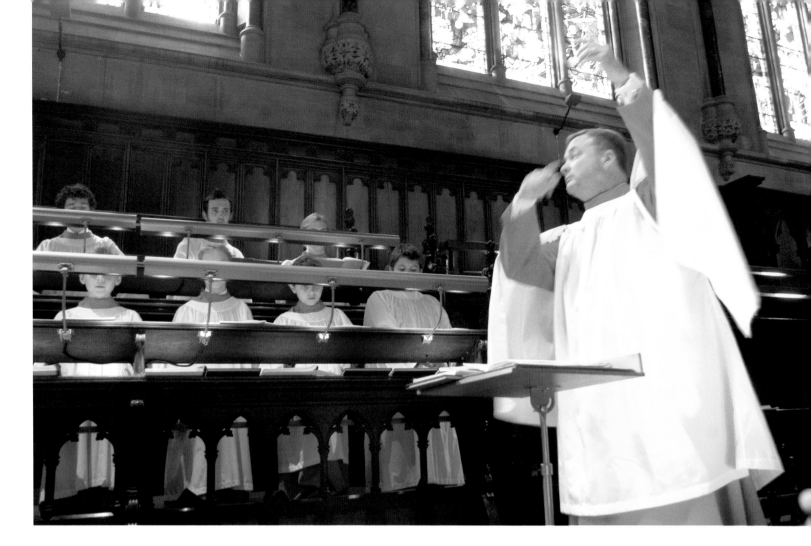

Bishop of Chichester, Dr Gunning, along with three others, provided the financial means for six choristers and their director to reside in Third Court. The choristers at that time were chosen by the Master and Senior Fellows.

Over the next century, other college choirs became established. At the turn of the nineteenth century, six lay clerks were employed to sing the lower voice parts in the services of all three main chapel choirs: St John's, Trinity and King's. The top line of the Choir at St John's was sung by the eight senior trebles of Trinity's choir: boys between the ages of nine and sixteen. In 1819 the choristers' education was entrusted to John Clarke Whitfield, Organist of both colleges 1798–1820 and University Professor of Music 1821–6.

On the arrival of Thomas Attwood Walmisley thirteen years later, the boys were receiving their education in a private school in Downing Terrace. The arrangement enabled them to sing at College services at 9.15 am on weekdays and 5 pm on Sundays. The Choir also sang on Sunday mornings for Easter, Whit- and Trinity Sundays. Walmisley, known for his 'great invention as a composer', provided an alternative to the usually monotone responses in the Cathedral service by

arranging the *Tallis Responses*. His notebooks make it clear that St John's Choir was treated as junior to Trinity and King's at this time, as they were never assigned *the* appropriate anthem (*There were shepherds*) on Christmas Day, although St John's did perform 'for HM The Queen Dowager' on Sunday 9 December 1843, when the Dean, unlike his contemporaries in the other two chapels, exhibited a little Johnian spirit in refusing to suspend the choral service!

St John's split from the other two choirs following Walmisley's death in 1856, although choristers from St John's and Trinity were educated together for another seventeen years. George Muswell Garrett established the newly independent Choir over a period of forty years, building on the foundations laid by Walmisley, whom he much admired. In 1888 the College instituted four choral scholarships, so enabling a fresher sound, more easily shaped by the Director of Music.

The development of the Choir in the twentieth century was presided over by five highly influential figures. In 1901 Cyril Bradley Rootham took on the task of providing music for six services a week. Shortly after arriving, he started the Choir tradition of singing from the top of the Chapel Tower at noon on Ascension

Day, in response to a debate at High Table with William Bateson and Joseph Larmor as to whether voices could be heard from that height. During the singing of Palestrina's *O Rex Gloriae*, Rootham observed the reaction of people below, and watched one important window: 'I particularly kept an eye on Larmor's windows, in his rooms in Second Court, and presently was rewarded by seeing his head come out, and look about to see whence the sound of voices came!'

It was also under Rootham that the Choir made its first recording, in 1927. It reveals a choir of high standard,

accompanied by strings and singing at a much slower tempo than that to which we are accustomed in the current era. The recording precedes all other known recordings of Cambridge choirs.

Robin Orr studied under Rootham, and succeeded him in 1938. Seen as cutting edge in his time, Orr's contribution to Anglican Church music has been undervalued in many respects, although his compositions in other fields have been more obviously appreciated. Later on he became Professor of Music in Cambridge (1965–76). During the war, Orr joined the RAF

55

Choirboys process from School to Chapel

Volunteer Reserve and, until Herbert Howells (see panel) stepped in, students maintained the Sunday services, with evensongs sung by a volunteer choir.

George Guest, in turn, was an organ student under Robin Orr, and took over when the latter decided to devote more time to composition in 1951. However, he also had a deep respect and a strong personal relationship with Boris Ord, who was at the height of his fame at King's College. Ord inspired the preoccupation with communicating the mood of the text in Guest's music-making, resulting in a choir which 'sings with its eyes'. In a presidential address to the Royal College of Organists, Guest stated: '…it is in the eyes of a conductor that a member of the choir finds inspiration … Boris Ord's eyes were magnets which drew members of his choir into a share of a quite unique musical experience.'

So it is that the 'St John's sound', with its free emotive quality, may have at its root the inspiration of a Kingsman.

Aided by the retirement of the last three lay clerks in 1948, the College increasing the number of Choral Scholars from six to twelve, and by fierce competition for chorister places, Guest changed the music of the choir for the better in a matter of a few years. However, the Schoolmaster Sam Senior retired in 1955, and the School, of at most two rooms, was no longer thought acceptable. Trinity had recently abolished their choristers' school, with a marked subsequent decline in their choir's standard, and the Fellowship at St John's were considering following their example. Guest gathered support for the Choir through correspondence in *The Times* and communication from various eminent musicians including Vaughan Williams, whose telegram from Rome instructed 'Save St John's Choir School at all costs'. The College Council finally voted in favour of maintaining the Choir, and a new school was established in 1955.

The College appointed Christopher Robinson from a highly prestigious job at Windsor to succeed Guest in 1991. He was able to continue the advances made by Guest, with regular BBC broadcasts, international tours

Left: Dr George Guest 1982

Below left: Christopher Robinson (courtesy of Martin Denny)

DR HERBERT HOWELLS CH CBE (1892–1983)

Born in Gloucestershire, Herbert Howells studied at Gloucester Cathedral in his teens before his self-taught skills in composition gained him a scholarship to study at the Royal College of Music in 1912. In 1916 he was diagnosed with Graves' disease and given a life expectancy of six months. Through treatment at St Thomas' Hospital London, he survived to marry Dorothy Dawe in 1920, with whom he had two children. Their son, Michael, died in 1935. Howells was coming to terms with the death when he wrote *Hymnus Paradisi*, possibly his greatest work.

With the arrival of the Second World War, students had to run the College music. Howells, then Director of Music at St Paul's Girls' School, came up to take Sunday services between 1941 and 1945. Apart from providing great support to the large College congregation, this renewed his interest in sacred music. His *Collegium Regale* (composed 1944–5), Gloucester (1946), St John's (1950) and St Paul's (1951) Evening Service settings are among the pieces which make him probably the most significant composer of twentieth-century Anglican rite. Howells was very much at ease at St John's, which elected him to an Honorary Fellowship in 1962; and it is a great tribute to the College that his daughter Ursula, the distinguished actress, left it his estate of rights of publication and royalties.

Dr Herbert Howells (© Clive Barda/Arenapal)

57

and acclaimed recordings. In 2003 he handed on a precious legacy of a choir with its unique sense of phrasing and natural musical expression to the current Director of Music, David Hill, formerly Organ Student at St John's and Organist at Westminster and Winchester Cathedrals.

The Choir still amazes freshers at their Matriculation Service and plays an important role in the daily life of the College. Its influence is now felt substantially in the wider community as well. Broadcasts have provided a platform for leading contemporary composers, including Tippett, Tavener, Bingham, Harvey, Rutter and Moore, while singers and Organ Scholars from St John's have moved on to reach the highest levels of their professions.

The achievement of the Choir under successive Directors of Music can be appreciated on the CD that accompanies this book.

6 THE LIBRARY AND ITS TREASURES

The College Library seeks above all to balance two important objectives – its commitment to the care of an exceptional collection, and the provision in a friendly and welcoming environment of up-to-date facilities. There is of course nothing new about the proper storage and provision of books at St John's. Bishop John Fisher's 1524 Statutes required that the College should 'posses and preserve a Library', and possession and preservation have marched in step ever since.

In the sixteenth century the Library was located in the wing immediately south of the Great Gate, on the first floor. By modern standards it housed a very small collection – some seventy books are noted in an inventory of 1558 – and for another sixty years or so nothing very much changed. But expectations grew and in a flurry of building work matched to acquisition it was transformed early in the seventeenth century into the largest and finest library in Cambridge. A splendid new building forming the northern flank of what became Third Court – today's Old Library – was financed substantially through the munificence of John Williams, Keeper of the Great Seal, Bishop of Lincoln and later Archbishop of York. Williams's monogram, I L C S (*Iohannes Lincolniensis Custos Sigilli*) can be seen on the western parapet to this day, together with '1624', the date at which the Library building was completed.

Thereafter, a series of major donations – ranging from the library of the Puritan divine William Crashaw to choice volumes from Charles I's Attorney-General, Robert Heath – rapidly filled the impressive dark oak bookcases made by Cambridge craftsmen. Crashaw's library, presented to the College via William Shakespeare's friend and patron the Earl of Southampton, is particularly

fine. In its heyday, the Library welcomed as visitors royalty, statesmen and distinguished guests from all over Europe, demonstrating through its collections the learning and scholarship of the wider university. Charles I, Charles II, Samuel Pepys and John Evelyn were among the many who walked down the great sweep of the Upper Library, 130ft from door to the oriel window overlooking the river – a walk unimpeded by the nineteenth-century cases and radiator covers which now run the length of the Library. And in those days there was no New Court (and, indeed, virtually no stained glass) to cut out the westering sun on a summer's evening. The scale of this monument to scholarship impressed the Stuart eye. Evelyn, who visited the Library in 1654, described it as the 'fairest in that university'.

A seventeenth-century shelflist in the Upper Library

The Upper Library, with Paul Dirac's Nobel Prize certificate

THE UPPER LIBRARY

Its collections remain of great significance. Indeed, the Old Library has become the first Cambridge college library to achieve designation by the Museums Libraries and Archives Council as 'of national and international importance'. There, using the most up-to-date facilities, readers may examine a wide range of books, manuscripts and other objects. The College holds 340 incunabula – works printed before 1500 – and of the 33,000 books in the Upper Library, the vast majority date from before the nineteenth century. The earliest printed book in the Library dates back to the very dawn of printing with movable type – a 1466 edition from Mainz of Cicero's *De officiis*. The earliest book from an English printer – William Caxton – is a 1481 translation of Cicero's *De senectute*. Indeed the Library holds two copies of this work. One of them, formerly owned by the Johnian Parliamentary general Sir Thomas Fairfax, comes from a rich collection of incunabula bequeathed to the College by an eighteenth-century Master, John Newcome, which also includes a copy of the 1474 edition of Ovid's works formerly owned by Lorenzo de Medici. Many volumes on the shelves of the Upper Library have an interesting provenance. Former owners include the Elizabethan magus Dr John Dee, and Queen Elizabeth I's Secretary and Treasurer Lord Burghley – both Johnians; Sir Walter Ralegh; and a notorious alumnus, Titus Oates (see Chapter 11). John Collins, Regius Professor of Physic, left a fine collection of sixteenth-century medical works at his death in 1634. The poet and diplomat Matthew Prior bequeathed around three hundred works, mainly relating to French history and literature, while Charles Otway, a Fellow of the College who died in 1721, accumulated several thousand English sermons, political pamphlets and tracts published during his lifetime. In 1806 the surgeon Thomas Gisborne bequeathed almost two thousand of his non-medical books.

The College holds several first editions of seminal scholarly works, not least Newton's *Principia* and Charles Darwin's *Origin of Species*, the latter annotated critically by the College polymath Samuel Butler. The Library also possesses a fine first edition of Johnian William Gilbert's *De magnete* of 1600, the first major scientific work produced in England and the book that introduced the word 'electricity' into the English language.

60

*The oriel window of the
Old Library, seen from
the Cam*

THE LOWER LIBRARY

Used until the nineteenth century for storage and accommodation, the Lower Library holds many treasures of its own. Among more than 270 medieval manuscripts in the collection are a tenth-century psalter from an unidentified Irish monastery; a thirteenth-century psalter with a magnificent series of forty-six full-page illuminations telling the Bible story from the Creation of the World to the Ascension of the Virgin Mary; a particularly early version of Chaucer's *Troilus and Creseide*; and Lady Margaret Beaufort's exquisite Book of Hours complete with an inscription in her own hand on the same opening as an illuminated depiction of St John and his Eagle.

Later manuscripts include the earliest version of Sir Philip Sidney's *Arcadia*; the autograph manuscript of Thomas Sackville's *Complaint of Henry Duke of Buckingham*; papers relating to the execution of Mary Queen of Scots; secret correspondence touching on the Restoration of Charles II; the travel journals of Edward

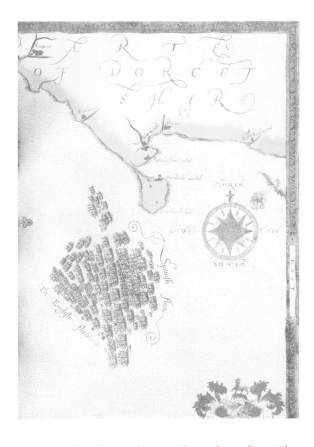

Henry Palmer in the nineteenth-century Levant; and several notebooks compiled by Victor Hugo, presented by the widow of a former Fellow, Professor Barrère.

The College is also fortunate to possess distinguished collections of personal papers. These are especially strong in the sciences – including papers of John Couch Adams, the Johnian co-discoverer of the planet Neptune; the eminent geophysicist Sir Harold Jeffreys – a Fellow for more than seventy years; the computer pioneer and Bletchley Park codebreaker Max Newman; and astronomer Sir Fred Hoyle (see panel in Chapter 8) who coined the term 'Big Bang'. In non-scientific fields, the Library holds the papers of novelist and artist Samuel Butler, the diaries of archaeologist Glyn Daniel, and the correspondence of Sir Cecil Beaton (see panels on each). The papers of the author Lyn Newman (née Lyn Lloyd Irvine) include extensive correspondence from the 1920s and 1930s with members of the Bloomsbury Group and others, including Clive Bell, Leonard Woolf, E M Forster, Julian Huxley and Bertrand Russell. Philanthropy at the turn of the eighteenth century is represented by important papers of the Johnian anti-slavery campaigners Thomas Clarkson and William Wilberforce. Also in the Collection are letters from Johnian politicians of different eras, including William Cecil and Viscount Castlereagh, and papers relating to Lord Palmerston.

Many fascinating items relate to Johnians with a more modest place in history. The undergraduate Alan Hiller served and died on the Western Front in the First World War and his letters provide a poignant insight into life in the trenches. John Colenso was Bishop of Natal from 1853 to 1883. In addition to his involvement in religious controversy (see Chapter 5), he devoted much of his time to the education of the Zulus, gave his support to the native Africans and opposed the British invasion of Zululand. His papers are rich in details of colonial life and administration. Stephen Nottcutt, who became an Ipswich solicitor, provides a glimpse of events at St John's in the 1880s through a fine sequence of undergraduate letters to his mother. The correspondence of Ernest Benians (Master 1935–52) also describes his years as a student in the College, while the diaries of T R Glover, Fellow, and for many years University Orator, shed light on personalities and College politics in the first four decades of the twentieth century. The early Victorian travel anecdotes of the antiquary John Carrighan, who journeyed through Europe to Constantinople; the English Surrealist poetry of Hugh Sykes Davies; Glyn Daniel's behind-the-scenes view of the popular 1950s TV show *Animal Vegetable Mineral*; and the eye-witness account by Henry Cantrell of Bonnie Prince Charlie's arrival at Derby in 1745 – a dramatic turning point in the history of both England and Scotland – all demonstrate the richness and diversity of papers held in the Library.

SIR CECIL BEATON CBE (1904–80)

After an undistinguished undergraduate career as a historian – by his own admission he spent a great deal of time socializing, acting in the ADC and Marlowe Society, and designing sets and costumes – Cecil Beaton made good use of great talent and a flair for self-publicity to establish himself as one of the finest society photographers of the twentieth century. In the course of a long and illustrious career he also won two Oscars for his costume design and art direction in the spectacular musicals *Gigi* and *My Fair Lady*. His candid diaries and extensive correspondence were presented to the College by his executors. Enjoying the patronage of royalty, nobility, actors, scholars, writers and film stars, Beaton moved in a world of duty and achievement, gossip and intrigue. A list of his correspondents reads like a roll-call for British and American high society in the mid-twentieth century, with letters from Sir Isaiah Berlin, Sir John Betjeman, Truman Capote, Sir Noel Coward, Marlene Dietrich, Dame Margot Fonteyn, Sir John Gielgud, Audrey Hepburn, Christopher Isherwood, Somerset Maugham, Nancy Mitford, Marilyn Monroe, Siegfied Sassoon, Dame Edith Sitwell, Sir Stephen Spender and Sir Peter Ustinov, among many others.

Beaton successfully developed his work to suit the temper of the times. He was fascinated by what has been called the 'Peacock Revolution', taking iconic photographs of the Rolling Stones, Twiggy and Jean Shrimpton. His appetite for novelty hardly slowed in old age. His biographer Hugo Vickers records that just before his death Beaton photographed 'Little Bo Bitch', a minor figure in the emerging punk rock scene.

Sir Cecil Beaton in his Bridge Street rooms in 1922 (courtesy of Sotheby's)

ARTEFACTS AND CURIOSITIES

Any ancient college library is also something of a museum, a home for objects and items associated with members of College down the centuries. Among these unexpected but evocative artefacts is the extensive photographic archive of everyday life at St John's from the 1870s onwards; the well-equipped *materia medica* cabinet of William Heberden, 'father of rheumatology' (complete with a mummified lizard and a desiccated mushroom two centuries old and half a metre across); the physicist Paul Dirac's Nobel Prize medal and citation; a Tudor comb; a 'lead skull'; Johnian rugger blazers from the nineteenth century; Sir Fred Hoyle's first telescope; and a life mask of William Wordsworth taken in 1815 by the artist Benjamin Haydon. Extensive collections of Greek and Roman coins are currently held on loan by the Fitzwilliam Museum while historic astronomical instruments from the College's former Observatory (see Chapter 8: Astronomy and Astronomers) are on loan to the Whipple Museum. One gem from the old Observatory does remain in the Library – a magnificent eighteenth-century long-case chronometer made by John Shelton.

Life mask of Wordsworth taken by Benjamin Haydon 1815

There is much to be seen in the Library's Exhibition Area where, over the past decade, displays have been mounted on subjects as diverse as College rooms; St John's in wartime; and College malefactors. Details can be found on the comprehensive Library website.

THE WORKING LIBRARY

Johnians of a certain vintage will remember working in the current Lower Library. The new Working Library, opened in 1994 and accessed through a large swinging door in Chapel Court, offers a very different experience. Welcoming and – despite its size – intimate, it provides flexible and accessible space, spread over six floors, with wings and corridors devoted to key works in every Tripos subject now taught in the University. It offers members of the College twenty-four-hour access to a collection of more than 100,000 textbooks, reference works and journals, all housed in an agreeable working

63

Right: The new College Library seen from Chapel Court

Below: The reception area of the Working Library

64

environment. Virtually every desk either has PC facilities or offers laptop connectivity to the internet, allowing access to a vast range of electronic journals, e-books and other online resources. Comfortable chairs, designated quiet areas, a popular Seminar Room, foreign-language newspapers, a fine audio-visual collection and some of the best library views in Cambridge, all enhance the learning experience. We may live and work in an electronic age, and the e-journal and the e-book are ever more apparent, but the use and borrowing of actual books shows no sign of slowing.

In a happy continuation of a long tradition, at least five hundred books are received as donations every year, the vast majority from members of College. Works specifically by Johnian authors demonstrate an impressive variety of scholarly and professional careers and experience.

Finally, a word on those on the other side of the counter – the Fellows and staff who have worked in the Library. Until the nineteenth century the ancient office of Librarian was held by a rapidly changing succession of, for the most part, quite junior Fellows. But from the 1880s onwards the Librarianship has been held by Fellows with a strong commitment to the development of the Collection. Some, like Hugh Gatty in the 1930s and 1940s, donated important collections of books and papers. And some – notably the medieval historian C W Previté-Orton and the classical scholar Guy Lee – held the office for upwards of twenty years. But it is the Sub-Librarians who hold the record for longevity in office. Charles Scott joined the staff in 1903, and retired in 1956. His successor, Norman Buck, appointed 'Library Boy' in 1929, also served on the staff for a further fifty-three years.

THE COLLEGE ARCHIVES

The College Archives contain the records of the growth and administration of St John's since its foundation in 1511. There is also a rich medieval archive of deeds and account rolls inherited from the Hospital of St John which preceded the College on the same site, and from other small and decayed religious houses whose properties formed a great part of its initial endowment. The Archives hold the Foundation Charter granted by the eight executors of Lady Margaret Beaufort on 9 April 1511, and still bearing their seals and signatures,

Left: Students at work in the Working Library

Below: The initial of the licence in mortmain granted to the College in 1526, showing St John the Evangelist, with chalice and serpent issuing from it

The seals of the executors of Lady Margaret Beaufort at the foot of the Foundation Charter, 9 April 1511

which brought to fruition their negotiations with the Bishop of Ely and the Crown in order to fulfil her will by transforming the Hospital into a college.

Over five centuries, the business of the College has produced a wealth of formal and less formal evidence of its life and functions: statutes, registers of membership, orders and minutes of its organs of government, accounts, records of its buildings, benefactions and the administration of property. Some of these records have a fascination far removed from the dryness of their titles. The annual accounts can throw a surprising amount of light on little-known details, such as the money paid by wealthier sixteenth-century undergraduates for using the College tennis court. The admissions registers, commenced systematically in 1630, record in most cases the places of origin, age, parentage and schooling of those entering the College, providing valuable information on social make-up and local connections. The history of the College's estates can be illustrated from many sources including some finely drawn and coloured maps. The estate papers of a hundred and more years ago throw light on such topics as the development of farm buildings, land use, and topographical subjects such as the planning of residential west Cambridge.

St John's is also fortunate to possess more personal records: eighteenth- and nineteenth-century 'examination books' record the order of merit in College internal exams, and the notebooks and correspondence left by individual tutors since the late nineteenth century highlight academic progress. Social life is reflected in the records of clubs and societies in the nineteenth and twentieth centuries, including those of the Lady Margaret Boat Club. The organization behind the renowned choral tradition of the College can be seen in the Choir Books 1856–1955, and letters of commendation for those leaving the Choir 1870–1920. There are also a few 'unofficial' records which fitfully illuminate former social conditions: a Johnian recently donated some kitchen and JCR suggestions books from which one can pinpoint the moment in 1941 when the cleaning of shoes in time for 9 am lectures was suspended owing to shortage of staff!

For centuries the College kept its Archives in chests and presses in the higher of the two chambers – the Old Treasury – above the Great Gate. In 1888 a new fireproof strong-room was constructed. In 1968 this was replaced by a muniment room which has subsequently been extended and equipped with dehumidification, fire-warning and fire-extinguishing systems.

COLLEGE PLATE

Recently described by an eminent goldsmith as 'containing some outstandingly beautiful and unique items', the College Plate collection comprises nearly two thousand individual pieces, ranging in size from candelabra to salt spoons. Candlesticks and cutlery are used in the Combination Room on a daily basis. Other items are brought into service for great College occasions. The oldest item in the collection is a Seal Top spoon, registered at the London Assay Office in 1551. The following are amongst other items of note:

The 25in. tall silver-gilt Booth Cup, marked London 1616–17, engraved with an elaborate design of scrolls, with monsters' heads, straps and jewels, and medallions of Jupiter, Diana and Venus embossed beneath them. Very frail, it is rarely brought out from the silver vault.

The silver-gilt Rosewater Dish and Ewer, of German origin, donated by Edward Villiers in 1671.

The 22in. tall silver-gilt Burghley Cup, marked London 1683–84, engraved with Chinese subjects, and donated by the fourth Earl of Salisbury, who succeeded to the earldom while he was a Fellow Commoner at the College. It is regularly displayed in the Combination Room.

The Brownlowe Sacramental Plate, marked London 1728–29, consisting of four chalices, two flagons and an alms basin, and regularly used in the Chapel during the celebration of the Eucharist.

The Horton-Smith Hartley Cup, 23in. tall including the wooden plinth, marked London 1936–37 and made by Omar Ramsden, the gift of a former Fellow who was a physician at St Bartholomew's Hospital, London. It has a silver-gilt description and a finial consisting of an eagle with its wings raised, standing on a globe surrounded by foliated cresting.

The collection also contains items by notable silversmiths such as Paul de Lamerie, Thomas Chawner, Gabriel Sleath and William Cafe.

Whilst most of the collection has been donated to the College, specific items have in recent years been

The Larmor Award: silver-gilt goblets by Michael Brophy 1984

Standing on the Combination Room table are the silver-gilt Burghley, Booth and Hartley Cups, with the silver-gilt Rosewater Dish, and a silver sconce on the panelled wall behind

specially commissioned to meet the daily needs of the Fellowship. To commemorate the appointment of the Rev. J S Boys Smith as Vice-Chancellor of the University in 1963–5, the College commissioned silver coffeepots from Gerald Benney. Similarly, the Vice-Chancellorship of Sir Harry Hinsley in 1981–3 was commemorated with the commissioning of a set of four silver water jugs from Frances Loyen.

The College also regularly commissions silver from recently qualified silversmiths to be presented as Larmor Awards (see Chapter 21). Recent silversmiths have included Howard Fenn, Rebecca de Quin, Adrian Hope and Clive Burr.

7 St John's and slavery

Two eminent Johnians – William Wilberforce and Thomas Clarkson – played leading roles in the British campaign to abolish first the slave trade, and then the actual institution of slavery in the British colonies. A third Johnian, Lord Chief Justice Denman, was an ardent opponent of slavery.

Wilberforce and Clarkson could not have been more dissimilar. Elfin-like, Wilberforce was sociable, quick-witted, and a staunch conservative. Tall and bluff, Clarkson had little small talk and the politics of a Whiggish liberal. What united them was an unshakeable belief in the moral repugnancy of slavery.

Wilberforce was not known for his studiousness at St John's where, however, he met fellow-Johnians Thomas Gisborne and Thomas Babington whose friendship and support were subsequently of value to him in the abolitionist campaign. Clarkson, on the other hand, was a diligent, disciplined student. In 1785 he won the Latin essay prize for senior bachelors. Its subject, 'Is it lawful to make slaves of others against their will?', had been set by Vice-Chancellor Peter Peckard, Master of Magdalene, who had himself denounced the slave trade in a University sermon the previous year. It affected Clarkson deeply. In 1787 he co-founded The Committee to Abolish the Slave Trade, becoming its chief organizer and researcher – 'a moral steam engine' Coleridge called him – and mobilizing public support throughout the country.

The campaign needed a political figurehead and Wilberforce, a popular, independent MP friendly with Prime Minister Pitt, was ideal – an evangelical, he was keen to embrace a moral cause. In 1787 Clarkson helped convince Wilberforce to make abolition his personal campaign.

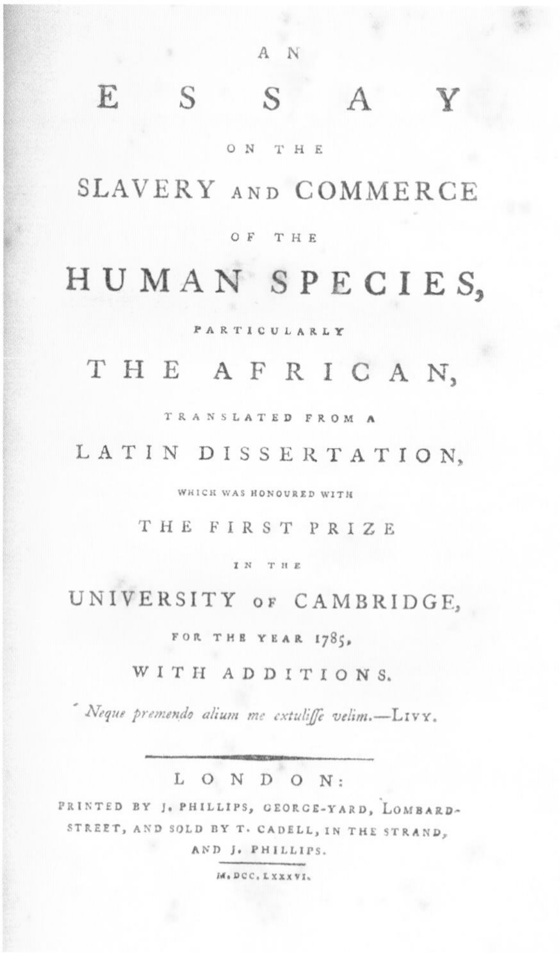

AN

ESSAY

ON THE

SLAVERY AND COMMERCE

OF THE

HUMAN SPECIES,

PARTICULARLY

THE AFRICAN,

TRANSLATED FROM A

LATIN DISSERTATION,

WHICH WAS HONOURED WITH

THE FIRST PRIZE

IN THE

UNIVERSITY OF CAMBRIDGE,

FOR THE YEAR 1785,

WITH ADDITIONS.

" Neque premendo alium me extulisse velim.—LIVY.

LONDON:

PRINTED BY J. PHILLIPS, GEORGE-YARD, LOMBARD-STREET, AND SOLD BY T. CADELL, IN THE STRAND, AND J. PHILLIPS.

M.DCC.LXXXVI.

Title-page to Clarkson's prize essay against slavery 1786

  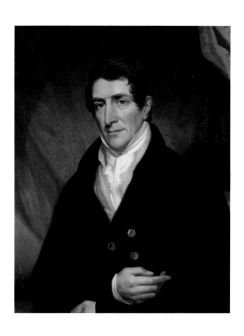

Left to right:

Portrait of William Wilberforce, 1759–1833, in the College Hall

Portrait of Thomas Clarkson, 1760–1846, purchased by the College from his widow

Portrait of Lord Chief Justice Thomas Denman, 1779–1854, by John James Halls (© National Portrait Gallery)

While there was wide public support for Wilberforce's efforts in Parliament, the spectre of revolution, and war with France, brought delay. Finally in 1807 an Act of Parliament abolished the British slave trade. Wordsworth celebrated this in a sonnet addressed to Clarkson, who had become a personal friend. Clarkson and Wilberforce's role in the movement gradually receded, but they both lived to see the success of the Abolition of Slavery legislation in 1833 – Wilberforce died within days of the third Commons reading of the Bill.

In 1832 the great American abolitionist William Lloyd Garrison helped organize the New England Anti-Slavery Society, and published the first issue of his anti-slavery newspaper *The Liberator*. With the passage of the British Reform Bill, he embarked for England to give a series of lectures largely devoted to indicting the American Colonization Society which, by promoting the settlement of free slaves in Africa, hoped to reduce their numbers in the States and thus help preserve the institution of slavery. He sought and obtained the blessing of the dying Wilberforce for his mission, walked in his funeral procession, and returned to the States armed with a letter condemning the Colonization Society signed by England's most prominent abolitionists, including Wilberforce – of whom Garrison saw himself as the chief American heir. In 1846, Garrison took the negro abolitionist Frederick Douglass to meet Clarkson shortly before the latter's death.

As Attorney-General in Lord Grey's administration,

Thomas Denman drafted much of the Reform Bill and defended its schedules in parliamentary debate. But for him, abolition of slavery was the most important of all reforms. His first major speech in the House of Lords in 1839 was in support of a Bill for the Better Suppression of the Slave Trade. By then, he had a personal as well as a moral interest. His son Joseph, Captain of a Royal Navy cruiser tasked with intercepting slavers off the coast of West Africa, had freed slaves and been sued, ultimately unsuccessfully, by the slave owner. Denman, who regarded slavery as 'the foulest stain that ever rested on the character of the country', published a number of abolitionist pamphlets and in 1848 successfully opposed a proposal to withdraw a naval squadron from interception duties off Africa.

At St John's, the Wilberforce Room boasts a fine mahogany table, the gift of Professor John Hope Franklin to mark his Fellowship of the College in 1962–3 – the first African American to hold Cambridge's Pitt Professorship of American History and Institutions. Cambridge has named roads after both Wilberforce and Clarkson. The bicentenary, in 2007, of the abolition of the British slave trade, sees an issue of commemorative stamps by the Royal Mail, with other national celebrations to mark this major historical event. The College is holding its own celebrations, together with Pocklington School, long associated with St John's, where Wilberforce was a pupil before entering the College in 1776.

8 SCIENCE AND DISCOVERY

The strength of the College in a wide range of scientific disciplines is amply demonstrated by the following record of achievement in astronomy, biological sciences and chemistry, earth sciences and exploration, electronics and computing, mathematics, and physics. The chapter concludes with portraits of Johnian Nobel Laureates.

Interestingly, whilst the natural sciences had been studied for centuries, it was not until 1851 that the Natural Sciences Tripos was introduced, as part of the growing Victorian appreciation of science and technology. Even then it was confined to BAs who had already distinguished themselves in mathematics and classics, hitherto the foundation of Cambridge learning. When, ten years later, it was opened to students reading for the BA itself, it rapidly overtook the Mathematical Tripos in size, not least owing to the growth of the Medical School from 1870. It took until 1966 for Medicine (see Chapter 14) to achieve its own Tripos.

Windows in the Palmerston Room, engraved in 1988 by David Peace and Sally Scott, celebrate the achievements of great Johnian scientists

*Right: Sir John Herschel
FRS 1792–1871 by Julia
Cameron (© Julia
Margaret Cameron
Trust)*

*Far right: The former
Observatory on the
Shrewsbury Tower
c.1860*

*Below right: John Couch
Adams FRS 1819–92*

ASTRONOMY AND ASTRONOMERS

For evidence of the strength of the College's
astronomical tradition one has only to look at Johnian
Presidents and Gold Medal recipients of the Royal
Astronomical Society (RAS) – Sir John Herschel, John
Couch Adams, Charles Pritchard, Sir Harold Jeffreys,
Raymond Lyttleton, Roderick Redman, Sir Fred Hoyle
and Kenneth Budden.

In fact, Johnian astronomy precedes both the
Astronomical Society (1820) and the University
Observatory (1823). An observatory was built on the
top of the Shrewsbury Tower in 1765, a site from which
the transit of Venus had been observed in 1761 – the first
for which a prediction had been widely known. Its
instruments included a transit and a quadrant for
determining star positions, a three and three-quarter
inch refracting telescope, and an astronomical clock by
Shelton, now in the College Library. Following
construction of the University Observatory its use
declined; the building fell into disrepair and was
demolished in 1859.

SIR FRED HOYLE FRS (1915–2001)

Fred Hoyle (1933: Fellow 1939–72; Hon. Fellow 1972) won the Mathematical Tripos Part III Mayhew Prize. Following a period of research under Paul Dirac (see below), he was elected Fellow for a thesis on quantum electrodynamics. During the war he worked for the Admiralty on radar and other projects. By 1946 he had formulated the concept that elements are formed in evolving stars and injected into space via supernova explosions. In parallel with Hermann (later Sir Hermann) Bondi and Tommy Gold (whom he had met during his Admiralty work), he developed the so-called 'steady state' theory of continuous creation, as against the 'Big Bang' theory (which he himself named). In the 1950s he gave a series of radio talks entitled *The Nature of the Universe*, subsequently published, which established his name firmly in the public mind as a major British scientific figure.

In 1958 he was appointed Plumian Professor of Astronomy and Experimental Philosophy in succession to Sir Harold Jeffreys, and it was from this position that he persuaded the University to establish in 1967 the Institute of Theoretical Astronomy of which he became the first Director. He resigned from both positions in 1972 when he felt unable to continue working at Cambridge. Hoyle was never afraid to advance controversial theories. He was critical of Darwinian evolution, which he claimed violated laws of probability. He disagreed with the 'primeval soup' theory of the evolution of life

on earth, arguing instead for a version of 'panspermia'. In his own field, individually and in collaboration with others, he produced seminal papers including work on the synthesis in stars of all nuclei from carbon upwards, and on the evolution through nuclear processing of low-mass stars into 'red giants'. He published prolifically, not only on astrophysics. He wrote, or had a hand in, a number of novels and children's stories, a play, an opera libretto, and space serials for television.

Sir Fred Hoyle FRS 1915–2001 (© Michael Ward, 1995)

Herschel graduated as Senior Wrangler in 1813, having been elected FRS while still an undergraduate. Elected Fellow of the College in 1816 he resolved to turn his attentions to astronomy, undertaking to complete projects begun by his father, Sir William Herschel. Recognizing that this required observations of the southern sky, he visited South Africa where, from 1832 to 1837, he made many important discoveries. His Johnian contemporary Fearon Fallows had earlier obtained appointment as HM Astronomer at the Cape of Good Hope, accomplishing in 1827 the Admiralty's plan to establish an observatory to complement the Royal Observatories at Greenwich and Edinburgh.

John Couch Adams graduated as Senior Wrangler, and was elected Fellow, in 1843. He formed and executed the intention of determining, from the observed irregularities of the motion of Uranus, the position in the sky of an unknown planet, but through the apparent dilatoriness of Airy (the Astronomer

Royal) and Challis (the Cambridge Professor of Astronomy) the discovery of the planet (Neptune) in 1846 was actually made from the analogous predictions of Le Verrier. Adams's life was filled with major mathematical achievements, both before and after his appointment as Director of the University Observatory in 1861.

Charles Pritchard graduated Fourth Wrangler in 1830, was elected Fellow in 1832, and later, as headmaster of Clapham Grammar School – where he took an increasing interest in astronomy – joined the RAS in 1849, becoming its President in 1866. In 1869 he was appointed Savilian Professor of Astronomy at Oxford, where he established the Oxford University Observatory. Awarded the Gold Medal of the RAS for work on stellar photometry and the Royal Medal of the Royal Society for work on stellar parallaxes, he was made an Honorary Fellow of St John's in 1886.

Sir Harold Jeffreys (see *Earth Sciences and exploration*

below) and Sir Fred Hoyle (see panel) feature elsewhere. Much of the scientific work of Hoyle's great friend Ray Lyttleton (Fellow 1937–95) was related to fluid dynamics. Lyttleton had a lifetime interest in comets – and cricket (how the fast bowler achieves swing in the flight of the ball being a topic of long, close scrutiny).

Roderick Redman (1923: Fellow 1931–75) became a research student under the supervision of Arthur Eddington at the University Observatory. After a period at the Dominion Astrophysical Observatory in Victoria, B.C., he returned to Cambridge as Assistant Director of the Solar Physics Observatory when he was still only twenty-six. Later, he became Professor of Astrophysics and Director of the Observatories, an entity formed by the amalgamation of the government-owned Solar Physics Observatory with the University Observatory. Redman's first task was to re-equip the Observatory with modern instrumentation – no easy task in the financial and industrial climate of the immediate post-war period, but one that he had achieved by 1955.

The most recent Johnian to be honoured by the RAS was Kenneth Budden (1933: Fellow 1947–2005), for many years College Director of Studies in Physics and University Reader in Physics. With a First in Physics, he went on to conduct ionospheric research at the Cavendish Laboratory. His abiding interest was in radio waves of very low frequency, a subject over which he obtained complete mastery. While deftly handling complex equations he had the great gift of explaining lucidly to others exactly what they meant in physical terms.

Astronomy is continued in the College today by Professor Roger Griffin (1954: Fellow 1962–65 and 1972–), whose pioneering cross-correlation technique to determine stellar radial velocities is used to study binary and multiple stars and their orbits. In the field of astrophysics, Professor Steve Gull (1968: Fellow 1976–79 and 1981–) has developed important imaging techniques, using Bayesian methods to factor out 'noise' from images of the night sky. These techniques have also proved useful in more down-to-earth applications such as reconstructing fuzzy police images of car number plates.

BIOLOGICAL SCIENCES AND CHEMISTRY

From their inception St John's has played a distinguished part in the story of the biological sciences and chemistry in Cambridge.

Amongst the best-known holders of the Professorship of Botany, created in 1724, was the Johnian J S Henslow (1796–1861), who had an inspirational influence on the young Charles Darwin and obtained a place for him as naturalist on HMS *Beagle*. Henslow also established the University Botanic Garden on its present site. Another outstanding Johnian was Frederick Blackman (1887: Fellow 1895–1947) who, as Reader in Botany, helped father the new area of plant physiology. He was succeeded in the Readership by another Johnian, George Briggs (1912: Fellow 1920–85), later Professor of Botany. Briggs collaborated with Haldane in 1925 to derive one of the classic equations of enzyme kinetics and went on to analyse the dark and light reactions of photosynthesis, the mechanism of salt accumulation in plant cells, and the movement of water. Woe betide anyone who thought him a horticulturist rather than a plant physiologist! One of his most distinguished Johnian pupils was the Australian Sir Rutherford Robertson (1936) who became Director of the Research School of Biological Sciences at the Australian National University and President of the Australian Academy of Science. Another was Dr Clifford Evans (1930: Fellow 1938–2006), Emeritus Reader in Experimental Ecology, whose many outstanding services to the College besides teaching included oversight of its ancient buildings. And mention must be made of another Johnian Professor of Botany, Charles 'Beetles' Babington (BA 1830: Fellow 1882–95), who had studied under Henslow and became a noted entomologist. His *Manual of British Botany*, first published in 1843, reached a tenth edition in 1922.

William Bateson (1879: Fellow 1882–1926), son of

73

ERASMUS DARWIN 1731–1802

Erasmus Darwin was corpulent, ungainly, and had a crooked stoop and a bad stammer. He was also attractive to women and one of the most remarkable men of his age. Admitted to St John's in 1750 in the footsteps of his father, he followed the traditional course of classics and mathematics and showed early promise as a poet. After three years he left for Edinburgh to study medicine, and by 1756 had established a successful practice in Lichfield. He was highly regarded and innovative in his treatments, and George III would have appointed him royal physician, but he declined.

Outside medicine, his fertile mind took him into a remarkably wide range of fields: physics, chemistry, geology, meteorology, agriculture and mechanical invention. His inventions included a copying machine, an artesian well, and a steering mechanism used in modern cars. He researched the formation of clouds. He published works on female education and supported the campaign against the slave trade. In the 1770s he helped to found the Birmingham Lunar Society which numbered Boulton, Priestley, Watt and Wedgwood among its members.

His volumes of verse enjoyed great popularity in their day and were much admired by his fellow Johnian William Wordsworth. The *Botanic Garden* of 1791 contained voluminous footnotes with many original observations on scientific and social matters. His major work on medicine and natural science, *Zoonomia, or the Laws of Organic Life* was published between 1794 and 1796. In rhyming couplets, this gave the first consistent, all-embracing hypothesis of evolution and greatly influenced his grandson Charles, whose first draft of the *Origin of Species* bore the same title. Erasmus Darwin's views brought him dangerously close to conflict with the Establishment, anxious about what it saw as anything seditious at the time of the French Revolution. In his final work, *The Temple of*

Nature (1803), he visualized life developing from primitive forms in the sea, moving to land, and evolving into human form:

> Organic Life beneath the shoreless waves
> Was born and nurs'd in Ocean's pearly caves;
> First forms minute, unseen by spheric glass,
> Move on the mud, or pierce the watery mass…

Portrait of Erasmus Darwin, 1731–1802, by Joseph Wright of Derby, in the College Hall

the Rev. W H Bateson, a reforming Master of the College, may be regarded as the founder of the science of genetics (it was he who coined the name in a letter to Adam Sedgwick in 1905). A dedicated Darwinist, he clashed with the prevailing school of biometricians who objected to his advocacy of discontinuous variation, rediscovered and championed the much earlier work of Gregor Mendel on transmission of heritable traits in plants and animals and revealed the existence of genetic linkage. The first British Professorship of Genetics was specially created for him in 1908 at Cambridge.

Almost fifty years later, Johnian W D (Bill) Hamilton (1957) read Part II (genetics) in the Natural Sciences Tripos, and fell under the spell of the great mathematical geneticist, Sir Ronald Fisher, the Professor of Genetics. Hamilton has been described by Richard Dawkins as 'a good candidate for the title of the most distinguished Darwinian since Darwin'. His work as a graduate student at University College London and the London School of Economics is perhaps his most famous: 'Hamilton's Rule' of inclusive fitness deals with the way in which genes for altruistic self-sacrifice will spread through a population, incorporating social behaviour into Darwinian theory. His later work was centred on parasites and their role in sexual selection (females looking for parasite-free males). He became a Royal Society Research Professor at Oxford, won a host of awards, including the Crafoord Prize of the Swedish Academy (equivalent to a Nobel Prize), and died, tragically, in 2000, of malaria contracted in Africa while searching for evidence that the AIDS virus originated in an oral polio vaccine.

Within living memory, the College has furnished two distinguished holders of the former Drapers Chair

The Chemistry Laboratory constructed at the rear of the College in 1853 for the use of George Liveing FRS 1827–1924

of Agriculture, Sir Frank Engledow (1910: Fellow 1919–85) and Sir Joseph Hutchinson (1920: Fellow 1957–88). Engledow was influenced by Udny Yule (see *Mathematics* below) in developing the quantitative statistical approach to biological data which was to characterize much of his future research. During the Second World War he rendered conspicuous service in advising on the nation's food supply. Thereafter he was much involved in the agricultural problems of developing countries. Before returning to Cambridge, Hutchinson did invaluable work as a geneticist with cotton growing research stations in both the West Indies

75

Sir Frederic Bartlett CBE
FRS 1886–1969

and East Africa, helping inspire a 'green revolution', and published widely on the genetics, taxonomy and economic botany of cotton. His Quaker compassion for the Third World and deprived peoples everywhere remained undimmed to his death.

In experimental psychology, St John's was for long pre-eminent worldwide. Much credit is due to Sir Frederic Bartlett (1912: Fellow 1926–69), who built on the legacy of W H R Rivers (see Chapter 14). Appointed first Professor of Experimental Psychology at Cambridge in 1931, he began with studies of perception and memory under controlled conditions, but from the beginning of the Second World War excelled in analysing the human skills required in repetitive work, not least those in the operation of complex military equipment. Under his auspices, in 1944 the Medical Research Council founded their Applied Psychology Research Unit at Cambridge, with his star pupil, Kenneth Craik, as its first Director.

Craik (1936: Fellow 1941–5) came to St John's as a graduate student. His research on visual adaptation and after-images was combined with fashioning scientific instruments and gadgets of all kinds. Elected a Research Fellow of the College, his scientific contributions to the military were of exceptional importance and famously included the development of a cockpit for analysing skill fatigue in airmen. Following his tragic death in a traffic accident, his parents founded the Kenneth Craik Memorial Lectureship, awarded annually by the College.

The oldest Chair of Chemistry in Cambridge dates back to 1702. George Liveing (1847: Fellow 1853–1924), who held it for forty-seven years, rented a cottage in today's Corn Exchange Street to run the first practical class. With his election to a Fellowship, the College built him a special laboratory behind New Court, replaced by the College bathhouses in 1922, and where the Cripps Building now stands. He later masterminded the new University Chemistry Laboratory in Pembroke Street and can be recognized as one of the earliest Adullamites in Cornford's *Microcosmographica Academica* of 1908 ('dangerous, because they know what they want … not

refined like classical men … they succeed in getting all the money that is going'). At his death aged ninety-six (he was knocked down by a lady cyclist from Girton while walking to his laboratory) he was still President of the College.

Biochemistry sprang as 'the illegitimate child of chemistry out of physiology' in 1898 with the appointment of Gowland Hopkins (later Sir Frederick Gowland Hopkins and Nobel Prize-winner) to teach chemistry to medical students at Cambridge. In 1923 Hopkins became the first Sir William Dunn Professor and one of his staff was Ernest Baldwin (1928: Fellow 1936–69) who wrote the first famous book for undergraduates reading the subject, *Dynamic Aspects of Biochemistry*. Among his Johnian pupils were the Nobel Prize-winner Frederick Sanger (see panel below) and Norman Heatley (see Chapter 14).

In more recent years, W G Palmer (1911: Fellow 1926–69), a right-hand man of Sir William Pope, Liveing's successor as 1702 Professor, wrote a definitive book on valency. F B Kipping (Fellow 1954–65) was the last perhaps of the 'classical' organic chemists. Frank Hollick (1929: Fellow 1935–2001) long held sway in zoology. Robert Hinde (see Chapter 21) was another distinguished member of the Zoology Department and A T Welford (1932: Fellow 1956–68), formerly Chaplain,

Dr Keith Johnstone with biology students Jack Westwood and Elizabeth Durkin at the Department of Plant Sciences, June 2006

was a luminary of the Department of Experimental Psychology until his departure for professorships in the Universities of Adelaide and then Hawaii.

Professor D H Northcote (Fellow 1960–76) taught biochemistry before becoming Master of Sidney Sussex College. Usha Goswami (Fellow 1990–7 and 2003–) was a member of the Department of Experimental Psychology prior to her appointment as Professor of Education. Reg Prince (Fellow 1960–), the late Ron Snaith (Fellow 1989–2000) and Paul Wood (Fellow 2000–) have continued the tradition in inorganic chemistry; Jim Staunton (Fellow 1969–; Emeritus Professor of Organic Chemistry) and Joe Spencer (Fellow 1995–) in organic chemistry. Chris Dobson (Fellow 2001–) is John Humphrey Plummer Professor of Chemical and Structural Biology. Professor (now Sir) David King was a Professorial Fellow (1988–95) in physical chemistry before leaving St John's to become Master of Downing (and later Chief Scientific Advisor to the Government).

In the life sciences, Ken Edwards (1966: Fellow 1971–87) taught genetics and cell biology until he was appointed Secretary General of the Faculties and later Vice-Chancellor of Leicester University. Richard Perham

(1958: Fellow 1964–; Master 2004–) retired as Professor of Structural Biochemistry in 2004 and Keith Matthews (1964: Fellow 1967–) as Reader in Pharmacology in 2003. Current Fellows include Ernest Laue (Professor of Structural Biology), Graham Burton (Professor of Reproductive Biology), Steve Edgley (Anatomy), Hugh Matthews and Ian Winter (Physiology) and Kate Plaisted (Experimental Psychology).

Keith Johnstone (Plant Sciences) recently received an award under the National Teaching Fellowship Scheme for innovative teaching in the biological sciences.

EARTH SCIENCES AND EXPLORATION

Victorian geologists were nearly all male, recognizable in the field by their plus fours, walking boots, hammer, compass, hand lens and map, hat, and oilskins if wet. Today's geologists are just as likely to be female, with men and women sporting a very wide range of field gear. This evolution has been accompanied by profound changes in the nature of what used to be referred to as geology, mineralogy and palaeontology, but is now more likely to be referred to as 'earth sciences' – the application of physics, chemistry and biology to

THE MAGNETISM OF ST JOHN'S

Over the centuries, many Fellows of St John's have been attracted to study magnetism. William Gilbert was a pioneer in the field. He postulated that the Earth itself is a giant dipole magnet, and predicted how the dip of a compass needle varies with latitude. Gilbert published his great treatise *De magnete* in 1600, a work that impressed Galileo. In the twentieth century Sir Harold Jeffreys studied all aspects of Earth structure, including the still challenging problem of how circulations within the metallic core generate the terrestrial magnetic field.

Sir Joseph Larmor investigated many electromagnetic phenomena, and discovered that if an orbiting system of electrically charged particles (all with the same ratio of charge to mass) is placed in a uniform magnetic field, the whole system precesses at a constant frequency. This led to a pre-quantum theory of the Zeeman effect, the splitting of atomic spectral lines in a magnetic field. The Larmor frequency of nuclear spins is what is measured in nuclear magnetic resonance (NMR) imaging, otherwise known as MRI. The Master, Richard Perham, and current Fellows Chris Dobson, Ernest Laue and Jim Staunton have studied enzyme reaction mechanisms and protein structure and folding using NMR spectroscopy.

The sources of magnetic fields are electric currents, and also the spin vectors of the electrons, protons and neutrons in an atom, which act as magnetic dipoles. How atomic magnets co-operate to produce the varied magnetic properties of solid materials, including ferromagnetism, is complicated. Charles Kittel (1936), well known for several physics textbooks, has researched widely in this area. Russell Cowburn (1990: Research Fellow 1997–2000: Professor of Nanotechnology at Imperial College), is developing ultrafast, nanometre-scale ferromagnetic circuit elements as possible competitors to electronic computing and data storage devices.

Paul Dirac's 1931 paper on magnetic monopoles is celebrated. Experimentally, no monopole has ever been seen, although the end of a long magnet is rather like one. However, Dirac showed that the quantum theory of electrons interacting with a pure monopole is consistent, provided the monopole's magnetic charge has a quantized strength. Dirac monopoles have point-like magnetic sources, so it is difficult to estimate their mass. In current theories of elementary particles, including electrons, quarks, gauge bosons and Higgs bosons, monopoles can appear in a new form, as heavy particles with a smoothed-out magnetic source. These monopoles have been classified, and their dynamics studied, by, among others, the former Master, Peter Goddard (see Chapter 21) and current Fellows Nick Manton (1971: Fellow 1997–) and David Stuart (Fellow 1999–). A few such monopoles may have been produced in the hot conditions shortly after the Big Bang.

GVILIELMI GIL
BERTI COLCESTREN-
SIS, MEDICI LONDI-
NENSIS,

DE MAGNETE, MAGNETI-
CISQVE CORPORIBVS, ET DE MAG-
no magnete tellure; Phyſiologia noua,
plurimis & argumentis, & expe-
rimentis demonſtrata.

LONDINI

EXCVDEBAT PETRVS SHORT ANNO
MDC.

The title-page to William Gilbert's De magnete (1600)

understanding the Earth and other terrestrial planets.

St John's has nurtured many notable earth scientists. One of the first and most distinguished was William Gilbert (1558: Fellow 1569 – see panel on 'The Magnetism of St John's'), whose great treatise *De magnete* laid the foundations of geomagnetism, the modern study of which has led to profound changes in our understanding of the Earth.

Born in 1891, Sir Harold Jeffreys was a Fellow for seventy-five years until his death in 1989. He made outstanding contributions to several fields of mathematics and science. In geophysics he wrote *The Earth: Its Origin, History and Physical Constitution* (1924), a treatise that systematized the subject for the first time; and he constructed the Jeffreys-Bullen tables that allowed the positions of earthquakes to be located from seismic records long before computers were invented. He was the first to claim that the core of the Earth is a fluid,

although he never accepted the idea of continental drift or plate tectonics, considering the interior of the Earth to be incapable of flow on the scale required.

J Tuzo Wilson, a Canadian, came to St John's in 1930 to study natural sciences and went on to a distinguished career in geophysics. Unlike Jeffreys, he realized that the continents had indeed 'drifted', and his work paved the way for the modern view of drift enshrined in plate tectonics. Among his achievements was his discovery of 'transform faults', particularly in the oceans (but also including the notorious San Andreas Fault of California) and their correct interpretation as features along which plates are sliding past one another.

Fred Vine (1959) made the most recent pioneering Johnian contribution to geophysics. Through his interpretation of the magnetic lineations of the ocean floor (the 'magnetic stripes'), discovered jointly with his supervisor as a research student, it became possible to

79

Sir Harold Jeffreys FRS 1891–1989 by Zsuzsi Roboz, 1984

*Left: Sir Vivian Fuchs
and Sir Edmund
Hillary in a tent en
route from the South
Pole to the Ross Sea
(Jon Stephenson, 1955–8
© Royal Geographic
Society)*

*Below: James Wordie
(left) helping to scrub the
galley floor of the
Endurance (Frank
Hurley, 1914–16 © Royal
Geographic Society)*

date most of the present-day ocean floor with remarkable precision, and to track the motions of the continents around the Atlantic and Indian Oceans.

The Johnian polymath J S Henslow became Professor of Mineralogy (1822–7) and subsequently of Botany (1827–61) in Cambridge. As previously mentioned, he recommended his friend Charles Darwin as naturalist on a planned two-year survey of South America aboard HMS *Beagle*, letting Darwin himself know of the position 'almost as an afterthought'.

Alfred Harker (1879: Fellow 1885–1939) graduated as a mathematician, but went on to study igneous rocks, of which his textbooks were classics for many years. 'Harker diagrams' still find a use in the interpretation of such rocks, and his painstaking unravelling of the complex geology of the younger igneous rocks of Scotland in particular led to new insights into how they were intruded. He left the magnificent Harker Collection, housed in the Sedgwick Museum, which includes specimens from all over the world. It is still being added to, for example with lunar specimens, and is much used by research workers.

Right: Max Newman
FRS 1897–1984
(© Elliott & Fry)

Below right: Sir
Ambrose Fleming FRS
1849–1945 (© Science
Museum, Science and
Society Picture Library)

J E Marr (Fellow 1881–1933; Woodwardian Professor 1917–30) was a pioneer in the study of geology and scenery, exemplified in his book *The Scientific Study of Scenery*. His interest in scenery leads on naturally to those Johnians who have combined their geological knowledge with geographical exploration. Foremost among these are Sir James Wordie and Sir Vivian Fuchs.

Wordie (Master 1952–9 – see Chapter 21) was responsible for establishing the first permanent British base on the Antarctic continent. Fuchs (1924) was the geologist in a team which Wordie – who had been his tutor – took to east Greenland in 1929. Later, leading the Commonwealth Trans-Antarctic Expedition (1957–8), he accomplished the first completely overland crossing of Antarctica. He is credited with determining that Antarctica's ice lies on top of a single landmass. His service as first Director of the British Antarctic Survey (1958–73) is marked by the Fuchs Foundation.

The Johnian zoologist Colin Bertram (1929: Fellow 1945–2001) was involved in considerable exploration activity. He participated in the British Graham Land Expedition of 1934–7 and wrote various works on Antarctica. He was Director of the Scott Polar Research Institute in Cambridge for several years, before becoming the College's Senior Tutor.

Two of the College's Honorary Fellows are earth scientists: Alec Deer (1934: Fellow 1939–50 and 1961–6; Hon. Fellow 1969), former Master of Trinity Hall and former Vice-Chancellor of the University; and Sir Mark Moody-Stuart (1960: Hon. Fellow 2001), former Chairman of Shell. A third, Lord Browne (1966: Hon. Fellow 1997), Group Chief Executive of BP, leads many geologists in their work of discovering and extracting petroleum.

The diversity of the subject is illustrated by the range of current Fellows' interests: Simon Conway Morris (evolution), Albert Galy (cosmochemistry), Nick McCave (climate change), Alan Smith (retired, global tectonics) and Andy Woods, Director of the BP Institute (fluid flow).

ELECTRONICS AND COMPUTING

St John's has a strong history in computing, and is proud to count Sir Maurice Wilkes as a Fellow (see panel). The EDSAC I computer, which performed its first calculation in May 1949, was the world's first stored-program computer to operate a regular computing service.

Wilkes's supervisor when he first arrived at the College was Max Newman (1915: Fellow 1923–45), a topologist who was head of the mathematical section

SIR MAURICE WILKES FRS (1913–)

Maurice Wilkes with EDSAC I in construction at the Cambridge Computer Laboratory (reproduced by kind permission of the Computer Laboratory)

Sir Maurice Wilkes counts himself one of those lucky people who find themselves in the right place and time to play a role in one of the great movements of their age, namely the early development of digital computers. He had come up to St John's as an undergraduate in 1931, taken the Mathematical Tripos, and worked for his PhD in the Cavendish Laboratory on experimental studies of the propagation of radio waves in the ionosphere. The possibilities of numerical computation in scientific research were becoming recognized, although digital computers lay far in the future, and it was widely thought that analogue computers would play a larger role than proved to be the case. Under the urging of Professor Lennard-Jones, whose interests lay in structural chemistry, the University agreed to the setting up of a new laboratory with wide terms of reference, a remarkable act of vision. Wilkes joined him as the first, and only, member of staff. War disrupted all plans and Wilkes went off to work on radar and operational research.

After the war, Wilkes found himself Director of the Laboratory. The first full-scale digital computer – the ENIAC – was already in operation in Philadelphia, but subsequent advances in computer architecture were such that everyone agreed successor machines would be built according to a new set of principles. Wilkes was invited to attend a course of lectures on these principles, and at the end of it a few of the students returned to their bases determined to build a machine along the new lines. The EDSAC built at Cambridge was the first of these to go into service anywhere in the world.

Sir Maurice is the author of *Memoirs of a Computer Pioneer* (1985)

(known as the 'Newmanry') at Bletchley Park during the Second World War (see Chapter 23). Newman realized that it might be possible to build electronic machinery to assist with the complex mathematical and statistical techniques required for code-breaking. For this purpose, his group at Bletchley, in conjunction with the Post Office Laboratories at Dollis Hill, built the Colossus – effectively an electronic digital computer that was pre-programmed to carry out a set of highly specific tasks in formal logic. (The existence of the Colossus was kept secret for thirty years after the war.) Newman can also claim credit for having first encouraged Alan Turing to work on problems of computability.

An earlier prominent figure in the field of electronics was Sir Ambrose Fleming, who came to the College as a student studying electricity and magnetism under James Clark Maxwell, gained a First in Natural Sciences in 1880, and was elected a Fellow in 1883 (later leaving for a chair at University College London). While working as a consultant for the Marconi Company, Fleming designed the transmitter that in 1901 was used to send the first transatlantic transmission, and in 1904 invented and patented the thermionic valve, often considered the beginning of electronics.

MATHEMATICS

The title of 'the first Johnian mathematician' probably belongs to John Dee, who entered St John's at the age of fifteen in 1542 and became a Fellow three years later, though he transferred to Trinity College in 1547. He is best known today as an astrologer and sorcerer and from the title of Peter Ackroyd's novel *The House of Doctor Dee*, but he was also a mathematician of European renown. His major mathematical work – a *Mathematicall Praeface* to Henry Billingsley's English translation of Euclid's *Elements* (1570) – is a masterly summary of the state of mathematical knowledge in the late sixteenth century.

The Johnian mathematician whose name is most widely known to mathematicians today is undoubtedly Brook Taylor (1701: Fellow 1704), the eponym of Taylor's Theorem in differential calculus. 'Taylor Series' made their first appearance in his textbook *Methodus incrementorum directa et inversa* (1715). He also made important original contributions to the mathematics of perspective. He is commemorated by a statue in the College Chapel, on the outside of the organ chamber.

James Wood (Master 1815–39) is not often thought of as a mathematician. But he made one remarkable contribution: the first published proof (in the *Philosophical Transactions* of the Royal Society for 1798) of the Fundamental Theorem of Algebra, that every polynomial equation over the complex numbers has a solution. Most mathematicians credit this theorem to Gauss, who published several proofs of it in the course of his life, but Wood's paper predates Gauss's first proof by one year.

James Joseph Sylvester, the most distinguished Johnian mathematician of the nineteenth century, was Second Wrangler in 1837. (The First and Third Wranglers of that year were also Johnians.) As a Jew, he was at that time unable to take his degree or be elected to a Fellowship and spent most of his career in London and the United States (at Johns Hopkins), where he is revered as one of the founders of American math-ematics. After the removal of religious restrictions at

THE LAST WOODEN SPOON

In former days, the Mathematical Tripos had its own terminology: those awarded First Class degrees were Wranglers; Second Class, Senior Optimes; Third Class, Junior Optimes; and the names of successful candidates were listed, in descending order. It was in this order that they received their degrees from the Vice-Chancellor, ending with the man who passed bottom. As the latter knelt to receive his degree, a large Wooden Spoon would be lowered from the gallery by his friends and suspended over his head. This, or a similar, custom was known to Byron who refers to the Wooden Spoon in *Don Juan* as: '… the name by which we Cantabs please/ To dub the last of honours in degrees'.

The recipient of the Wooden Spoon in 1909 was C L Holthouse of St John's, a keen oarsman who had rowed for three years in the LMBC May Boat. As this was to be the last year under the old descending-order system, his friends commissioned a splendid spoon, decorated with the College coat of arms and the LMBC motto 'Si Je Puis'. Its handle consists of a Lady Margaret oar and scarlet blade bearing an epigram in Greek inviting the viewer to shed a tear over this, the very Last Wooden Spoon. Carefully preserved by C L Holthouse, it eventually found its way to the College, where it hangs in the Small Combination Room.

The Last Wooden Spoon

83

Oxford and Cambridge, he was elected to the Savilian Chair at Oxford. Before that, in 1880, St John's had elected him to an Honorary Fellowship. He made contributions to all areas of mathematics, but especially to algebra.

In the early twentieth century, two of Cambridge's three Chairs in Mathematics were held by distinguished Johnians: the Lucasian by Sir Joseph Larmor (see Chapter 21 and the panel on 'The Magnetism of St John's') and the Lowndean by H F Baker (1883: Fellow 1888–1956). Baker, the leading British geometer of his day, held the Lowndean Chair from 1914 to 1936, and was succeeded by another Johnian, Sir William Hodge (1923: Fellow 1930–3). Baker's six-volume *Principles of Geometry* was published between 1922 and 1938. He is remembered for having dismissed as a crank a young Indian clerk who wrote to him enclosing strange mathematical formulae. The following year, the Indian had better success in writing to G H Hardy, the Sadleirian Professor: his name was Srinivasa Ramanujan, one of the most original mathematical minds of the twentieth century. Larmor's successor in the Lucasian Chair was another Johnian, the Nobel Laureate Paul Dirac (see panel below).

One of the founding fathers of modern statistics, G Udny Yule (1913: Fellow 1922–51) is best remembered for his pioneering work on how to measure correlations between different sets of data. Thanks to his teaching St John's became a producer of distinguished statisticians, including Sir Maurice Kendall (1926 – after whom the Kendall correlation coefficient is named) and Sir David Cox (1942).

Louis Mordell (1907: Fellow 1945–72), born in Philadelphia, was one of the most distinguished number theorists of the twentieth century. The first half of his career was spent away from Cambridge, culminating in his tenure of the Fielden Chair of Pure Mathematics in Manchester, from which he returned to Cambridge (and to St John's) in 1945 as Sadleirian Professor. His successor at Manchester was another Johnian, Max Newman (1915: Fellow 1923–45), a topologist perhaps best known for his wartime work as head of the 'Newmanry' at Bletchley Park (see *Electronics and Computing* above).

Sir Harold Jeffreys (1910) held a Fellowship continuously for almost seventy-five years, from 1914 to his death in 1989 – probably a record for any Oxbridge college. His great expertise was in theoretical geophysics, and in particular seismology (see *Earth Sciences* above) but he also made important contributions to the foundations of probability theory.

St John's today continues to be one of the strongest colleges in mathematics, taking around fifteen undergraduates each year, of whom some five, six or seven will go on to Part III of the Mathematical Tripos or other postgraduate study. Of the seven Fellows currently teaching in mathematics – Matthias Dörrzapf, Peter Johnstone, Nick Manton, Richard Samworth, David Stuart, Yuri Suhov, Andrew Woods – four (including three Professors) were undergraduates at St John's. It is safe to say that at any given time the College's student population includes one or two people who will go on to similarly distinguished academic careers in mathematics. Perhaps the present student body includes someone who will rival or even surpass the exploits of those described above.

Physics

No fewer than five Nobel Prizes for Physics have been won by Johnians or Johnian Fellows: Paul Dirac (1931), Sir Edward Appleton (1947), Sir John Cockcroft (1951), Sir Nevill Mott (1977), and Abdus Salam (1979). Their achievements are detailed below. Another Nobel Laureate, Allan Cormack (Medicine, 1979) also started out as a Johnian physicist, working in the Cavendish.

Dirac was elected to the Lucasian Chair in 1932, in recognition of his pioneering work on the mathematical foundations of quantum theory. To Cambridge's credit, the election came one year before the Nobel Prize. Other Johnian physicists of distinction include Sir Joseph Larmor (see Chapter 21), Sir Mark Oliphant (Fellow 1934–7), and Sir Roger Penrose (1952). At

Sir Edward Appleton
GBE KCB FRS
(© The Nobel
Foundation)

Cambridge in the 1930s, Oliphant worked with Rutherford on experiments that led to the discovery of the tritium isotope of hydrogen, a fundamental step in the production of nuclear bombs with very high explosive yields. Involved in the Manhattan Project during the Second World War, he later regretted this and became a founding member of the Pugwash Movement, describing himself as 'a belligerent pacifist'. An Australian, he was a founding father of the Australian National University in Canberra, and Governor of South Australia from 1971 to 1976.

Penrose is well known for his popular writing about science as well as for his important research contributions in the field of mathematical physics. He first came to St John's as a graduate student in pure mathematics. Under the influence of Dirac amongst others, his research turned to physics. He continued at St John's as a Research Fellow from 1958 to 1961, working on cosmology. This work led to his calculation in the 1960s of many of the important features of black holes, including (with Stephen Hawking) the proof that all matter within a black hole collapses to a singularity. As a mathematician, Penrose is also known for discovering the phenomenon of Penrose tiling: pairs of shapes that tile the plane only aperiodically. One such tiling is displayed at the entrance to the College Library.

Physics remains important to today's College as a core subject within the Natural Sciences Tripos and a major research interest. Annually about eight underg-

raduates specialize in physics after the broad-based first year natural sciences course. This pool feeds primarily physics in the higher parts of the four-year Tripos, but also astrophysics, materials science and engineering. Physics also thrives at graduate level, with some four or five students emerging with PhD degrees each year, many continuing to post-doctoral work in Cambridge and elsewhere. An impressive list of Johnian physicists hold positions in many universities in the UK and abroad, including the former Master, Peter Goddard (see Chapter 21).

Cutting-edge research is well-represented in current activity, most notably in quantum physics, nanotechnology and organic electronics. Johnian physicist Sir Richard Friend, Cavendish Professor of Physics, has conducted pioneering research into the physics and engineering of semiconductor devices made with carbon-based semiconductors, which has revolutionized understanding of the electronic properties of molecular semiconductors. Co-founder of two Cambridge-based research companies, Cambridge Display Technology and Plastic Logic, he patented the first organic polymer light-emitting diode, a technology that is used, for example, in cell phone displays.

NOBEL LAUREATES

Sir Edward Appleton GBE KCB FRS (1892–1965)
Service in the Royal Engineers gave Edward Appleton (1911) ample opportunity for experiment with wireless valves in the First World War, after which he returned to work at the Cavendish Laboratory on the propagation of radio waves, being elected Fellow of the College in 1919. His research culminated in 1924 in experimental proof of the Kennelly-Heaviside layer. Appointed Professor of Experimental Physics at King's College London in 1925, his experiments continued and led to the discovery of a higher reflecting layer, known initially as the Appleton layer. He and his successor as Director of Studies in Physics at St John's, Douglas Hartree (1915: Fellow 1924–7) devised the Appleton-Hartree formula giving

the velocity and attenuation of radio waves in the ionosphere. He was elected FRS in 1927.

In 1936 he became Jacksonian Professor of Natural Philosophy at the Cavendish and was re-elected Fellow of St John's. In 1939 he was appointed Secretary of the Department of Scientific and Industrial Research, a key post in the direction of scientific resources during the Second World War. Knighted in 1941, he was awarded the Nobel Prize for Physics in 1947. In 1949 he became Principal and Vice-Chancellor of Edinburgh University, a position he held until his death. He gave the Reith lectures on 'Science and the Nation' in 1956.

Sir John Cockcroft OM KCB CBE FRS (1897–1967)

John Cockcroft studied at Manchester prior to service in the First World War as a signaller with the Royal Artillery. After a period as engineering apprentice with Metro-Vickers, he won a scholarship to St John's and took a First in mathematics in 1924. Recommended to Rutherford at the Cavendish he gained a PhD in 1928, meanwhile helping Vickers with calculations of magnetic fields in power generation. Working with E T S Walton, he developed a high-voltage, high-energy beam which split atoms of lithium, leading to a new era of nuclear physics. Elected FRS in 1936, he became Jacksonian Professor of Natural Philosophy in 1939.

Meanwhile at St John's, as Bursar, he oversaw the rebuilding of the Gatehouse (which had been affected by roof damage and death watch beetle) as well as the construction of Chapel and North Courts.

Involved by Sir Henry Tizard in 1938 in the development of radar, he persuaded large numbers of physicists to spend time at coastal radar stations, and in 1940 he joined Tizard on a mission to Washington to exchange defence scientific information. Later that year, he became Chief Superintendent of the Air Defence Research and Development Establishment. In 1943 he was sent to Canada to build the heavy water reactor at Chalk River and thereafter was deeply involved in nuclear work, returning to the UK to direct the Harwell Laboratory from 1946 to 1959. When the United

Kingdom Atomic Energy Authority (UKAEA) was created in 1954, Cockcroft became the first Member for Research. He was closely involved in the creation of the International Atomic Energy Authority (IAEA) in 1955, and with the early years of CERN, Geneva. He won the Atoms for Peace Award in 1961.

He was the first Master of Churchill College, from 1959 till his death. He won the Nobel Prize for Physics, with Ernest Walton, in 1951, and was awarded the OM in 1957.

Professor Paul Dirac OM FRS (1902–84)

Paul Dirac, Lucasian Professor of Mathematics from 1932 to 1969, is numbered alongside Newton and Einstein as one of the greatest physicists of all time. The son of a Swiss schoolmaster who had settled in Bristol, and an English mother, his father's requirement that he speak at table in perfect French may have resulted in his legendary taciturnity.

Dirac first graduated from Bristol in electrical engineering aged nineteen in the midst of the Depression. Unable to get a job, he remained at Bristol and took a degree in mathematics as well before beginning research at St John's in 1923 on atomic physics, then in an incomplete and paradoxical state. In 1925, as a graduate student, he made his first major discovery: building on his insight into the deeper structure of Heisenberg's newly formulated quantum mechanics, he solved many of the central problems of

Above left: Sir John Cockcroft OM KCB CBE FRS (© Elliott & Fry)

Above: Paul Dirac OM FRS – bronze bust by Harald Isenstein, cast in 1973 from a 1939 plaster original

Sir Nevill Mott CH FRS
*(© The Nobel
Foundation)*

atomic theory which had been baffling theoretical physicists for the previous decade. He said in later years that nothing ever gave him as much satisfaction as this first major discovery.

By 1928 the major problem was how to reconcile quantum mechanics with Einstein's theory of relativity. Dirac solved this problem by formulating what became known as the Dirac Equation for the electron. Dramatically, this equation predicted the existence of an antiparticle for the electron, the positron, which was found experimentally in 1932.

With these developments, quantum mechanics was in an essentially complete form. Dirac's enormous contributions to it were acknowledged by his election to the Royal Society in 1930 and to the Lucasian Professorship in 1932, and by the award of the Nobel Prize for Physics for 1933, which he shared with Erwin Schrödinger. He continued to lecture and work on theoretical physics until shortly before his death in 1984.

Professor Sir Nevill Mott CH FRS (1905–1996)
One of the giants of twentieth-century physics, Nevill Mott (1924) played a major role in the development of solid state physics from its infancy in the 1920s through to his Nobel Prize-winning work of the 1970s and his final work on high temperature superconductors in the 1990s. In the late 1920s he worked in Copenhagen with Niels Bohr and in Manchester with Lawrence Bragg before election to a Fellowship at Gonville and Caius in

1930. At the age of twenty-eight he moved to Bristol as Professor of Theoretical Physics, switching from nuclear to solid state physics and building up Bristol as one of the leading groups in this field. Concerned by the arrival of atomic energy, he was one of the founders in 1946 of the Atomic Scientists' Association, and was active for many years with the Pugwash Conference.

Elected Cavendish Professor of Physics in 1954, he made many changes and pressed, with eventual success, for reform of the Natural Sciences Tripos. Fellow of Gonville and Caius from 1954, he was Master from 1959 to 1966. Thereafter, he took up the new field of non-crystalline semiconductors, producing the enduring concepts and models and, in co-authorship, the text which defined the field. In 1977 he won the Nobel Prize for this work. He was elected an Honorary Fellow of St John's in 1964.

Professor M H F Wilkins CBE FRS (1916–2004)
Maurice Wilkins entered St John's in 1935 but missed a First in physics in 1938, perhaps because of much time spent with the Cambridge Scientists' Anti-War Group. Unable as a result to take a PhD at Cambridge, he did so at the University of Birmingham, working under a young Dr J T Randall (later famous for the cavity magnetron for radar). Wilkins joined the atomic bomb Manhattan Project, moving to Berkeley, California, in 1944. He returned to the UK, disturbed by the dropping of the atomic bombs on Japan, and determined to take up biological work. He rejoined Randall, now head of an MRC biophysics unit at King's College London, and began a study of DNA, chiefly by means of X-ray diffraction. It was a fateful choice – DNA was still not widely recognized as the genetic material – but his work attracted the interest of James Watson and Wilkins's friend Francis Crick in Cambridge. The troubled story has been widely told of how Randall brought Rosalind Franklin into King's in 1951 also to study DNA, how relations between her and Wilkins turned sour, and how Crick and Watson combined brilliant model-building with the X-ray results of Wilkins and Franklin to arrive

87

88

in 1953 at the famous double-helical structure of DNA. Wilkins latterly (2003) gave his own version in his autobiography, *The Third Man of the Double Helix*. Rosalind Franklin died tragically early of cancer in 1958 and the Nobel Prize in Physiology or Medicine was awarded jointly to Crick, Watson and Wilkins in 1962. Disenchanted with nuclear weapons, Wilkins joined the Pugwash group of scientists and the Campaign for Nuclear Disarmament, and was President of the British Society for Social Responsibility in Science from 1969 to 1991.

Dr Frederick Sanger OM CH CBE FRS (1918–)

Frederick Sanger came up to St John's in 1936, taking a First in Part II (biochemistry) in 1940. As a Quaker, he was a conscientious objector during the Second World War. He worked for his PhD on lysine metabolism and nutrition, and in 1943 began studying the chemistry of the protein hormone insulin. Over the next ten years he worked out novel methods of determining the amino acid sequence of the hormone, revolutionizing understanding of the chemistry of all proteins. For this, he was awarded the Nobel Prize for Chemistry in 1958. In 1962 he became one of the co-founders of the newly established MRC Laboratory of Molecular Biology in Cambridge, and turned his attention to the study of nucleic acids. Again he devised novel techniques, this time for determining the sequence of the nucleotides that make up the chains of RNA and DNA. This

culminated in the first genome sequence, that of a bacterial virus, φX174, rapidly followed by others. The award of a second Nobel Prize for Chemistry (jointly with Paul Berg of Stanford and Walter Gilbert of Harvard) came in 1980. Later automated, and in the hands of others, Sanger's DNA sequencing methodologies were famously employed in the determination of the human and other genome sequences at the Sanger Centre at Hinxton, created by the Wellcome Trust and MRC and duly named after him. Sanger is one of only four people to have been awarded the Nobel Prize twice. A modest and unassuming man who has inspired admiration and affection worldwide, he has been showered with honours. His great work is commemorated in St John's in the etched glass windows in the Palmerston Room.

Professor Allan Cormack (1924–1998)

Allan Cormack, Nobel Laureate in Medicine and Physiology, was one of the developers of CAT scanning, which allows information on the entire three-dimensional region scanned by an X-ray beam to be imaged. After graduation from the University of Cape Town, he spent four years at St John's working with Otto Frisch on the properties of helium 6 before returning to take up a lectureship in the Cape Town Physics Department. Asked to spend part of the week at the Groote Schur Hospital to deal with radioactive materials, he began to think about how most of the information in an

Far left: Maurice Wilkins CBE FRS (© King's College, London)

Centre: Frederick Sanger OM CH CBE FRS (© The Nobel Foundation)

Above: Allan Cormack (© The Nobel Foundation)

Abdus Salam FRS by Anthony Morris 2001

Professor Abdus Salam FRS (1926–96)

One of the leading theoretical physicists of the twentieth century and the first Muslim to win a Nobel Prize, Abdus Salam was born in the Punjab, then in India. After an outstanding academic career at Government College, Lahore, in 1946 he gained a scholarship to Cambridge. The withdrawal of another Indian student provided a last-minute place for him at St John's, where he gained a First in Part II of both the Mathematical and Physics Triposes.

In 1949 he began research on Renormalization Theory, the means by which extremely accurate experimental predictions are obtained from quantum field theories that would otherwise produce meaningless infinities. His work in this technically difficult but crucially important area gained him an international reputation and resulted in his election as a Research Fellow of St John's in 1951. However Abdus Salam was committed to returning to Lahore, by then in Pakistan, and he spent the next three years there as a professor, returning to St John's in the long vacations. But, even with this contact, he found it impossible to continue with research, and so in 1954 he came back to Cambridge as a lecturer, moving to Imperial College as Professor of Theoretical Physics in 1957.

The central theme of his research was the search for a unified theory of the fundamental forces of nature. His greatest triumph, perhaps the greatest triumph in fundamental physics in the last fifty years, was the discovery of a theory which successfully unified electricity and magnetism with the weak nuclear force (the force responsible for radioactivity) into a single theory. For this he shared the 1979 Nobel Prize in Physics with Sheldon Lee Glashow and Steven Weinberg.

An equally outstanding achievement was his creation of the International Centre for Theoretical Physics in Trieste, Italy, which made it possible for leading scientists working in developing countries to continue with ground-breaking research, in a way he had found impossible. Establishing the Centre took all of the charisma, irrepressible enthusiasm and astounding capacity for hard work that made Salam a great physicist.

X-ray was being wasted. While on sabbatical at Harvard he was invited to join the Physics Department of Tufts University where he remained until his retirement.

When he realized that tomography as used in astronomy and oceanography could be applied to X-ray analysis, he was surprised that he was unable to find a solution in existing literature and decided to work out the problem himself. Having done this, he had little interest in the engineering aspects, and the first commercial CAT scanner was patented by an Englishman, Godfrey Hounsfield, in 1968. The two men shared the Nobel Prize in 1979, meeting for the first time in Stockholm.

9 INNOVATION, BUSINESS AND FINANCE

ST JOHN'S INNOVATION CENTRE

As one drives into Cambridge from the north, it soon becomes clear that this is not just another Fenland market town. Close to the city boundary, signs point to 'Research Park', 'Science Park' and 'Innovation Park'. The Innovation Park in question was founded twenty years ago by St John's, and remains centrally important in the explosive growth of entrepreneurial activity in science and technology which has distinguished Cambridge not only regionally, but nationally and even internationally. The so-called 'Cambridge Phenomenon' was first identified in 1985 when there were 360 high-technology companies in the area; a decade earlier there had been only twenty, while today there are around 1,500.

In 1984 Christopher Johnson (Fellow 1970–) took a well-earned sabbatical from his post as Senior Bursar of the College, and visited several science parks in the USA. At the beginning of the 1970s, Trinity College had founded the first science park in Cambridge on their land to the west of Milton Road in the north of the city: a group of buildings housing science and technology-based companies, each large enough to have their own premises. Chris had an idea that a similar development might prove a worthwhile investment for St John's, on nearby land owned by the College since the sixteenth century. He returned from Salt Lake City inspired to start a rather different venture, in which small office and laboratory units provided space and a nurturing environment for fledgling companies formed to exploit ideas which had evolved from the laboratories and tearooms of the University, and with the key concept of leases which were easy for these new companies to initiate, vary or terminate as their fortunes changed.

Left: Chris Johnson, who developed the concept of the Innovation Centre following a study tour in the United States

Opposite: St John's Innovation Centre has played a major role in the growth of entrepreneurial activity in the Cambridge region

In 1997 the first tenants moved into the new St John's Innovation Centre, and from then onwards the College progressively developed the surrounding land, with the addition of further buildings and extensions to the Centre itself. Walter Herriot, honoured with the OBE in 1999 and with the Queen's Award for Enterprise Promotion in 2006, was a local bank manager before he became Director of the Innovation Centre in 1990. One of the godfathers of the Cambridge high-technology boom, Walter has been involved with early-stage businesses since the 1970s.

The Centre now occupies some 8,000 sq.m in two buildings, and houses around sixty companies employing 700 people. Although some of these are spin-outs or start-ups from the University, this is by no means the rule;

most of the small companies which choose the Centre as their home have emerged from the scientific and technological ferment in the Cambridge area which feeds on, and in turn nourishes, the work of the University. Over a five-year period the survival rate for companies in the Centre has been about ninety per cent, compared to fifty per cent for other similar businesses in the Cambridge area, and forty-five per cent for businesses generally in the UK. The Centre provides facilities in the form of meeting and conference rooms, a restaurant and standard business services. Most importantly, the Director and his staff provide a wide range of advice and support not only to tenants but also to many of the other small companies in the Cambridge region. Some 200 of these use the Centre as a 'virtual incubator'. The Centre also acts as an 'enterprise hub' for the Regional Development Agency, and acts as a European Innovation Relay Centre providing business links between the region and thirty European countries. In a typical year, through these and other activities, around 1,000 companies have some contact with the Centre.

The high level of visibility which the Centre enjoys in the region, and the evidence that companies based in the Centre have high success rates, are two reasons why space there is highly sought after. St John's Innovation Centre continues to act as a magnet for high-technology entrepreneurs, and was identified in a recent survey as the location where by far the highest number of new companies chose to be sited. The Centre will continue to provide a valuable contribution to the endowment income of the College, and also to play a nodal role in the Cambridge high-technology community.

BUSINESS AND FINANCE

From the likes of Sir Charles Parsons (1873), the inventor of the steam turbine and founder of the major engineering company of the same name, and H G Pye (1920), who was at the forefront of early radio, many Johnians have had distinguished careers in the business world.

Recent and prominent names from the energy industries include those of Sir John Hill (1945), former

Lord Browne of Madingley, Group Chief Executive of BP (courtesy of BP plc 2006)

Chairman of British Nuclear Fuels; Sir Mark Moody-Stuart (1960: Hon. Fellow 2001–), former Chairman of Shell and currently Chairman of Anglo American; Lord Browne (1966: Hon. Fellow 1997–), the current Group Chief Executive of BP; and Sir Christopher Laidlaw (1940), former Deputy Chairman of BP Oil and Chairman of ICL.

Johnians from the world of finance include the current Governor of the Bank of England, Mervyn King (Fellow 1972–7: Hon. Fellow 1997–); Sir Brian Corby (1949), formerly Chief Executive and then Chairman of Prudential; Sir John Quinton (1950), a former Chairman of Barclays; Alan Lord (1947), formerly Deputy Chairman and Chief Executive of Lloyds of London (and previously Chairman of Dunlop); Gavyn Davies (1969), Chief International Economist with Goldman Sachs who went on to become Chairman of the BBC; W Richard Holmes (1971), Chairman and CEO of American Express Bank; Sir Douglas Wass (1941), former Chairman of Nomura International; Lindsay Tomlinson (1969), CEO of Barclays Global Investors Europe; Damon Buffini (1981)

The Innocent Smoothie founders: Adam Balon, Jon Wright, Richard Reed

and Graham Wrigley (1981) of the private equity firm Permira; Howard Covington (1971), Chief Executive of New Star Asset Management and Mark Coombs (1979), Managing Director of Ashmore Investment Management.

Businessmen from the world of manufacturing, transport and engineering include Keith Orrell-Jones (1958), former Chairman of Smiths Group and FKI and Group Chief Executive of Blue Circle Industries; Marcus Beresford (1961), former Chief Executive of GKN; and Mike Clasper (1971), former Chief Executive Officer of BAA.

From the property arena come Aubrey Adams (1967), Group Chief Executive of Savills, and John Weston Smith (1951), who stood down as Chief Operating Officer of British Land in 2006 after thirty-five years with the company.

Those from media and the arts include Lord Bernstein (1956), formerly Chairman of Granada Group; Stephen Hill (1979), formerly Chief Executive of the Financial Times Group and more recently of Betfair; and Lord Rowe-Beddoe (1958), Chairman of the Wales Millennium Centre and formerly Chairman of the Welsh Development Agency from 1993 to 2001.

But this is not a static picture, and new names continually come to the fore, such as the young Johnian entrepreneurial trio of Adam Balon (1991), Richard Reed (1991) and Jon Wright (1991) who have formed Innocent Ltd, makers of the Innocent Smoothie.

The College's alumni in the worlds of business and finance, of whom those named can be no more than an illustration, form a distinguished and wide-ranging body that provides a strong and valuable bridge between the College and the wider economy.

10 THE HUMANITIES

The College's considerable strengths in the teaching of the humanities are shown in the following vignettes of ten main disciplines.

ANTHROPOLOGY

'Arch and anth' at St John's today draws people into anthropology from a notable variety of backgrounds. The undergraduate intake has no 'typical' school subject profile. Those coming to do an MPhil or doctoral research in anthropology add their diverse experience to the pool in College. The subject benefited in the past from the breadth of interests and curiosity brought to it by people like W H R Rivers (coming from medicine and psychology, and effectively the founder of anthropology at the College: see Chapter 14), Gregory Bateson (1922: Fellow 1931–6), coming from biology, and Louis Leakey (from his African upbringing among Kikuyu). More recently the subject has benefited from versatile Johnians such as Robert Hinde (on ritual and communication, social relationships and gender: see Chapter 21), Sir Jonathan Miller (1953) on imitation, ritual and the history of medicine, and Adam Kendon (1952) on non-verbal communication, Australian Aboriginal sign languages and Neapolitan gesture. Sir Jack Goody (1938: Fellow 1961–; Emeritus William Wyse Professor of Social Anthropology) exemplifies in his own research and writing the wide scope of social anthropology as the comparative study of human societies and cultures – from fieldwork in northern Ghana on inheritance, the transmission of myth and oral tradition, to comparisons of household and kinship in Africa and Europe, and his analyses of the impact of writing in society and culture. Gilbert Lewis (Fellow 1972–), working in New Guinea, studied village reasoning about misfortune, illness and treatment.

Change certainly confronts anthropology with fresh subjects and challenges. Among more recent Johnian contributions come the first characterization of the concept of 'informal economy' for development studies, from Keith Hart (1961); the work by Daniel Miller (1973) on material culture in Britain and Jamaica, shopping, and the study of street culture; Steven Hooper (1974) directing the Sainsbury Research Unit for the Arts of Oceania, Africa and the Americas; Helen Watson (Fellow 1991–) on women's lives in urban poverty in Cairo, on religious identity and sectarian violence in Ulster; and the work of Simon Coleman (1982: Fellow 1990–2) on a charismatic Christian movement in Sweden and contemporary pilgrimage.

In the undergraduate Part II, the option of writing a dissertation in place of a paper provides the opportunity for developing an independent project, perhaps including some 'field' experience. Many find it one of the most challenging and enjoyable parts of their course. One notable Johnian dissertation was on 'Initiation to the [College rugby] Red Boys' – a work of fearless observation. The Tutors were banned from reading it.

ARCHAEOLOGY

St John's has a worldwide reputation as one of Cambridge's centres of excellence in teaching and research in archaeology. Since the foundation in 1851 of the UK's oldest Chair of Archaeology, five of the eleven Disney Professors have been Fellows of the College: the first, John Marsden (1851–65), his successor Churchill Babington (1865–1880), and all three of the most recent

95

Emma Pomeroy (BA 2003) digging Neolithic remains in Pupicina Cave, Croatia in 2001. The Cave, excavated by Dr Preston Miracle from 1995 to 2002, has provided key evidence about the end of the Ice Age and the adoption of agriculture in southeastern Europe.

incumbents, Glyn Daniel (1974–81), Colin Renfrew (1981–2004), and Graeme Barker (2004–).

Glyn Daniel's career is portrayed in Chapter 21. In *Some Small Harvest* (1986), he reflected that he had taught archaeology to over 250 people in his lectures and supervisions from 1946 to 1974, including 'ten professors, countless lecturers, four directors of British Schools abroad, directors and staff of many museums, and half a dozen Fellows of the British Academy'. His pupils included Colin (now Lord) Renfrew, his successor in the Disney Chair, and a former Master of Jesus College, Cambridge, who also presented an acclaimed BBC series, and has written many influential books on archaeological theory. Another pupil was Barry Cunliffe, Professor of European Archaeology at Oxford.

The College's best-known archaeology graduate of the first half of the twentieth century was Louis Leakey (1922: see panel). Following in his footsteps, and in an enduring contribution of Johnian archaeology, John Alexander (Fellow 1976–) has strongly nurtured indigenous African archaeology, teaching an entire new generation of African archaeologists. His work has been recognized by an honorary doctorate from Khartoum University.

Graeme Barker's field is prehistoric archaeology. His excavations of Niah Great Cave in Sarawak have dated the appearance of anatomically modern humans in South-East Asia to some 45,000 years ago, the first reliable data for the chronology of the expansion of our species outwards from Africa. Johnian Fellow Preston Miracle's work in Croatia has provided new insights into the spread of farming across Europe.

Each year, the College takes three or four students for 'arch and anth', and has two or three MPhil and several PhD students in most years, so at any one time there are up to a dozen archaeology students at St John's. Field trips to the Dordogne are currently organized for second-year undergraduates, and students also undertake several weeks of independent fieldwork in a variety of locations.

Graeme Barker recalls that in switching from Classics to Archaeology following a chance meeting with Colin Renfrew and Glyn Daniel, he discovered that he had become a member of the 'Johnian

DR LOUIS LEAKEY FBA (1903–1973)

The son of missionaries, Louis Leakey was brought up in Kenya until the age of sixteen, close to the Kikuyu tribe into which he was initiated. He came to St John's in 1922, reading French and Kikuyu, and then archaeology and anthropology. As a Fellow from 1929 to 1934, he led various expeditions to East Africa which established a sequence of early cultures, publishing the results in *Stone Age Africa* (1936) and other works. A regrettable failure to document and identify sites damaged his scientific reputation; this and scandal over his personal life put paid to his career at Cambridge, and in 1937 he returned to Kenya to conduct an ethnological study of the Kikuyu.

A member of the Kenya CID during the Second World War and after, he gave warning of Mau Mau activities, publishing *Mau Mau and the Kikuyu* (1952) and

Louis Leakey with Homo habilis *fossils 1970*
(© The Leakey Foundation)

Defeating Mau Mau (1954). He was court interpreter at the trial of Jomo Kenyatta.

From 1941 he was curator of the local Nairobi museum and in 1947 organized the first Pan-African Congress of Prehistory, which helped restore his reputation. From the 1950s, he and his wife made significant discoveries in the Olduvai Gorge in modern Tanzania. Many hominid fossils were found, including those of *Homo habilis* in 1964. Although his theories and discoveries were often controversial, Leakey altered our understanding of the path of human evolution.

Amongst several wildlife initiatives, he was a strong supporter of game parks, and backed the work of Jane Goodall with chimpanzees. His son is the anthropologist Richard Leakey.

Connection', an informal network of archaeologists from the College, founded by Glyn Daniel, which remains one of the most stimulating and influential archaeological communities anywhere in the world.

Classics

In the 1960s a classical scholar of the College might be targeted with an invitation he (it was the 1960s) could not refuse: doing the Burghley verses, a set of Greek and Latin compositions to be conveyed to the Marquess of Exeter (at Burghley) and to the Marquess of Salisbury (at Hatfield). Three centuries earlier *every* Scholar of the College had been obliged to put one of the psalms into Latin for their Lordships' benefit. It is nice to imagine Richard Bentley (BA 1680), the College's and probably Britain's greatest classical scholar of all time (and subsequently a famously wily and tempestuous Master of Trinity), dashing off his lines.

St John's has always been regarded as one of the strongest classical colleges, and is one of the few that

retains a thriving Classical Society. From time immemorial John Crook has hosted its meetings – talks, parties, play readings (usually Aristophanes) the staple diet – in the book-lined rooms which for generations of Johnians have been the home of classics in the College. There have been memorable characters among the dons. Three who come to mind are the formidable vegetarian J E B Mayor (1844: Fellow 1849–1910), Professor of Latin immediately before A E Housman, and celebrated editor of Juvenal; T R Glover (1889: Fellow 1892–6, 1901–43), at the height of his powers between the wars as Public Orator and Baptist preacher, who believed that education should equip a man for life not the library, and is reputed to have kept sherry out of the College trifle for decades; and Guy Lee (BA 1940: Fellow 1945–2005), gentlemanly author of a notoriously racy translation of Ovid's *Amores*, who could never be manoeuvred into preceding a pupil from his study to his keeping room.

Others rose to the giddy height of President of the

College: for a long period Martin Charlesworth (Fellow 1923–50); R L Howland (1924: Fellow 1929–86), an Olympic shot-putter; John Crook (1939: Fellow 1951–, and Emeritus Professor of Ancient History) and Malcolm Schofield (1960: Fellow 1972–, and Professor of Ancient Philosophy).

But most Johnian classicists don't turn into Fellows. In our time, for example, Mike Brearley (1960) became England cricket captain and a psychoanalyst, and Sasha Behar (1987) an actress with the RSC and on *EastEnders*. Others have joined the noble and indispensable army of schoolteachers – not least T E Page CH (BA 1873), founder of the Loeb Classical Library, and Bob Lister (1971), who for well over a decade has been turning others into teachers on the Cambridge PGCE course. Nowadays St John's has more graduate students and is increasingly international: a recent third-year was Israeli, another Japanese. There isn't much verse composition, but gender studies flourish. Johnian classicists still love their Homer and Virgil.

ENGLISH

Writing of English studies before the creation of the Tripos, E M W Tillyard describes 'Ascham and Cheke, the great Johnians of the sixteenth century' as 'the first Cambridge scholars to include English in their scope'. Johnians have thus been at the forefront of the scrutiny of English from its very beginnings in Cambridge.

Inevitably, those who taught English at the introduction of the Tripos in 1917 came from different disciplines: the first Johnian English Fellow, Hugh Sykes Davies (see Chapter 21) began life as a classicist. Gradually, however, a new type of scholar emerged in line with more general changes in the study of English, with literary theory playing a part in the curriculum alongside the traditional study of authors and texts. Whereas, earlier in the century, English dons might have taught across the entire range of the Tripos, teaching became more focused on Fellows' particular strengths. George Watson, with special interests in political literature and critical theory, also co-edited *The Cambridge*

Bibliography of English Literature. Current Teaching Fellows in English include Professor John Kerrigan (whose research interests span tragedy since antiquity, Renaissance literature, Romanticism and modern poetry), Richard Beadle (who has published on medieval and early modern literature, the history of the book, and drama), and Yota Batsaki, who specializes in the English and French novel, Enlightenment political and aesthetic theory, literary theory, and the relationship between literature and sculpture. Together with the Junior Research Fellows in English occasionally admitted by the College, they cover a broad spectrum of the teaching syllabus.

Despite the increasing pressure of examinations and results, roundedness and breadth is something which St John's seeks to develop in its English students. Since its inception, English has maintained a small but distinctive presence in the College, and many English students have been distinctive in their own ways, too. St John's has a strong tradition of turning out dramatic and literary talent from the serious to the seriously quirky (see Chapters 15 and 18). Journalism also has received its share of attention from resident Johnians, with one establishing *The Cambridge Student* in the 1990s, a newspaper which has challenged the long-standing dominance of *Varsity*. Each year, the students who graduate in the subject continue to prove that studying English at St John's offers an outstanding opportunity to explore the delights and the potential of literature.

GEOGRAPHY

Johnian geographers trace their ancestry to the year 1600 when Samuel Purchas graduated from the College. Purchas, who was born in Thaxted and became Rector of St Martin's, Ludgate, once claimed he had never travelled more than a hundred miles from his birthplace and yet encompassed the whole world in his geographical writings. *Purchas His Pilgrimes* (1625), described by the *Encyclopaedia Britannica* as a compilation of information that was 'often injudicious, careless and even unfaithful', nevertheless includes what is sometimes the only use of

97

sources now lost, and remains an inspiration to generations of armchair Johnian geographers.

After the University appointed its first Lecturer in Geography in 1888, the subject quickly evolved from exploration and map-making to regional studies, spatial modelling and the study of cultural landscapes. At St John's, an early twentieth century influence was Sir James Wordie (Master 1952–9: see Chapter 21), the leading scientist on nine polar expeditions. The first Teaching Fellow was Ben Farmer (1934: Fellow 1948–96), an expert on South Asia, and it was he and Glyn Daniel (see *Archaeology*) who founded the Purchas Society in 1947. The diversity of geography in the College is well represented by the list of Fellows over the past half century: Clifford Smith (1961–70: Latin America), Jack Langton (1970–3: Britain's Industrial Revolution), Tim Bayliss-Smith (1973–: development and Melanesia), Robin Glasscock (1977–: medieval historical geography) and Neil Arnold (1997–: glaciology).

The Purchas Society thrives to this day, and has filled the Combination Room with alumni on two notable occasions. The first was Ben Farmer's retirement in 1986, when he was presented with a book largely written by his former students – *Understanding Green Revolutions*. The second was a dinner to mark the fiftieth anniversary of the Society in 1997, where alumni included the first Johnian women geographers.

Among those who gathered to celebrate Ben Farmer's leadership were David Harvey (1954), author of *The Limits to Capital*, *The New Imperialism* and many other books, who has been called the world's most cited academic geographer; and the geomorphologist David Stoddart (1956), Professor of Geography at Berkeley. Johnian geographers continue to make their academic mark – Emma Mawdsley (1989) was recently appointed to a Cambridge lectureship – and are well represented in many worlds including research, education, local government, journalism, business and indeed sport, where Rob Andrew (1982) represents Johnian geography.

HISTORY

In his memoirs, Rev. J S Boys Smith wrote of the 'exceptionally strong entry in History' in the years before the Second World War: the names he gives are a roll-call of later history Fellows of the College – Hinsley, Miller, Robinson, Thistlethwaite – as well as some who achieved fame in other places and spheres such as Sir John Habakkuk (1933), Principal of Jesus, Oxford, and the first Cambridge man to become Vice-Chancellor of Oxford; Nagendra Singh (1934), President of the International Court of Justice; and S W Templeman (1938), Lord of Appeal.

Sir Harry Hinsley (see Chapter 21) fostered the study in Cambridge of the history of international relations. Edward (Ted) Miller (1934: Fellow 1939–65; later Professor of Medieval History at Sheffield and Master of Fitzwilliam) published widely on medieval England and wrote a history of St John's (*Portrait of a College*, 1961). After war service, in which he was awarded the DFC, and a period in the Colonial Office, R E (Robbie) Robinson (1939) returned as a Fellow in 1949 and from 1966 to 1971 was Smuts Reader in Commonwealth History, following which he took up a chair at Oxford. Frank Thistlethwaite (1934: Fellow 1945–61; founding Vice-Chancellor of the University of East Anglia) specialized in North American history.

The College can claim a pioneering role both in the study of imperial and Commonwealth history and in the subsequent expansion of the subject into the history of the Third World. E A Benians (Master 1933–52) was joint editor of the eight volumes of the *Cambridge History of the British Empire* (1929–59). E A Walker (1936) was Vere Harmsworth Professor of Imperial History 1936–51 and Fellow 1936–68. In 1953 Nicholas Mansergh (see Chapter 21) came to the College as the first Smuts Professor of Commonwealth History. R E Robinson (see above) was joint editor of the influential *Africa and the Victorians* (1961), said to have 'offended all the right people'. He was succeeded by John Iliffe (Fellow 1971–), Professor of African History from 1990 to 2006.

A supervision in College 2006

For British political history, the College has been well served by Henry Pelling (1939: Fellow 1966–97), and by Peter Clarke (1960: Fellow 1980–2000), who became Master of Trinity Hall. Well known, too, are Peter Hennessy (1966) and David Cannadine (Fellow 1975–77). Current College historians – including Peter Linehan, Mark Nicholls, Ulinka Rublack, Simon Szreter, Sylvana Tomaselli and Robert Tombs as well as a number of Research Fellows – cover a wide range of European and British history from the history of the Reformation in Europe to questions of changing family size in nineteenth-century Britain. As always, undergraduates – of whom the College takes some seven or eight each year – go into diverse careers, particularly the City, law, public service, teaching, literature, and the media.

MODERN LANGUAGES

Legend has it that the Modern Languages Tripos, as remembered by generations of students since the 1950s, was designed by a Professor of German and a Johnian, W H Bruford (1912: Fellow 1951–66). There was certainly something Germanic about its central precept – that the language, literature, history and thought of a national culture at a particular time should be studied as an integral whole.

Bruford's successor in the College, J P Stern (1941: Fellow 1955–72), was a Czech émigré who had flown in Lancasters as a tail gunner during the War. He was a combative figure who pursued his German studies with rigour and determination, and he left such a deep impression on the College that when he moved to the Chair of German at UCL, almost a decade was allowed to elapse before another Fellow for German was recruited – David Midgley (Fellow 1980–).

The College's high reputation for Italian studies was the achievement of Patrick Boyde (1953: Fellow 1966–), renowned for his wide-ranging Dante scholarship and his magnificently illustrated lectures on Italian art. Now retired as Professor of Italian, he maintains a high profile in College life as a grandfather figure to the graduates, and has been succeeded by someone who shares his interest in the connections between literature and science, Pierpaolo Antonello.

French – and the general oversight of the subject – was meanwhile sustained for many years by Edward James (Fellow 1955–), who was commemorated by an undergraduate speaker at his retirement dinner in 1993 as 'the Trinity incarnate': supervisor, Director of Studies and Tutor in one. A succession of talented young teachers – Naomi Segal (Fellow 1988–93), Rupert

Wood (Fellow 1994–9) and Victoria Best (Fellow 1999–) – has sustained undergraduate enthusiasm for the subject ever since. So the traditional strengths of the College in French, German and Italian have been maintained, and discreetly augmented in 1993 with the addition of Manucha Lisboa, University Lecturer in Portuguese.

At the same time the old Tripos model of Bruford's day has continued to evolve under changing circumstances, incorporating elements of cinema studies (since that has become a chief embodiment of the cultural canon in our time) and assimilating the irrepressible rise of Spanish. Linguistics has meanwhile also risen to academic respectability, and has acquired a Tripos of its own, the brainchild of another Johnian, Peter Matthews (1954: Fellow 1980–). And while the status of modern languages as a subject in the nation's schools gives foreign ambassadors periodic cause for concern, St John's continues to recruit extremely talented young linguists from a wide variety of backgrounds whose successes in Tripos in recent years have not gone unnoticed by the College Tutors.

PHILOSOPHY

The Moral Sciences Tripos, when established in the mid-nineteenth century, covered the whole range of human sciences including psychology. Psychology continued to be taught as a sizeable element in the Tripos until 1952, when the growing subject of Experimental Psychology was administratively disentangled from Philosophy and acquired its own Part II. Before this, the psychological strand of the Tripos was strongly represented at St John's, where the Director of Studies in the 1930s and 1940s was Sir Frederic Bartlett, the first Professor of Experimental Psychology at Cambridge. The de facto change in the Tripos to a more philosophical focus was recognized in the College in 1947 when Rev. J S Boys Smith became Director of Studies. (The change of focus was not acknowledged in the name of the Tripos until 1969, when 'Moral Sciences' gave way to 'Philosophy'.)

As a philosopher, Boys Smith's interests lay in metaphysics, of an idealist character, philosophy of religion, and ethics. His intellect and integrity impressed all those who knew him. And the same can be said of his successor, Renford Bambrough, who took over as Director of Studies in 1959 and continued in the role for over thirty years. Bambrough began his academic career as a classicist, specializing in ancient philosophy. The central metaphysical and ethical questions raised by Plato and Aristotle remained the focus of his work, but he was also much influenced by contact with John Wisdom, Professor of Philosophy at Cambridge through the 1950s and 1960s, and by the writings of Wittgenstein. A major philosophical concern was to defend the possibility of objectivity in ethics, aesthetics and religion against the subjectivist and relativist trends of modern thought. His rigour and *gravitas* impressed themselves upon generations of Johnian philosophers. He was an influential figure in the College in other ways, too, serving successively as Tutor, Dean and President.

Jane Heal, whose interests are in the philosophy of mind and language, joined the College in 1986 and took over direction of studies when Renford Bambrough retired. She was promoted to a personal chair in the University in 1999 and was the first woman to be elected as President of the College, a post she held from 1999 to 2003. She was joined in 2002 by Serena Olsaretti, who works in political thought. With them St John's continues to be one of the major Cambridge colleges for philosophy.

SOCIAL AND POLITICAL SCIENCES

The College's contribution to the development of the social, political and behavioural sciences has been significant. W H R Rivers, one of the earliest scholars to focus on and indeed help to establish social anthropology as a discipline, was a Fellow (see Chapter 14). More recently, Peter Townsend, who prepared a classic study of poverty in Britain, was an undergraduate member of the College, and Anthony Atkinson, who has advised the Government on welfare aspects of public policy, especially relating to income inequality and social inclusion, was a Fellow from 1967 to 1971. Sir Jack Goody (1938: Fellow 1961–) is another Johnian with an international reputation who has contributed to important aspects of comparative social analysis; and Robert Hinde, former Master (see Chapter 21) is prominent in the scientific study of human conflict and its resolution.

St John's was among the first Cambridge colleges to elect a sociologist to a Fellowship – David Lockwood, a leading figure in the expansion of the subject in British universities in the post-war period, held a Fellowship from 1960 to 1968. During that time he made major contributions to the study of social inequality and the social and political implications of economic change. John Barnes, the first Professor of Sociology in Cambridge, was an undergraduate at St John's and Fellow from 1950 to 1953. He made a seminal contribution to the theory and empirical study of social networks that help shape both sociology and social anthropology, and there has been recent renewed interest in his work insofar as it informs understanding of the nature and formation of 'social capital'.

The College currently takes about four undergraduates each year to read the Social and Political Sciences Tripos (SPS). The subject also attracts a number of undergraduates from other fields of study after their first and second years. Christel Lane (Fellow 1991–: economic sociology) and Sylvana Tomaselli (Fellow 2004–: political theory) devote themselves to supervision in SPS, and other Fellows assist in specialist subjects.

THEOLOGY AND RELIGIOUS STUDIES

The oldest Professorship in the University – in Divinity – was, like the College, a gift of Lady Margaret (in 1502) and the study of theology has been central to the life of the College since the very beginning. Today, the Theology and Religious Studies Tripos is one of the most wide-ranging of undergraduate subjects with papers in history, philosophy, languages, religion and the human sciences, biblical studies and all the major world faiths. In recent years the core disciplines of traditional Christian theology (biblical studies, doctrine, philosophy and Church history) have been supplemented with the study of Judaism, Islam, Hinduism and Buddhism, as well as more innovative and interdisciplinary papers including an exploration of 'Jewish and Christian responses to the Holocaust', 'Self and salvation in Indian and Western thought', and 'Image and icon in the Christian tradition'.

Sadly, the contemporary Johnian theologian cannot just roll out of bed like his or her predecessors and cross the street to the nineteenth-century Divinity Building. The Faculty is now located in a much-admired contemporary building (by Edward Cullinan Architects, who designed the College Library) on the large Arts complex on the Sidgwick Site.

Undergraduate theologians in St John's have been fortunate down the years in being actively involved with a community that includes a lively group of postgraduates and a vibrant Theological Society. In recent years papers have been given on a diverse range of subjects including the origins of radical Islam, the 'secret' of C S Lewis's *Narnia* stories, and the life and theology of the artist Caravaggio. In addition, this community is supplemented from time to time by holders of the Naden Research Associateship in Divinity, a coveted post-doctoral position which has been held by a number of prominent academics including both the current Regius Professor and the Lady Margaret's Professor of Divinity.

Recent theology graduates from the College can be found in quite diverse environments, from the corridors of the Victoria and Albert Museum to Bosnian refugee camps, from the Cannes film festival to the world of international relations, following careers in journalism, law, media, teaching, the music industry and academia.

101

11 Politics and Public Service

Prime Ministers

The post of Chief Minister or Prime Minister, though known by different names over the centuries, has been filled by five Johnians – with very mixed success.

In the Tudor period, the office of Lord Treasurer was one of many key jobs held by William Cecil, first Baron Burghley (1520/2–98). He came up to St John's in 1535 and spent six years here, immersed in classical learning. Cicero, it seems, provided the model for Cecil's later statesmanship. Cecil's big political break came in 1558 with the accession to the throne of Princess Elizabeth, already his patron. Appointed secretary of state on the first day of her reign, he acted as her chief minister for the next forty years, securing the Protestant succession in the process.

Burghley looked after his own family succession too. His son by his second marriage, Robert Cecil (1563–1612), who must have followed his father to St John's some time around 1580, also followed him into government. Little wonder that people spoke of a *regnum Cecilianum*. After Burghley's death in 1598, Robert Cecil became a pivotal figure in the transition from the dying English Queen to the new Scottish monarch, who succeeded as James VI and I in 1603. By 1605, when Robert was made Earl of Salisbury, he was clearly pre-eminent at court and remained so until his own death. The country then managed without a Johnian at the helm for over two centuries. Nor did the brief premiership of Frederick Robinson, first Viscount Goderich (1782–1859), redeem the situation. Born into a landed family in Yorkshire, he was up at St John's from 1799 to 1802, showing a diligence which later made him a useful wheelhorse in government. At the Treasury he

acquired the nickname 'Prosperity Robinson'. In August 1827 the recently ennobled Goderich was asked to form a government himself. Alas, it all ended in tears. When he started complaining about his burdens, the King took it as a resignation; and, after only five months in office, Goderich was asked to find his own successor, whereupon he started crying, and the King lent him a handkerchief. After this shambles, a quarter of a century elapsed before the next Johnian Prime Minister – George Hamilton-Gordon, fourth Earl of Aberdeen (1784–1860). Like his near contemporaries Goderich and Palmerston, he had begun his political career as a Pittite; indeed, as the orphan's guardian, William Pitt had paid the fees at St John's from 1800. His studies temporarily interrupted in 1801 by his inheritance of the earldom (and its debts), and terminally interrupted in 1802 by the Grand Tour, the gilded youth was launched on a long political career.

Above left: William Cecil, Lord Burghley, Lord Treasurer to Elizabeth I

Above: Robert Cecil, Earl of Salisbury, Secretary of State to Elizabeth I and James I

LORD PALMERSTON (1784–1865)

Harry Temple succeeded as third Lord Palmerston in 1802 while an undergraduate at Edinburgh University – then at its academic peak. Cambridge was another matter. Palmerston came up as a gentleman for a gentleman's education, choosing St John's for its 'remarkably good society', meaning that it was full of peers' sons like himself, and good for political networking.

Palmerston's political career thus began at St John's. Since his title was an Irish viscountcy, he could sit in the House of Commons. Soon elected as a Pittite, he took office in 1809 but in the 1820s became separated from his old friends – the 'stupid old Tory party'.

From 1830, when the Whigs came to power, Palmerston was to be in and out of the Foreign Office for the next twenty-five years. Robust and patriotic, he actually preferred bluffing to fighting, and displayed more overt morality in his policies than in his notorious sex life. A Johnian influence can be detected in his use of gunboat diplomacy to enforce the abolition of the Atlantic slave trade.

Palmerston offered moral support, if little else, to liberal nationalists throughout Europe. He said that Britain's role called for 'a good deal of judicious bottle-holding' – a technique he had doubtless observed at St John's.

Palmerston's late flowering made him the obvious choice to succeed Aberdeen as Prime Minister in 1855: already seventy, and

still in office at eighty. He intuitively spanned the political divide, heading a coalition between traditional Whigs and popular radicals. He thus made the Gladstonian Liberal Party possible after his death, though it was Disraeli who inherited his legacy in foreign affairs. Ambiguous to the end, Palmerston's final words were: 'Die, my dear Doctor, that's the last thing I shall do!'

Viscount Palmerston, Prime Minister 1855–8; 1859–65

Half a century later, after Sir Robert Peel's death, Aberdeen found himself leading the Peelites himself and brought them together with the Whigs in 1852 in a coalition ministry. Its bright promise, however, was suddenly blighted by the outbreak of the Crimean War.

The reluctant Prime Minister was persuaded to soldier on by Queen Victoria, who dreaded that she might instead get his Whig colleague, Palmerston. She was right. When Aberdeen finally resigned in 1855, his final duty was to help Palmerston to form a new government. It was the *regnum Johnianum*.

OTHER HISTORICAL FIGURES

St John's has never been a strongly 'political' college, but among its alumni are several figures who have left a mark on British history. The poet and ambassador Sir Thomas Wyatt built a career at the court of Henry VIII, surviving

dangerous associations with Anne Boleyn and Thomas Cromwell, and two imprisonments in the Tower of London. Lord Burghley and the Earl of Salisbury were joined at the Elizabethan Privy Council table by Thomas Howard, Earl of Suffolk and Lord Chamberlain from 1603, and by Thomas Sackville, Earl of Dorset and Lord Treasurer under James I. A man of parts, Sackville co-wrote the first modern English play *Gorboduc*. A generation later, Thomas Wentworth, Earl of Strafford, served as Charles I's Lord Deputy in Ireland in the 1630s, and his name became synonymous with the autocracy of the King's personal rule. Paying the price for Charles's unpopularity, Strafford was attainted by Parliament and beheaded in 1641.

Three Johnians played leading parts in the developing opposition to Charles I – Algernon Percy, Earl of Northumberland and Lord High Admiral of England; Sir

TITUS OATES (1649–1705)

The College has inevitably produced one or two scoundrels. There was James Dawson, hanged drawn and quartered as a traitor after the 1745 Rebellion; William Ewin the usurer, 'the most hated man in Cambridge'; and James Hackman, Army officer turned clergyman who shot his actress lover outside Covent Garden in 1779. No Johnian career, however, can compare in infamy with that of Titus Oates.

Oates migrated to St John's from Caius in 1669 and left Cambridge without a degree, embarking on a career spectacular for its selfishness, cruelty, and economy with the truth. Inside five years he contrived to throw away a curacy, a post as a household chaplain, and a career in the Royal Navy. Converting to Catholicism in 1677, Oates travelled on the Continent, returning to London, and to the Church of England, with lurid tales of a widespread conspiracy fomented by Jesuits to murder King Charles II. His bold charges, given credence in Parliament and at Court, gripped the imagination of the capital. From 1679 to 1681, at least thirty-five innocent men were executed for their alleged parts in an entirely fantastical plot. Belatedly, London came to its senses. In a sensational trial, Oates was convicted of perjury, imprisoned for life, flogged, and set in the pillory, where the London mob pelted him enthusiastically with eggs and rotten fruit. Released in 1688, his later years were marked by fresh religious conversions, a marriage of convenience, a conviction for assault, and enduring poverty. It is hard to say a good word for him, but he believed at least some of his own tall stories, and, over time, convinced himself that he was a saviour of the English nation, waging battle against her political and religious enemies.

Titus Oates in the stocks, and his signature

Thomas Mauleverer, who signed the King's death warrant; and Thomas Fairfax, Commander-in-Chief of the Parliamentary armies through the later stages of the English Civil War. An accomplished general, the latter was eulogized by John Milton:

> Fairfax, whose name in arms through Europe rings,
> Filling each mouth with envy or with praise,
> And all her jealous monarchs with amaze,
> And rumours loud that daunt remotest kings.

Matthew Prior emulated the achievements of Thomas Wyatt both as poet and ambassador, while Thomas Thynne, Viscount Weymouth, served at the centre of British politics as Secretary of State in the 1750s and 1760s, taking a robust approach to the Falkland Islands crisis of his day. In the nineteenth century, St John's produced a Foreign Secretary of genius, Castlereagh (see panel). Edward Law, Earl of Ellenborough, who graduated in 1809, was unimpressed by some aspects of life in the University: 'From what I saw of them at Cambridge,' he wrote many years afterwards, 'the persons I least respect are Fellows of Colleges.' For all that, he ended up as Governor-General of India at the conclusion of the First Afghan War. George Villiers, Earl of Clarendon, Palmerston's close ally, was Viceroy of Ireland in the aftermath of the potato famine, and later Foreign Secretary during the Crimean War.

VISCOUNT CASTLEREAGH (1769–1822)

Castlereagh is remembered as one of the leading statesmen of nineteenth-century Europe. Generous, honourable, but deeply depressive, he fought his demons and shaped, during ten years as Foreign Secretary, the enduring continental settlement which resulted from the Congress of Vienna following the Napoleonic Wars. He also played a prominent role in the negotiations which brought to a close Britain's 1812 War with the United States. As Leader of the House of Commons and in effect a deputy Prime Minister under the Earl of Liverpool, he took a tough line on illegal assemblies after the so-called Peterloo Massacre in 1819 and rejected moves towards parliamentary reform. At the

Viscount Castlereagh

same time he took an enlightened stance on Catholic emancipation and negotiated anti-slavery treaties with Spain, Portugal and the Netherlands. The dual role proved too much for one man. A colleague described the burdens that Castlereagh carried as 'enough to destroy the health of Hercules'. His health and sanity gave way under the strain and in 1822 he committed suicide.

Shelley in his satirical *Mask of Anarchy* spoke for radicals of the period in his memorable couplet: 'I met Murder on the way,/ He had a mask like Castlereagh'. The judgment of posterity has been kinder. Castlereagh has won the plaudits of many who have studied his statesmanship. Henry Kissinger was one among many admirers.

105

One should not be parochial. For instance, members of the College played a prominent part in the early history of New Zealand. Alfred Domett served as Prime Minister in 1862–3, while Sir James Allen was Acting Prime Minister, and the country's effective leader, for two years during the Great War. Allen's colleague Sir Francis Bell went one better, serving as Prime Minister, albeit for only a couple of weeks in May 1925. Dr Manmohan Singh (see Chapter 19) now holds the same office in India.

Below: Thomas Wentworth, Earl of Strafford 1593–1641

Below right: General Lord Fairfax 1612–71

PUBLIC SERVICE

Throughout the nineteenth and twentieth centuries, St John's has produced an impressive number of distinguished public servants. These have included, amongst British Permanent Secretaries, Sir Douglas Wass at HM Treasury (1974–83), Sir Kevin Tebbit at Defence (1998–2005), Sir Michael Scholar at the Welsh Office and the Department of Trade and Industry (1993–2001), and Sir Tim Lankester at Overseas Development and the Department of Education (1989–95). Sir Michael and Sir Tim are currently Heads of Oxford colleges – St John's and Corpus Christi, respectively. Sir Roy Denman, Second Permanent Secretary in the Cabinet (1975–7), became Director-General for External Affairs at the EEC Commission (1977–82) and Ambassador of the European Communities in Washington (1982–9). Sir Bryan Hopkin was Chief Economic Adviser to the Treasury (1974–7) and Sir David King, the Government's Chief Scientific Advisor, is a former Fellow of the College. Sir Nigel Crisp (now Lord Crisp) was Chief Executive at the NHS and Permanent Secretary at the Department of Health from 2000 to 2006. Sir Robin Catford was Secretary for Appointments to the Prime Minister and Ecclesiastical Secretary to the Lord Chancellor from 1982 to 1993.

In HM Diplomatic Service and the Colonial Service,

Lord Caradon was Permanent UK Representative at the United Nations (1964–70), following an earlier distinguished career as a colonial administrator in Cyprus and elsewhere. Rt Hon. Sir Percy Cradock (1946: Hon Fellow 1982) was Ambassador in Peking (1978–83) and the Prime Minister's Foreign Policy Adviser (1983–92). Sir Bryan Cartledge (Hon. Fellow 1985) was Ambassador to the Soviet Union (1985–8), and is a former Principal of Linacre College, Oxford. Sir Robin McLaren was Ambassador to China (1991–4), and Sir John Margetson was Ambassador to the Netherlands (1984–7). Sir Richard Posnett was Governor of Bermuda from 1981 to 1983. Johnians currently head or have recently headed two consulates-general in the United States – Sir Philip Thomas in New York and Judith Slater in Houston.

In other branches of public service, Air Chief Marshal Sir Roger Palin was Commander-in-Chief RAF Germany (1989–91) and Air Member for Personnel (1991–3). Sir David (now Lord) Rowe-Beddoe was Chairman of the Welsh Development Agency (1993–2001) and is currently Chairman of the Wales Millennium Centre. Sir David Wilson (Hon. Fellow 1985) was Director of the British Museum (1977–92) and Sir Neil Chalmers directed the Natural History Museum from 1988 until 2004, when he became Warden of Wadham College, Oxford.

In other spheres, Sir Giles Shaw MP was Minister of State at the Home Office and the DTI and subsequently Chairman of the House of Commons Select Committee on Science and Technology (1992–7). Lord Whitty, a former General Secretary of the Labour Party and Government Minister, is Chair of the National Consumer Council. Sarah Teather MP, elected for Brent East in 2003, is on the Liberal Democrat front bench. In the world of non-governmental organizations, Dr Peter Williams was Director of the Wellcome Trust from 1965 to 1991.

In the academic world, St John's has produced a

CAMBRIDGE UNION SOCIETY

LENT TERM, 1959

EIGHTH DEBATE

TUESDAY, 24th FEBRUARY, 1959
at 8.15 p.m.

"This House rejects the Christian Religion's claim to be a power for active good in a troubled world"

Proposed by Mr. J. D. LEAHY, St. John's College.

Opposed by Mr. C. S. TUGENDHAT, Gonville and Caius College.

Mr. H. SYKES DAVIES, St. John's College, will speak third.

Rev. Canon MERVYN STOCKWOOD, Christ's College,
will speak fourth.

FOR THE AYES	*Tellers:*	FOR THE NOES
Mr. L. MARKS, Sidney Sussex College.		Mr. D. E. LEA, Christ's College.

King's College.
19th February, 1959.

JULIAN GRENFELL,
President.

number of Vice-Chancellors, and at the present time no fewer than eight Heads of Houses in Oxford and Cambridge are Johnians.

The foregoing inevitably omits many distinguished public servants both in this country and overseas. But it powerfully suggests the breadth of the contribution which Johnians have made, and continue to make, to public administration and public service.

This Notice of Debate in the Cambridge Union in 1959 shows that St John's was not always on the side of the angels

12 ECONOMICS

In the late nineteenth century economics was taught in Cambridge only as part of the Moral Sciences and History Triposes. The year 1903 saw the foundation of the Economics Tripos, the prime mover being a Johnian, Alfred Marshall (see panel). The number of students in the early years was small – only two in 1909–10 – but they were privileged to sit at the feet of an inspiring teacher. According to the biographical essay by Marshall's student John Maynard Keynes, 'the pupil would come away with an extraordinary feeling that he was embarked on the most interesting and important voyage in the world.' Marshall saw economics as 'an engine for the discovery of concrete truth' and Keynes's judgment, made in 1933, that 'this engine, as we employ it today, is largely Marshall's creation' remains, for parts of the discipline, substantially true even now. Marshall was driven by a Victorian high moral purpose – to uncover the causes of poverty – and his combination of analytical invention and rigour with a strong commitment to improve human welfare through influence on public policy has characterized many of the Johnian economists who followed him in the ensuing century.

One such was Jagdish Bhagwati, who arrived from Bombay to read economics in 1953. One of his supervisors, C W Guillebaud, who had been a teaching Fellow in the College since the Twenties, greeted him with the words, 'You know Indians never do well at Cambridge'. This challenging pedagogical method evidently worked well, because in his second undergraduate year Bhagwati wrote a seminal paper, published in 1958, on 'immiserizing growth' – growth of a country's productive capacity which, by worsening its terms of trade, makes the country worse off. He went on

to become both one of the world's foremost theorists of international trade and one of its most influential policy advocates. Like Marshall, he has spent much of his life arguing the case for free trade, playing, in the words of his star pupil, Paul Krugman, a 'large if subtle role in keeping protectionism from becoming respectable'.

Another Indian who disproved the Guillebaud thesis was a near-contemporary of Bhagwati, Manmohan Singh (see Chapter 19) who graduated at the top of the class-list in 1957 and, after a distinguished career as an academic economist, turned to policymaking, first as the Governor of India's central bank, then Finance Minister and finally Prime Minister. Singh's sequence of economic reforms from 1991 onwards is widely credited with lifting India's rate of economic growth to one of the highest in the world.

At the time that Bhagwati and Singh came to the College, the other economics Fellow was R C O (Robin) Matthews (1949: Fellow 1950–65) who, after a spell at Oxford, returned to Cambridge in the late Seventies to take Marshall's Chair of Political Economy and the Mastership of Clare. Matthews is best known to economists for his important contributions to the study of economic growth, but he is known also, and conceivably to a wider audience, as one of the world's leading composers of three-move chess problems.

Three other economics Fellows of the College who have combined Marshall's flair for theory with a commitment to public policy deserve mention. A B (later Sir Tony) Atkinson, a leading authority on public economics and the distribution of income and wealth and a veteran of many government commissions, was a Teaching Fellow in the late Sixties who, after a spell

ALFRED MARSHALL 1842–1924

Alfred Marshall, the son of a cashier at the Bank of England, spent most of his academic life as a Fellow of St John's. Enrolled as a mathematician (he was Second Wrangler in 1865) he moved, through philosophy and social ethics, to economics, which he saw as the discipline that studies the moral basis for human behaviour and social organization. Sir Partha Dasgupta (Fellow 1985–) notes:

> As Professor of Political Economy from 1884 to 1908, Marshall took economics away from the Moral Sciences Tripos and in 1903 founded a new Tripos in Economics and Politics, a move that was decisive in making Cambridge the leading centre of economics in the world for over five decades. His *magnum opus*, *The Principles of Economics*, first published in 1890, laid the foundations of modern economics. The treatise was so thorough and original that for many decades it was common among economists to say that 'it is all in Marshall'.

He was in fact the originator of many of the fundamental concepts of modern economics, including marginal analysis, consumer surplus, the definition of elasticity, and the effect of market imperfections on output. In his later works – *Industry and Trade* (1919) and *Money, Credit and Commerce* (1923) – he made important contributions to the theory of money and international trade.

Alfred Marshall 1842–1924 by Sir William Rothenstein

away from Cambridge, briefly succeeded Matthews as Professor of Political Economy. Mervyn King (see panel), Teaching Fellow in the early Seventies, was another authority on public economics. He turned to public service in the Nineties and was appointed Governor of the Bank of England in 2003. Finally, Sir Partha Dasgupta, Professorial Fellow since 1985, is one of the world's leading exponents of welfare, development and environmental economics and of the economics of undernutrition.

St John's aims to teach the student of economics how to use the analytical framework of the subject (the 'engine' that Marshall referred to) to think about important questions such as 'Why are some countries rich and others poor?' The ability to reason as an economist, to assess economic evidence, and, more generally, to distinguish good arguments from bad ones stands the student in good stead in later life even if he or she does not become a professional economist.

Some Johnian graduates become academic economists, examples being Bhagwati and Singh, and Sir Charles Carter (1938), who, after a spell in prison as a conscientious objector during the Second World War (he was a life-long Quaker), became Professor of Applied Economics at Queen's University, Belfast, was then appointed to the Chair of Political Economy at Manchester, and, in 1964, became the founding Vice-Chancellor of Lancaster University.

Others have made careers in government service, two notable examples being Sir Bryan Hopkin (1933) and Sir Tim Lankester (1961), both Honorary Fellows of the College. Hopkin was Head of the Government Economic Service and Chief Economic Advisor to the Treasury from 1974 to 1977, while Lankester, after graduate work at Yale and a spell at the World Bank, became Private Secretary to two Prime Ministers (Callaghan and Thatcher) and subsequently Permanent Secretary at the International Development and Education Ministries.

Still others, probably the largest number, work or have worked in the City of London. The best known of these is perhaps Gavyn Davies, who graduated in 1972 and, after two years of graduate work in Oxford, became economic adviser at 10 Downing St from 1976 to 1979. He then joined a City firm as an economist, eventually becoming Chief International Economist and Managing Director of Goldman Sachs. After chairing a Commission of Inquiry into BBC funding, most of the recommendations of which were rejected by the Government, he was appointed Chairman of the BBC in 2001, only to resign in 2004 after the Hutton Inquiry criticized the Corporation for its editorial processes in the matter of a broadcast on the *Today* programme by another Johnian, Andrew Gilligan.

A REMINISCENCE BY PROFESSOR MERVYN KING, GOVERNOR OF THE BANK OF ENGLAND

My five years as a Teaching Fellow for the College from 1972 until 1977 were one of the happiest periods of my academic career. Following in the footsteps of economists such as Aubrey Silberston and Tony Atkinson, I was made welcome from the first day and soon discovered the truly international nature of the Fellowship – I was the only economist teaching in the College who was not from New Zealand. John Llewellyn, now a leading City economist, and Nicholas von Tunzelmann, the eminent economic historian, were my colleagues. My memories are of friendship – which continues to this day – with so many Fellows from many disciplines. Academic studies, sport, music, and a host of other activities, mixed naturally in the College. So it is highly appropriate that this volume has 'excellence and diversity' in its title.

My own research at the time focused on taxation and corporate finance. I worked for the Cambridge Growth Project, directed by Richard Stone who was later to win the Nobel Prize. An inspiring figure, Stone wore matching bow ties and socks and inhabited an office with a large table in the centre of the room piled with papers over which we could just see each other during seminars. I also joined a project led by another inspiring economist, James Meade, who also became a Nobel Laureate. The Meade Commission produced its Report on reform of the tax system in 1978 and our experiences on the Commission resulted in John Kay and I writing *The British Tax System*. And I seem to remember that I coxed the Fellows' Boat to its oars in 1973.

Professor Mervyn King, Governor of the Bank of England
(courtesy Bank of England)

13 ENGINEERING

Engineering at St John's, which each year welcomes fifteen or so new students, has an enviable reputation which goes back to the nineteenth century (see panel on Charles Parsons).

Harry Marsh (1955: Fellow 1963–71) recalls school advice to apply to St John's 'because Harry Rhoden was Director of Studies for engineering.' Rhoden (1930: Fellow 1941–72) joined the Metropolitan-Vickers Electrical Company in Manchester, developing a lifelong interest in turbines and compressors. In 1938 he returned to Cambridge as a Demonstrator in Engineering. For over thirty years he had a powerful influence on engineering in Cambridge and on hundreds of engineering students at the College itself. In the Engineering Department, he was at the heart of the teaching of thermodynamics, while at the College he built up a team of Fellows and supervisors across the spectrum of engineering disciplines. Many of these would go on to become Professors of Engineering at universities across the UK and abroad. For year after year, students from St John's dominated the class lists for the Mechanical Sciences Tripos.

The strength of engineering teaching in the College can be judged by a brief review of some of Rhoden's colleagues – Alexis Brookes (1931: Fellow 1948–2002), Stephen Harris (1938: Fellow 1962–72 and later Professor of Engineering at the University of Lancaster), John (now Sir John) Horlock (1946: Fellow 1954–7, 1967–74; Hon. Fellow 1988–), who became Professor at Cambridge, Vice-Chancellor of Salford and later of the Open University and Pro-Chancellor of UMIST), Michael Horne (1939: Fellow 1957–60 and later Professor of Civil Engineering at Manchester) and Kenneth Pascoe (1938: Fellow 1960–94).

In recent years engineering Fellows have included John Matthewman (1957: Fellow 1972–: computer applications), Ian Hutchings (Fellow 1975–: Professor of Manufacturing Engineering), Tom Hynes (Fellow 1987–: aerodynamics of jet engines), Janet Lees (1994: Fellow 1998–: concrete structures), Dick McConnel (Fellow 1979–: composite, steel and concrete structures), Duncan McFarlane (Fellow 1996–: automation systems), Ricky Metaxas (Fellow 1987–: computational electromagnetics and electroheat) and Mark Welland (Fellow 1986–: Professor of Nanotechnology). Former Professorial Fellows include Steve Williamson (1989–97, now Professor of Electrical Engineering at Manchester) and Robert Mair (1998–2002, now Master of Jesus, Cambridge).

In each generation, many of the Teaching Fellows have had experience of working in engineering in this or other countries. John Horlock, for example, worked on aero-engines as a design and development engineer for Rolls-Royce, and Stephen Harris used the opportunity presented by sabbatical leave to work in the team erecting the Sydney Opera House, a famously challenging task.

Among many Johnian engineering alumni who have made their mark in the construction and other industries is Ian Liddell (1957), who became a founding partner of Buro Happold in 1976 and is Cambridge Visiting Professor in the Principles of Engineering Design. His innovative design for the cable net and flat fabric roof of the Millennium Dome gained him several awards. In 2000 he was appointed CBE.

Harry Marsh is currently leading the College's contribution to the St John's College–Gatsby Schools Project (see Chapter 3).

THE HON. SIR CHARLES PARSONS OM KCB FRS (1854–1931)

The Hon. Sir Charles Parsons OM KCB FRS 1854–1931 (seated right) with the LMBC 3rd Lent boat 1876

developed a four-cylinder high-speed steam engine he had invented during his time in Cambridge.

This was the first of many inventions including the multi-stage reaction turbine; the first geared marine turbine; cavitation-free marine propellors; and axial fans and compressors. He was also an electrical engineer of genius, with inventions embracing a fan-ventilated rotor on electric generators; a three-phase alternator; and an alternator with rotating field magnets. He also held numerous patents on optics, including optical glass casting and searchlight reflectors.

Parsons, who can rightly be called the father of the steam turbine in the UK, founded the business of C A Parsons Ltd on Tyneside, which thrived as an independent power-producing company for a hundred years.

Parsons is probably the greatest engineer that the College has ever nurtured. The youngest of the six sons of the third Earl of Rosse, one-time President of the Royal Society, he received his early education from private tutors. One of his brothers wrote, 'Everything was provided at home to develop natural ability and mechanical taste, which my brothers possessed to a great degree … they were practical engineers before they reached the age for … attending college.'

After Trinity College Dublin, Parsons came in 1873 to St John's where he greatly enjoyed his time and was an enthusiastic member of LMBC. Passing out as Eleventh Wrangler, he spent three years as apprentice at Sir William Armstrong's works in Newcastle, and then joined Kitson and Co of Leeds, where he

The steam-driven Turbinia which Parsons drove at high speed through the Fleet at the 1897 Spithead review – a commercially successful publicity stunt

14 LAW AND MEDICINE

Opposite: The John Hall Law Library is a prominent feature of the new Library

Right: SPY cartoon of Sir Edward Marshall-Hall QC MP 1858–1927

LAW AT ST JOHN'S

Among the earliest eminent Johnian lawyers were two judges, Sir Robert Heath (1594) and Sir Soulden Lawrence (MA and Fellow 1774), who bequeathed a large library of legal works to the College. Thomas Denman (1796) was appointed Lord Chief Justice in 1832, having been Attorney-General during the passage of the Reform Bill. He was strongly opposed to the slave trade (see Chapter 7).

For junior members in modern times the centre of College law is supervision. Many have memories of being kept alert, in spite of a cold afternoon's sport followed by the heat of his gas fire, by the penetrating gaze of Meredith Jackson (1921: Fellow 1946–86; see Chapter 21). Many will recall too the genial good nature of Kenneth Scott (1936: Fellow 1943–84) and Warwick McKean (Fellow 1976–85), the deadpan humour of 'Dennis' Bailey (1919: Fellow 1931–80), as well as the tireless devotion and support of John Hall (1945) who set high standards, above all in the written work he so meticulously marked. He was the backbone of College law from his election to a Fellowship in 1955 until his death in 1992. For twenty years or more, students of legal history benefited from the benign but demanding supervision of the top legal historian of his day, Professor Toby Milsom (Fellow 1976). More recently, Jack Beatson (Fellow 1994) was Rouse Ball Professor before becoming the first academic to be appointed directly to the High Court in 2003. Sir Richard Aikens (1967: Hon Fellow 2005) was appointed a Judge of the High Court in 1999.

Notable among Johnian scholars who 'got away' is Glanville Williams (Research Fellow 1936–42), one of the academic giants of the twentieth century. More recently Peter Kunzlick (Fellow 1985–8) now holds a chair at

A REMINISCENCE BY THE HON. FRANK IACOBUCCI, RETIRED JUSTICE OF THE SUPREME COURT OF CANADA

During my lifetime I have received no better advice than that given me by two of my law professors at the University of British Columbia, both Johnians: to apply to St John's to pursue graduate studies. In 1962 I enrolled in the international law section of the LLB course, subsequently embarking on the Diploma. Cambridge's international law faculty was outstanding, with names like Lord McNair, R Y Jennings, Kurt Lipstein, Clive Parry, Derek Bowett and Eli Lauterpacht.

One of the many dedicated law Fellows at St John's was John Hall, who became a dear friend. He visited my wife and me in Canada on several occasions, and we never passed up an opportunity to visit him. Malcolm and Eva Clarke have also become close friends.

Prominent among my memories of law activities are the moot court competition, which I judged, and some Winfield Society events.

In my second year, the College asked me to be a supervisor in international law. This position was very important for me since I needed the money! Moreover, it was my first taste of teaching, which ultimately led to my career as a law professor at the University of Toronto.

Although a graduate student, I participated in Association Football and the May Bumps. This experience gave me a stronger feeling of connection with the College, and also led to a treasured continuing friendship with one of my team-mates.

My time at the College was both enjoyable and transformative. In that respect, while at the College, I met my future wife, Nancy (New Hall). In short, my association with St John's is one of the great blessings of my life.

Nottingham Trent, and Robert McCorquodale (Fellow 1988–95) and Takis Tridimas (Fellow 1995–97) hold chairs at Nottingham and Southampton respectively.

Three holders of the Goodhart Chair in the Law Faculty have been Fellows. Guido Calabresi (1980), who became Dean of the Yale Law School before his appointment to the United States Court of Appeals; Reinhardt Zimmerman (1998), now Co-Director of the Max Planck Institute, Hamburg; and Lord Mustill (1951: Hon. Fellow 1992 – and Fellow 2003–4 – see panel by Lord Hope).

Johnian law graduates have excelled not only in the law but also in other fields. In the world of modern finance they include Stephen Hill (1979), Damon Buffini (1981), Graham Wrigley (1982), and the College's current Senior Bursar, Chris Ewbank (1980).

Current students benefit from a sharp sense of the world beyond from David Fox (Fellow 1999–: land law), who started legal life in Otago, Richard Nolan (Fellow 1993–: equity), who returned from City practice and Ben Parker (Fellow 2001–: tort) from Oxford University. Christine Gray (Fellow 1997–: international law) was the first woman to be appointed to a law Fellowship at St John's and, in 2006, only the second woman to be appointed to a Chair in law in the University. Professor Malcolm Clarke (1961: Fellow

David Beamish (1970), the Johnian lawyer who was Mastermind *champion in 1988, and one of the few champions never to have passed on a question (courtesy of David Beamish)*

1970–) supervises the law of contract: he found it a difficult subject as an undergraduate in the College in the 1960s and, he says, still does!

The community of Johnian lawyers is held together by the Winfield Society which arranges talks, often by former Johnians, on current issues of law and practice. Its Annual Dinner commonly attracts a hundred or so Johnians, past and present; and its year ends with a punt party to which Fellows are invited – although only a few have the courage to attend!

MEDICINE AT ST JOHN'S

It was not until 1966 that a separate Medical Sciences Tripos was established at Cambridge, yet the study of medicine as an independent discipline at St John's goes back to the very earliest days of the College: Fellows 'skilled in the medical art' were specified in the Statutes as being exempt from the requirement to enter Holy Orders.

Illustrious Johnian medics through the centuries have included Sir Edward Alston (1612), father of Sarah, Duchess of Somerset, and President of the Royal College of Physicians (RCP); and Sir Noah Thomas, Physician to George III, whose splendid portrait by Romney as a fine, portly gentleman, hangs in the Hall. The *Zoönomia* of Erasmus Darwin (see Chapter 8) included a system of pathology. William Heberden (1725: Fellow 1731–1801), the outstanding clinician of

JOHNIAN LAW LORDS:
A REMINISCENCE BY THE RT HON. LORD HOPE OF CRAIGHEAD (1959)

As one who read classics, not law, at the College and whose entire career in the law had until then been spent in Scotland, I had the unique distinction on becoming a Lord of Appeal in Ordinary of joining four other living Johnians who had also done so – all of whom, like me, have been honoured by being admitted into the College's Honorary Fellowship. They were Lords Brightman, Templeman, Griffiths and Mustill. Ours is a remarkable record. Our number among the Law Lords was not equalled during our time by any other college in either Cambridge or Oxford.

The characters of each of these judges could not have been more different. Brightman, who died in 2006, was the archetypal chancery lawyer: reserved, painstakingly accurate, the perfect gentleman. Templeman was remorseless in his pursuit of counsel during the argument but utterly charming when it was all over. Griffiths, a talented and successful sportsman, gave the wholly misleading impression that he was simply an amateur among the professionals. Mustill was a hugely energetic, irrepressible extrovert, who found it impossible to restrain his enthusiasm for debate whatever the subject matter.

Lords Brightman, Templeman and Griffiths had all seen service during the war – Brightman in the Royal Navy, Templeman in the Gurkha Rifles and Griffiths in the Welsh Guards. As was typical of their generation, this experience played at least as great a part in shaping their characters as their time studying law in the College as undergraduates. They had all retired before I reached the House of Lords, but I had the pleasure of sitting with Lord Griffiths as a retired judge and with Lord Mustill before he too retired, although sadly not with both at the same time.

I now find myself the last in the line of Johnian Law Lords. The appellate jurisdiction of the House of Lords will end when it is transferred to the Supreme Court in October 2009. I look forward to the line of Johnian Supreme Court justices that will surely follow in my footsteps in that court. But for the present we can reflect with gratitude on what those four members of the College achieved at the highest level in our judicial hierarchy.

David Hope
13 April 2006

SIR PERCY WINFIELD FBA (1878–1953)

Percy Winfield (1895) took a First in law and was called to the Bar in 1903. Wounded in action in 1918, he recovered well enough to return to the College as a Fellow, becoming Rouse Ball Professor of English Law from 1928 to 1943.

Following *Chief Sources of English Legal History* (1925) and *Province of the Law of Tort* (1931), he wrote a definitive guide, *Textbook of the Law of Tort* (1937), which went to five editions under his hand and made a major impact throughout the United Kingdom and beyond.

Those who heard him lecture would recall his lean and erect figure, dry humour, and willingness to devote time and trouble to any who sought his help or advice. Of all Johnian academics, it is the work of Winfield that has had the greatest impact on the law of England.

Sir Percy Winfield KC FBA 1878–1953 (© Elliott & Fry)

A Winfield Society dinner of 1994 showing (front row): Lord Brightman, Lady Brightman, Lord Templeman, Professor Malcolm Clarke, Lord Mustill, Professor Robert McCorquodale, Mrs McCorquodale (© Eaden Lilley)

Right: Sir Noah Thomas FRS FRCP 1720–92 by George Romney

Below:William Heberden, 1710–1801, was responsible for the delineation of many diseases

his time – described by Samuel Johnson as 'the last of the distinguished physicians' – was responsible for the delineation of many diseases including angina pectoris and night blindness as well as his eponymous 'nodes'. His son, William Heberden the Younger (Fellow 1788–96) became Physician to George III in 1809. Thomas Gisborne (1744), three times President of the RCP, left a large part of his library to the College.

Sir Donald MacAlister (1873: Fellow 1877–1934) played a large part in preparing the *British Pharmacopaeia*, became President of the General Medical Council and Chancellor of the University of Glasgow. Sir Humphrey Rolleston (1883: Fellow 1889–1944), President of the RCP and Regius Professor of Physic, co-authored the massive *System of Medicine* and edited the twelve-volume *British Encyclopaedia of Medical Practice*. Lionel Penrose (1919) was a pioneer in several areas of mental illness, including the cause of Down's syndrome. Another psychiatrist, William Sargant (1925), was a strong supporter of physical as opposed to psychotherapeutic techniques. Grantly Dick-Read (1908) did much to promote natural childbirth, his books becoming bestsellers around the world. Lord (Max) Rosenheim (1924), President of the RCP, was the driving force behind the unification of the membership examination for the three UK Royal Colleges, and the foundation of the Faculty of Community Medicine.

As the first Professor of Radiotherapeutics (later Regius Professor of Physic), Joseph Mitchell (1928: Fellow 1936–87) made many advances in the field of cancer therapy, and was one of the motivators behind the new School of Clinical Medicine in Cambridge. His successor was Professor Norman Bleehen (Fellow 1976–). More recent alumni include Dr (now Sir) Jonathan Miller (1953), son of Emanuel Miller (1911), also a Johnian and distinguished psychiatrist, after whom the College's Emanuel Miller Prize is named.

Among former Teaching Fellows, mention should be made of Fergus Campbell (Fellow 1955–93), famous for the sessions in which he tried to hypnotize junior and senior members, and Alexander Monro (1937:

A REMINISCENCE BY PROFESSOR JON RHODES (1967)

I shouldn't really be writing this. The 'best years of my life' involved barely adequate contact with *Gray's Anatomy*, and my skeleton was rarely out of its box except to be ghoulishly admired by non-medical pals. An obsession with rowing had a lot to do with this. On my second morning at St John's I was sitting in a queue outside the rooms of Stephen Harris – the kindly engineer who was the medics' tutor. A rowing medic in the year above told me the importance of signing up to do anatomy dissections in the mornings. These could not be missed whereas other practical sessions were more relaxed! The morning anatomy dissectors could easily be recognized by the waft of formaldehyde that accompanied our entry into the lecture theatre.

Anatomy supervisions were with Xander Monro. The format was consistent – a generous glass of sherry, all lights turned off except for a dim brass table lamp and we would sit around a group of bones spread across the green baize table cloth whilst he drew some aspect of anatomy for us. He had a many-coloured biro with which he gradually built up a complex and, to me, abstract, drawing that combined with the dull lighting and the sherry to have a powerful soporific effect.

Physiology supervisions were by Fergus Campbell, a world authority on the mechanism of colour vision, a charming character despite what must have been extreme discomfort from a spinal deformity that kept his face almost parallel to the ground. His supervisions were inspirational. He was also an enthusiastic amateur hypnotist and gave brilliant public demonstrations which drew packed houses.

Fellow 1966–86), for many years the principal teacher of anatomy. David Dunn (1957: Fellow 1984–7), was one of the earliest to convert to keyhole surgery and a great rowing man.

Each year, the College admits thirteen to fifteen medical students and an average of two veterinary students. Over the past half-century, it has produced some 650 doctors and ninety vets. About a quarter of the doctors have gone into general practice, and about one in five into surgery (mostly general and orthopaedic). The Cambridge course continues to have a strong scientific emphasis and a 'traditional' structure, with the three-year BA followed by three years of clinical training, though all students are now introduced to clinical methods in the first two years.

Under an initiative sponsored by Ann-Louise Kinmonth (Fellow 1997–), University Professor of General Practice and College Director of Clinical Studies, St John's supports an annual medical student exchange with Yale, for medical students there who wish to learn about general practice in England. The College also facilitates an annual seminar for post-doctoral research training fellows in primary care across England and Scotland.

The College has a thriving Medical Society, and also hosts the prestigious annual Linacre Lecture, founded in 1534 by Henry VIII's physician. Recent Lecturers have included Nobel Laureates Baruch Blumberg, Sydney Brenner and Sir John Sulston.

A REMINISCENCE BY DR SUE HEENAN (1982)

Due to my discovery of life on the water during my first Michaelmas Term, I was anything but the model student. Despite Professor Perham's hints, there was little he could do to improve my infrequent attendance at the Downing site, and the biochemistry lab in particular. If there wasn't an outing, then I didn't need much of an excuse to take a detour en route to lectures via the Copper Kettle or Fitzbillies. In my second year I tried out for the Blue Boat, a good decision on the sporting front but less so on the medical side of things. I became a Blue, a life-changing experience, but failed my biochemistry practical and didn't shine in other areas, necessitating some stern words from my tutor, Dr Leake. Fortunately all was not lost and I finally saw the light, putting some of my basic science knowledge to use in my work as a radiologist.

W H R RIVERS (1864–1922)

A descendant, according to family tradition, of the midshipman who shot the sniper responsible for Nelson's death, Rivers was educated at the University of London and St Bartholomew's Hospital. He played a fundamental role in the establishment of experimental psychology and social anthropology as academic disciplines. Following his election to a Fellowship at St John's in 1902, he undertook pioneering research into sensory perception with Sir Henry Head and was made Director of the University's Psychology Laboratory. Between 1898 and 1915 he undertook several anthropological expeditions, performing pioneering experiments in cross-cultural psychology, developing the genealogical method for the study of social organization, and setting new standards of ethnological accuracy.

In 1916 he received a commission in the Royal Army Medical Corps and was posted to Craiglockhart Hospital for Officers, near Edinburgh. Here he played a key role in developing techniques to heal shell-shocked soldiers. His patients included the poet Siegfried Sassoon, for whom Rivers became a loved and revered father figure. *To a Very Wise Man* (1919) was Sassoon's poetic tribute to him. More recently Rivers has been portrayed in Pat Barker's award-winning *Regeneration* trilogy.

After the war, Rivers returned to St John's, threw himself into College life, and won the admiration and affection of a new generation of students. He died in 1922. Thirty years later Sassoon would write: 'I should like to meet Rivers in "the next world". It is difficult to believe that such a man as he could be extinguished.'

*W H R Rivers
1864–1922*

DR NORMAN HEATLEY OBE (1912–2004)

Norman Heatley graduated from St John's in natural sciences in 1933 and stayed on to research for a PhD in biochemistry, later moving to Oxford. He died in 2004 aged ninety-two, the last surviving member of the team which in the early 1940s developed penicillin – the 'miracle drug'. In fact it was Heatley's work on the means of extracting and purifying penicillin from the culture fluid which provided

*Dr Norman Heatley
at work on penicillin*

the route to effective production, and many believe that he should have shared the Nobel Prize given to Fleming and others. Some compensation came in the honorary doctorate in medicine which he was awarded by Oxford in 1990 – the first given in Oxford's 800-year history; in Honorary Fellowships from Lincoln College, Oxford and from St John's; and in an OBE. Friends and colleagues described him as modest to a fault. But he had the great satisfaction of knowing that he was a key part of the team that gave the world its first practical antibiotic, saving the lives of thousands of allied troops during the Second World War and countless millions of patients all round the world since then.

Tho: Wiatt Knight.

15 LITERARY ST JOHN'S

Opposite: Drawing of Sir Thomas Wyatt c.1504–42, by Hans Holbein the Younger (courtesy of The Royal Collection © 2006 Her Majesty Queen Elizabeth II). Courtier and diplomat, Wyatt was largely responsible for introducing the sonnet into English literature

> That Age is best, which is the first,
> When Youth and Blood are warmer;
> But being spent, the worse, and worst
> Times still succeed the former.

We do not know whether Robert Herrick (1613) wrote one of the best known of English lyric poems (*To the Virgins, to make much of Time*) during his time at St John's. Even if he did not, it has, from its familiar first line – 'Gather ye Rose-buds while ye may' – a marked and perennial applicability to the many ways in which students choose to spend their charmed time in Cambridge, whether their ambitions are academic, altruistic, athletic, artistic, or, like the poet's, primarily hedonistic. In the event, Herrick found St John's too expensive a setting in which to pursue his lavish life-style, and migrated to more affordable quarters at Trinity Hall, as he went on to become (to Swinburne at least) 'the greatest song-writer ever born of English race'. Many writers have passed the way of the older Oxford and Cambridge colleges over the years, and St John's has been more fortunate than most in the number it has fostered, of whom two, William Wordsworth and the Victorian polymath Samuel Butler, have left us memorable impressions of the undergraduate life of their times.

The educational principles upon which Bishop Fisher first established the College reflected the Christian humanist teachings of a close friend, the great Dutch scholar and writer Erasmus. The earliest Statutes required of undergraduates a high level of literary and linguistic cultivation, inasmuch as they were prohibited from conversing in a language other than Greek, Latin or Hebrew, though the vernacular might be used (quietly, so that immoderate laughter should not disturb others) in the privacy of their own rooms. The sixteenth-century beneficiaries of the original humanist curriculum were numerous and distinguished, and the intellectual *cachet* of the College soon exceeded that of any other foundation. Amongst the earliest was Thomas Wyatt (1516), the courtier-poet and diplomat who lived, dangerously, in the entourage of Henry VIII, and in whose writings the sonnet form finds its first true voice in English. Amongst the earliest Fellows were outstanding classical scholars such as Sir John Cheke and Roger Ascham (see Chapter 1), who were also the most notable stylists of the time in English prose. The first was tutor to Edward VI and the second to Elizabeth I, so that it is scarcely too much to say that the later Tudor dynasty itself was effectively Johnian-educated. The close of the century saw a change of atmosphere and the emergence of a new breed of writer in the shape of the acerbic and controversial 'university wits' such as Robert Greene and the innovative proto-novelist Thomas Nashe. Greene, a dramatist as well as a pamphleteer, is noted amongst other things for the earliest allusion to an up-and-coming actor-playwright called William Shakespeare ('that upstart crow, beautified with our feathers'), whose misfortune it was not to have had a university education. Nashe's eulogy of the College in his preface to Greene's *Menaphon* (1589) is probably an accurate reflection of its standing at the time, notwithstanding the rakehell reputations of the pair:

> … that most famous and fortunate Nurse of all learning, Saint *Iohns* in *Cambridge* … an Vniuersity within it selfe,

122

shining so farre aboue all other houses, Halles and hospitals whatsoeuer, that no Colledge in the Towne was able to compare with the tithe [*tenth*] of her Students.

A seventeenth-century report, probably reliable, asserts that Shakespeare's greatest contemporary, Ben Jonson, studied at the College for a time before being obliged to return to London to assist in his stepfather's bricklaying business. Jonson's reputation cast a long shadow over seventeenth-century English poetry. Herrick was arguably his most gifted follower, but other Cavalier poets associated with the College in its Royalist era also made their mark. The popular political satires of John Cleveland (Fellow, 1634) were in a mode in which Dryden, Pope, Swift and another Johnian, Charles Churchill, went on to excel, and his verse has worn better than that of the abstruse metaphysical musings of Edward Benlowes (1620) in his formidable but eccentric long poem *Theophila*. Cleveland's squib on the Scots particularly pleased the notoriously anti-Caledonian Dr Johnson: 'Had Cain been Scot, God would have changed his doom,/ Not forced him wander, but confined him home.' Equally popular were the satires of Matthew Prior, whose witty and engaging occasional verses are still anthologized. Prior was the son of a joiner, but his academic potential was noted by a

benefactor who found him working as pot-boy in a London tavern. He made the best of Cambridge opportunities, becoming a Fellow in 1688, and later a diplomat, ambassador and secret agent in the negotiation of the Treaty of Utrecht (1713), subsequently known as 'Matt's Peace'. His contemporary Richard Bentley (BA 1680) is chiefly known as one of the greatest of classical scholars, which no doubt gave him the confidence to publish an edition of Milton's

Left: Ben Jonson 1572–1637

Below: The portrait of Matthew Prior FRS, 1664–1721, by Alexis Simon Belle, which hangs in the Hall. It was probably painted in Paris in 1712/13 when Prior was Minister Plenipotentiary to the Court of Louis XIV

WORDSWORTH AT ST JOHN'S

William Wordsworth (1770–1850) came up in 1787 accompanied by William Cookson, a Fellow of St John's, who apparently hoped that his Fellowship would pass to this promising young man. It was not to be. Wordsworth devotes a whole Book of *The Prelude* to 'Residence at Cambridge', and tells a tale which is not unfamiliar to undergraduates arriving at Cambridge from unsophisticated provincial backgrounds. We see him finding his way, sometimes agreeably, but always with reservations. 'Beside the pleasant Mills of Trompington / I laughed with Chaucer', he writes, and seems to have enjoyed his idle moments as much as students of any age. But there was 'a strangeness in my mind, / A feeling that I was not for that hour, / Nor for that place'.

Professor John Beer (1948) writes:

As a sizar – a position that marked him as a poor man and socially inferior – Wordsworth occupied unprepossessing rooms – 'my abiding-place, a nook obscure' as he puts it – and we cannot even be sure exactly how they lay. We know they were above the kitchens, from which he could hear a 'humming sound', and also what he could see from his window:

> And from my bedroom I on moonlight nights
> Could see right opposite, a few yards off,
> The antechapel, where the statue stood
> Of Newton, with his prism and silent face.

The portrait of Wordsworth on Helvellyn *by H W Pickersgill, which hangs in the Hall. A leading Romantic poet, famed for his* Lyrical Ballads*, published with Coleridge in 1798, Wordsworth lived most of his life in the Lake District. He became Poet Laureate in 1843*

123

A quick reading leaves one with the image of a young Wordsworth gazing directly into Newton's marble face; once one visits the site, however, it becomes clear that no such direct line of sight was possible. But the idea of Newton, his 'mind for ever / Voyaging through strange seas of Thought, alone', remained as a potent reminder of what the intellect could achieve. In the end, much as he respected the emergent learning, it was through literary endeavour that Wordsworth would make his way. But his experience of exclusion did not make him a violent revolutionary either. Instead, his memory of the social equality that he had known in Cumbria, now backed by an awareness that even in a class-ridden Cambridge 'something there was holden up to view / of a republic', led to his distinctive poetic philosophy, combining a respect for what could be achieved by the individual intellect with his belief that 'we have all of us one human heart'. His College experience had no doubt played its part in shaping that double sense of things.

Paradise Lost with many of his own 'corrections' and 'improvements', whilst at the same time engaging in a protracted and colourful feud with the Fellows of Trinity, where he continued to occupy the Master's Lodge for many years after they thought they had legally ejected him.

Some aspects of Cambridge undergraduate mores remained much the same in the eighteenth century as they had been in the seventeenth. Herrick's contemporary Simonds d'Ewes (1618), later a distinguished antiquary, was scandalized upon coming up by the prevalent 'swearing, drinking, rioting and hatred of all piety and virtue' that he encountered around him. Not long before Wordsworth arrived in 1787 the anxious and reclusive Thomas Gray of Pembroke (and Gray's *Elegy*) had been alarmed to find himself in a town where the bucks 'set women upon their heads in the streets at noonday, break open shops, and game in the coffee houses on Sundays.' Modern readers of Wordsworth may find it difficult to imagine him in powdered wig and dressed in the dandyish student fashions of the time. In the *Prelude* he candidly describes himself raising too many glasses to the memory of Milton when he visited the poet's rooms in Christ's, and staggering back to St John's to arrive late for chapel. The reasons why Wordsworth later said of Cambridge that he 'was not for that hour, or for that place' are complex, involving the prevailing intellectual climate and the field of study.

A sadder story attaches to another Johnian poet of the Romantic era, Henry Kirke White (1785–1806), who applied himself all too assiduously to the existing curriculum. The son of a Nottingham butcher, his precocious *Clifton Grove*, published when he was eighteen, induced admirers who included William Wilberforce and the poet Robert Southey to help fund a Cambridge education for him. Setting himself the highest academic goals, and egged on by a singularly insensitive and impercipient tutor, White worked himself to death, succumbing to consumption in his room (F8 Third Court) not long into his second year, and leaving behind a widespread reputation for glittering

promise tragically cut short, which lasted into the early twentieth century. During his short time at St John's White would probably have met another poor sizar whose name, which he changed from Brunty to Brontë as soon as he arrived in 1802 (probably in order to disguise his impoverished Irish origins) will always resonate where English literature is read. How far the Rev. Patrick Brontë's own poems and fictional tales influenced the formation of the masterpieces which each of his three daughters were to write remains a subject for perennial debate.

The nineteenth-century College to which Samuel Butler came in 1854 could be a place of serious intellectual endeavour and academic competition. The exclusive debating club known properly as the Cambridge Conversazione Society, but popularly as the 'Apostles', was founded in St John's in 1820, and its liberal attitude to unprejudiced and sincere enquiry through debate (as distinct from the oratory prevailing at the Union) left a lasting mark on the intellectual complexion of Cambridge for well over a century. *The Eagle*, the first college magazine to emerge at either Oxford or Cambridge, was started in 1858, with Butler as an inaugural contributor. From the start it was primarily a literary journal, a character which it preserved for many decades whilst at the same time taking on the recording function of conventional college publications. But the aspect of undergraduate life at St John's on which Butler concentrates in *The Way of All Flesh* is connected with the 'Labyrinth' or 'Wilderness' of run-down rooms occupied by the poorest and least well-connected students, which was demolished in the 1860s to provide space for the new Chapel:

In the Labyrinth there dwelt men of all ages, from mere lads to grey-haired old men who had entered late in life. They were rarely seen except in hall or chapel or at lecture, where their manners of feeding, praying and studying were considered alike objectionable; no one knew whence they came, whither they went, nor what they did, for they never

SAMUEL BUTLER (1835–1902)

Grandson of a bishop; successful at Shrewsbury and St John's; coxing LMBC to Head of the River in 1858 – all the ingredients were there for the mainline Church career desired by his clergyman father. But Samuel Butler wanted to be an artist and rebelled. He attended classes at the Cambridge School of Art, quite contrary to his father's wishes. Eventually it was decided that he should be packed off to the colonies, primed with £4,000, to make his fortune. The choice fell on New Zealand where he made a success of sheep-farming and conducted some exploration of virgin territory. At the same time he read Darwin's *Origin of Species* (1859) and returned with a tidy profit and a sceptical mind.

Although he was still not fully financially independent, his father conceded that he should attend art school in London, and he began to paint. From this early period comes *Family Prayers* (1864), which now hangs in the Green Room where the Fellows foregather before Hall. It shows a paterfamilias presiding over a subservient household, a scene which prefigures his bitter critique of Victorian family life in the book for which he is probably best remembered, *The Way of All Flesh*.

In 1870 he published *Erewhon, or Over the Range* which laid the foundations of literary notoriety. Grafted on to memories of the New Zealand district which he had explored, this tells of a topsy-turvy society where, for example, citizens are punished severely if they contract diseases. In a famous chapter, Butler warned of a quasi-Darwinian evolution of machines towards world mastery. Further works showed growing antipathy to organized religion.

Alps and Sanctuaries (1881), a travel account illustrated with his own sketches and paintings, reveals his love of Italy. On his father's death in 1886 he came into an inheritance which allowed him to live half the year there. Always intellectually restless, he stirred

contemporary classicists with the claim in *The Authoress of the Odyssey* (1897) that Homer was a woman; and in 1899 published *Shakespeare's Sonnets Reconsidered* as a gesture of solidarity with Oscar Wilde. *The Way of All Flesh*, published posthumously in 1902, had been written in the 1880s, but put away to avoid offending his family. It was instantly famous.

After his death, St John's acquired the splendid Samuel Butler Collection – a large accumulation of his papers, photographs (an art form with Butler), music and paintings, together with numerous printed editions of his works.

Samuel Butler

125

showed at cricket or the boats; they were a gloomy, seedy-looking confrerie … I have seen some of these men attain high position in the world of politics or science, and yet still look of the Labyrinth and Johnian sizarship.

The Dorset dialect poet, polyglot and philologist William Barnes was one of the older men who lived in the Labyrinth in the late 1840s, having entered his name on the College books in 1838 as a 'ten year man' who, under an ancient statute, would qualify for his degree by

virtue of residence for three terms in his final two years. Like Wordsworth, he was never at home in Cambridge, and the deep provincial roots of his finely crafted lyrics – widely admired by contemporaries and by scholars today – proved to be a formative influence on the work of Thomas Hardy.

Literary Modernism arrived at St John's in the shape of the controversial philosopher and poet T E Hulme (1902, sent down 1904), the influence of whose ideas on twentieth-century writing and art was to be

ST JOHN'S HUMORISTS

The Johnian instinct not to take life too seriously has produced several kings of modern comedy.

James Keith O'Neill Edwards, who entered the College as a Choral Scholar in 1938, became a household name in the 1950s and 1960s as the flamboyantly moustachioed 'Professor' Jimmy Edwards. His principal television role was as the headmaster in the deeply politically incorrect sitcom *Whack-O!* (first aired in 1956), set in a rapidly declining public school and featuring plots which customarily involved flagellation (hence its title). Edwards also starred in the 1959 film *Bottoms Up!*, based on the television series. On radio he is best remembered as the lugubrious Mr Glum in *Take It From Here* and as a regular panellist in *Does the Team Think?* Founder of the Handle Bar Club for men with large moustaches, he died in 1988.

Jonathan Miller had already trodden the boards in revue at St Paul's School by the time he arrived at St John's to read medicine in 1953, and was soon causing a stir with Footlights: the *Daily Telegraph* critic described the main 1955 Footlights show as 'primarily a vehicle for Jonathan Miller, who made his name a year ago. He has developed a fantastic talent to such a pitch in the last twelve months that he is infinitely more like Danny Kaye than Danny Kaye himself.' Miller and fellow Cambridge graduate Peter Cook teamed up with Dudley Moore and Alan Bennett (both from 'the other place') to create the legendary satirical show *Beyond the Fringe*, first performed at the Edinburgh Festival Fringe in 1960 before taking the West End by storm in 1961 and transferring to New York the following year. Miller left the cast at the end of 1963, and the New York show survived his departure by only four months, closing in April 1964 – by which time he had moved on to fresh fields.

Douglas Adams died preposterously young in 2001 at the age of forty-nine, leaving behind a rich body of humorous work headed by the *The Hitchhiker's Guide to the Galaxy*, originally broadcast on radio in 1978 and revamped for television in 1981. A quarter of a century later the show retains

its cult status, and the mere mention of the number 42 still has true believers clutching their sides with mirth. Like Miller, Adams appeared in Footlights smokers, having cut his comic teeth with the Cambridge University Light Entertainment Society, for whom his only recorded performance was a performance to the inmates of Chelmsford Prison. George Watson, who taught him, wrote: 'His mind was a lumber room, wholly disorganized and richly stocked.'

Perhaps lower-profile but indisputably the most globally important Johnian humorist is David Nobbs (1955), whose prolific output of comedy writing – primarily for television – includes the classic *Fall and Rise of Reginald Perrin*, first broadcast on BBC1 in 1976. The eponymous Perrin – played by Leonard Rossiter – is a dysfunctional middle-aged and middle-management executive at Sunshine Desserts, who episode by episode inches closer to the end of his tether. 'I can't be bothered by this – life's too short!' he explodes during a meeting to discuss marketing strategy for the Exotic Ices campaign (though not before having proposed the slogan, 'I love to stroke my nipple/ With a strawberry lychee ripple'). Sadly, a call in the 2003 edition of *The Eagle* for Nobbs to be elected an Honorary Fellow, on the grounds that he had made more people laugh out loud than any other Johnian in the College's history, seems – so far at least – to have fallen on deaf ears.

Douglas Adams on the set of the sci-fi comedy series The Hitch Hiker's Guide to the Galaxy *1980 © BBC*

Right: T E Hulme 1883–1917 (© George Beresford/Getty Images)

Far right: Richard Eberhart, 1904–2005, at St John's c.1927. A Pulitzer Prize-winning poet, he was elected an Honorary Fellow of the College in 1986

far out of proportion to the slimness of his published oeuvre (which included a *Complete Poetical Works* consisting of five short items). Hulme's vigorous rejection of Romanticism created many of the preconditions for the advances in poetic expression achieved by T S Eliot and Ezra Pound, and his writings on aesthetics adumbrated the tendencies towards abstraction and geometric form in modern art. The circumstances under which his name was removed from the College's books after a brief return into residence in 1912 were accompanied by allegations of scandal. Following his death in action on the Western Front in 1917, some of his writings were published by the art critic Herbert Read, one of the few English writers to recognize the importance of the Surrealist movement. (Another was a friend of Read, the newly appointed Fellow in English at the College, Hugh Sykes Davies: see Chapter 21.) Of the same era was the

distinguished American poet Richard Eberhart, some of whose earliest verse was published in *The Eagle*. A memorial engraved with one of his poems is planned for the College grounds.

The post-war era has seen writers and writing of all kinds flourish at or under the aegis of the College. It is worth remarking that both of the University's weekly student newspapers, *Varsity* (1947–) and *The Cambridge Student* (1999–) were founded by Johnians, Harry Newman (MLitt 1949) and G Ien Cheng (BA 2000), both of them affiliated students from the United States. Under a unique endowment designed to encourage creative writing combined with travel abroad, the College administers an annual Harper-Wood Studentship for English Poetry and Literature (open to applicants from all colleges), which since its institution in 1950 has attracted many distinguished recipients, including the poets Thom Gunn, Jean Hanff Korelitz and Michael

A REMINISCENCE BY FREDERIC RAPHAEL

In October 1950, sporting my new gown, I was allotted a garret on A staircase in Third Court: lattice windows onto the Cam and the Bridge of Sighs. I was never more privileged. Was I as industrious as a Scholar should be? Asked by old Professor Anderson, who had covered my verses with chiding red ink, where in the corpus of Latin poets I had found a particular phrase, I said, 'I made it up, sir.' He sighed. 'We don't do that.'

I called all dons 'sir', though Guy Lee (a young, grey-haired Latinist, and a lifelong friend) winced at such ageing deference. Renford Bambrough, in his late twenties, had become an evangelical Wittgensteinian. I was converted, not least because I could never compete in the classics with my fellow-Scholar John (later Professor) Sullivan, a working-class Liverpudlian. Bicycle clips were more common than flat caps in 1950s St John's.

Hearties and arties were jeeringly opposed. When drunk, I was provoked into throwing a frying pan at a menacing member of the LMBC first boat. Pat Hutton, a fellow arty, said the next morning, 'Freddie, you're hell when you're drunk.' I said, 'In that case, I shall confine myself to being hell when sober.' I would. My college acting career culminated in playing Samson in *Samson Agonistes* in the Chapel, where I learned that consonants count for more than volume when in an acoustic nightmare.

In my fourth year, for which the College generously extended my scholarship, I and Tony (later Professor) Becher and David Gore Lloyd (whose early death primed my television series, *The Glittering Prizes*) rented 'unlicensed digs', where my girlfriend came to live with me. I had no idea that Guy Lee met Renford one day and said, 'Do you know about this beautiful black-haired girl Freddie Raphael is living with out on Montague Road?'

Renford said: 'No.'
Guy said: 'Neither do I.'

The College had in its tutelage the Harper-Wood Studentship, to enable would-be writers to go on their travels. I was given it after a curt interview by Hugh Sykes Davies, and wrote my first novel, in Paris, while the money lasted. One of my sons once said to me, 'Who would you be if it weren't for Cambridge?' No idea.

The front cover of Frederic Raphael's Glittering Prizes *with actor Tom Conti wearing a Johnian scarf against the background of New Court (© Penguin)*

Hofmann, the philosopher Roger Scruton, opera director David Pountney and novelists Amit Chaudhuri and Giles Foden.

Contemporary Johnian writers who have made a name for themselves include the novelists Piers Paul Read, Jonathan Smith and Jennifer Egan, Faber poet Charles Boyle, Royal Court playwright Jez Butterworth and leading chronicler of the Turf, Sean Magee. But any selection of names is invidious. Perhaps the last word is best left to Frederic Raphael (see panel), whose TV series *The Glittering Prizes* (1976) went on to become a novel that for many accurately captures the unsettling mix of creativity, ambition, competition and intense personal relationships that characterize modern under-graduate life in Cambridge; and does it with an acerbity calculated to put the romantic fantasy of *Brideshead Revisited* in its place: 'So this is the city of dreaming spires,' remarks the hero's girlfriend, visiting for the day. 'Theoretically that's Oxford,' he replies. 'This is the city of perspiring dreams.'

16 Art in St John's

Deposition from the
Cross *by Anton Raphael
Mengs (1728–79), from the
Antechapel*

Earlier chapters have shown something of the College's impressive collection of historical portraits – not least those of Lady Margaret over the High Table in Hall and the stern features of Bishop Fisher on the adjacent wall. Other portraits in the Hall include those of Wordsworth, Wilberforce and Castlereagh, admired by Johnians of all generations, though few tend to remember what are perhaps the finest of all – a Romney of Sir Noah Thomas, Physician to George III, and one of Erasmus Darwin by Joseph Wright of Derby. Further striking likenesses – including those of Elizabeth I, James I and the Countess of Shrewsbury – are part of a collection of Tudor and Stuart grandees in the reception rooms of the Master's Lodge; and a whole series of portraits of Masters of the College lines the stairs to the Combination Room.

In the Antechapel hangs a distinguished *Deposition from the Cross* by Anton Raphael Mengs – the gift of an alumnus in 1841. A very different work is to be found in the Green Room where Fellows assemble before Dinner. This is *Family Prayers* by Samuel Butler, whose talents as an artist were as formidable as his skills as a writer. The painting is one of considerable psychological depth and anticipates the dispraise of Victorian patriarchy shown in *The Way of All Flesh*. Butler's watercolours, of which the College owns several, are of great delicacy; and he was also a formidable photographer, with an acute eye for telling detail.

The College Library contains a number of fine busts, including those of Dirac, Marshall-Hall, Herschel and Wordsworth. A bronze head of Sir Cyril Cripps is to be found in the Porter's Lodge which bears his name.

Modern works of art are not easily found in the

College, though there is an evocative John Nash landscape (*A view of a pond in a rural landscape near Cambridge, 1962*) and a fine bronze owl by John Skelton; and the Fisher Building has prints by Sir Terry Frost and others. Some former College members will remember that Jim Ede of Kettle's Yard would frequently loan paintings to undergraduates to display in their rooms. Adrian Padfield (1960) recalls that after visits to Ede he would 'as often as not walk back to John's with an Alfred Wallis under my arm' and comments that he and others 'had no idea at the time of the real generosity and trust that was involved.' Recently, the College has hosted a Kettle's Yard Fellow, Marian Coutts, whose work included fine photolithographs of the Combination Room.

The west windows of the Palmerston Room are engraved by David Peace and Sally Scott with symbols representing the achievement of Nobel Laureate Paul Dirac and eight other great Johnian scientists (see Chapter 8). These range from William Gilbert to Frederick Sanger, whose research into the chemical structure of insulin and DNA won him the Nobel Prize in 1958 and 1980. One of the east windows, engraved by the same artists, commemorates the economist Alfred Marshall with curves of supply and demand.

Art of a very different kind is to be found in the series of wall paintings discovered some eighty years ago in the south-western corner of Second Court, in what is now part of K4. These date from the late seventeenth century and represent an allegory of the five senses. Various theories have been put forward to account for this unusually adventurous decoration of a College room, but there is as yet no agreement as to who might have been responsible.

Architecture is a lively discipline in the College, with a Professorial Fellow, Deborah Howard, and a Teaching Fellow, Frank Salmon, and a steady stream of architecture

Family Prayers by Samuel Butler which hangs in the Green Room where Fellows assemble before dinner

Portrait of James I in the Master's Lodge

students who play a prominent role in the creative life of the College, not least in designing the setting for May Balls. Amongst architectural alumni, Sir Hugh Casson (1928) is well known not only for his work as Director of Architecture for the Festival of Britain, but for his intimate and observant watercolours. He was the architect of the first master-plan for the Sidgwick Site and designed the so-called 'Raised Faculty Building' (Casson, Conder and Partners 1959–61). Among his portraits of Cambridge colleges, the depiction of St John's is delightful. The College is also proud of its association with Sir Nikolaus Pevsner, the renowned architectural historian who was a Fellow of the College from 1950 to 1955, and subsequently an Honorary Fellow. Apart from the famous series of county architectural guides – the *Buildings of England* – Pevsner's works include such classics as *The Englishness of English Art*.

The Annual Art Competition reveals a wide range of artistic talent, with students submitting works in a variety of media.

131

Right: Print by Sir Terry Frost RA (1915–2003), in the Fisher Building

Overleaf: This photograph of the New Court Gate won first prize in the College life section of the College Art Competition 2005 (courtesy of Sean McHugh)

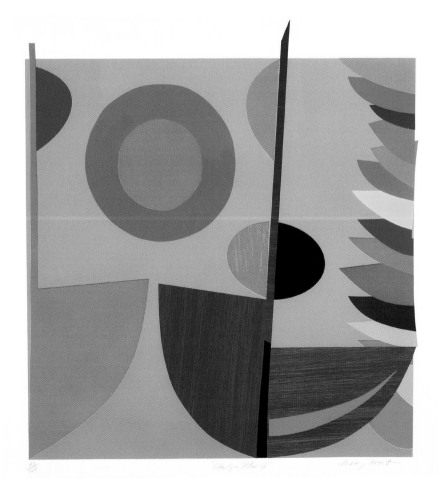

17 MUSIC IN ST JOHN'S

Simon Keenlyside as Billy Budd, English National Opera, 2005 (Tristram Kenton/Lebrecht Music & Arts)

Though the strength of the musical tradition in St John's naturally owes a great deal to the existence of the Chapel Choir (see Chapter 5), non-Chapel musical events have a vivid life of their own through the flourishing College Music Society, one of the largest and most active in Cambridge, assisted by professional and other musicians in the Fellowship, and taking advantage of the College's excellent facilities both for practice and performance. The Society, which sets out to provide performance opportunities for all musicians within the College, presents a year-round programme of high standard, ranging from lunchtime and 'late-night' recitals to charity concerts and formal events such as the annual Combination Room concert, and recitals in the Master's Lodge. It also contributes strongly to a highpoint of the Johnian musical year – the May Concert, long held in the Hall, now in the Chapel.

The Society has a variety of vehicles – a College Orchestra (the pick of College players, with help from outside); the St John's Singers; string and woodwind ensembles; and individual instrumentalists and solo singers. Recent years have seen many distinguished performances of both classical and modern works including Vivaldi's *Gloria*, Mozart's *Coronation Mass*, Beethoven's Eighth Symphony, Sibelius's Seventh, Bernstein's *Chichester Psalms* and Copland's *Appalachian Spring*.

One group which has established a reputation far beyond the confines of the College is 'The Gentlemen of St John's', an *a cappella*, close-harmony group drawing strongly on the Choral Scholars of the College. The bow-tied, dinner-jacketed 'Gentlemen', who have recorded prolifically, have sung at the Three Choirs Festival, serenaded the Duke of Edinburgh, and toured

JONATHAN HARVEY (1958)

Jonathan Harvey came to St John's on a music scholarship, and is an Honorary Fellow of the College. A lecturer at Southampton 1964–77 and a Reader at Sussex 1977–80, he was appointed Professor at Sussex from 1980, moving to a chair at Stanford in 1995 and later becoming Visiting Professor of Music at Imperial College, London. He has composed over a hundred works.

In the early 1980s, Harvey was invited by Pierre Boulez to work at the Institut de Recherche et Coordination Acoustique/Musique (IRCAM), a collaboration that has so far resulted in seven pieces for the Institute, and two for Boulez's Ensemble Intercontemporain. His work employs both classical instruments and electronics. A striking example of the latter is the tape piece *Mortuos Plango, Vivos Voco* (1980), made from recordings of the great bell of Winchester Cathedral and of a boy's singing voice. He has composed for orchestra (his *Madonna of Winter and Spring* of 1989 was recently performed by the Berlin Philharmonic under Sir

Simon Rattle) and for many smaller forces (four string quartets), as well as producing works for solo instruments. He has written many widely performed unaccompanied works for choir, as well as a large-scale cantata for the Millennium BBC Proms, *Mothers shall not Cry*. His opera *Inquest of Love*, commissioned by English National Opera, was premiered in 1993; his third opera, *Wagner Dream*, commissioned by Netherlands Opera, is to be premiered in 2007.

Jonathan Harvey's work has a transcendental quality, revealing influences from plainsong to Stockhausen, and he has drawn on Hindu and Buddhist as well as Christian themes for inspiration. One of his most interesting recent pieces is the *Bird Concerto with Pianosong* (2001), which he wrote on leaving Stanford, and which combines electronic and instrumental resources in a brilliant spectrum of sound. In 2003, he wrote a piece for the College choir – *The Royal Banners Forward Go* – for the Lent Meditation.

Holland. They are in strong demand at College events of all kinds.

A relative newcomer is Jazz@John's, a society which sets out to provide the best in quality jazz, funk and soul, attracting well-known performers and achieving sell-out evenings. A recent Lent Party Event staged five bands in one night, with blues, funk, soul, Motown, bossa nova, R'n'B, gypsy jazz and even Russian folk music.

Johnians who have gone on to achieve distinction as professional musicians include Simon Keenlyside (1983), David Pountney (1969), Richard Suart (1974) and Robert King (1982); and there is a long list of distinguished organists who began their careers as Organ Scholars.

Johnian composers include Robin Orr (Organist from 1938 to 1951, with a break for War service) and Jonathan Harvey (see panel), a music scholar and Honorary Fellow of the College, whose work has been extensively played and toured by major contemporary ensembles.

A Johnian chorister, Harry Gregson-Williams, has composed music for films including *The Lion, The Witch and The Wardrobe;* and on a very different note, tenor Allan Clayton (2000) was selected to sing the National Anthem in front of 80,000 fans at the 2005 Cup Final in Cardiff's Millennium Stadium.

Left to right:

The 'Gentlemen of St John's'

Allan Clayton sings the national anthem at the Cup Final, Cardiff, 2005

Jazz in the College gardens

18 THEATRICAL ST JOHN'S

Theatrical activity in St John's is not always easy to trace, because the written records are scanty, whether they be ancient archival references to College plays in the sixteenth century or sporadic reviews in *The Eagle* of productions by the Lady Margaret Players in more recent times. Moreover, theatrically inclined Johnians have inevitably inclined towards the major University dramatic groups, some going on to careers in the profession. Sir Cecil Beaton (1922: see panel in Chapter 6) left without graduating and soon found fame as a society photographer and set designer, having occupied much of his time at Cambridge in mounting productions at the ADC, featuring himself *en travestie* as, for example, Princess Angelica in Thackeray's *The Rose and the Ring* in 1924. Another figure from the same world was Ian Hay (John Hay Beith: 1895), the popular comic novelist and playwright of the First World War and inter-war years who collaborated with P G Wodehouse in staging some of his stories.

Sir Derek Jacobi (1957: Hon. Fellow 1987; see panel), starred in Marlowe Society productions at the Arts Theatre in 1958 (Marlowe's *Edward II*, broadcast by the BBC) and 1959 (*Henry IV Parts 1 and 2*), before becoming familiar to millions as Claudius and Cadfael. Sir Jonathan Miller (1953: Hon. Fellow 1982) began the strand of his career that culminated in *Beyond the Fringe* alongside Frederic Raphael in the Footlights revues of 1954 (*Out of the Blue*) and 1955 (*Between the Lines*), the first

Cambridge shows of this kind to transfer to the West End. More recently, Johnians who have gone on to acting careers include Sasha Behar (1987 – see Chapter 10, *Classics*) and Jamie Griffith (1993 – stage name Jamie Bamber), who writes:

'I had a great time at St John's juggling my time between playing rugby, studying languages and doing lots of productions for the ADC and the Lady Margaret Players. On leaving Cambridge I went to LAMDA for a year and then straight on to a number of TV jobs including a large role in *Hornblower*. Theatre work included Prince Hal at the Bristol Old Vic, and now I am in my fourth year playing Apollo in *Battlestar Galactica* – a huge critical hit in the States.'

It is evident from the early Statutes of the College that drama was both part of the academic curriculum and a form of entertainment for the College community. From the 1520s to the general suppression of all theatrical activity at the outbreak of the Civil War the variety of plays reflects the humanistic learning for which the College was noted, as well as its contacts with the world of the professional Elizabethan and Jacobean

theatre. The 1545 version of the Statutes laid down that plays were to be performed at certain times each year, for which funding would be provided. The Fellows were to take it in turn to be master of ceremonies and to produce the plays, and could be fined if they failed to do so. The plays, some of which were composed by Fellows or students, were presented in Hall, and were at first in Latin or Greek. The earliest archival references are to productions of the 1520s entitled *Microcosmos* and *Mundus Plumbeus* by a Fellow, Thomas Arthur, which, to judge by the titles, are likely to have been morality plays of the traditional medieval type. Classical drama soon entered the repertoire with a version of Aristophanes' *Plutus* (1536), and by the mid-century there were Greek-style tragedies on biblical subjects such as *Jephtha* and *Absolon*. In 1579 English history became the subject in the shape of Thomas Legge's *Ricardus Tertius*, the first recorded example of a chronicle play of the type soon to be perfected by Marlowe and Shakespeare. Towards the end of the century, and in common with the professional theatre of the time, plays on Italianate subjects became fashionable (such as *Machiavellus*, 1597), and for the first time we hear of plays being given in English, often ribald satires on the townsfolk of Cambridge. It was in this environment that the Johnian playwrights Robert

Greene and Thomas Nashe (see Chapter 15) first learnt their trade. Others interested themselves in staging and special effects: the mysterious Dr John Dee (BA 1545), alchemist and astrologer, acquired his reputation as a magician when, as part of a production of Aristophanes' *Peace* at Trinity, he caused a gigantic winged scarab beetle with a man on its back to fly across the stage.

The trilogy known as the *Parnassus Plays*, staged in the Hall at St John's between 1598 and 1601, was discovered to exist in manuscript in recent times, and though they are probably not representative of University drama generally, their adventitious survival gives a unique glimpse of the literary and theatrical preoccupations of Elizabethan undergraduates. The comic involvements and temptations of two young men are depicted in *The Pilgrimage to Parnassus*, Parnassus itself being the BA degree. In further adventures the young men go on to seek preferment and various other means of livelihood on the Continent and in London, but disillusioned and discouraged by the outside world, they eventually come back to Cambridge in *The Returne from Parnassus*. The authors (probably two) are unknown, but their easy and informed allusions to the poetry and plays of the time (Spenser, Nashe, Marlowe, Jonson and Shakespeare are commented upon amongst others)

The original cast of Beyond the Fringe *1964: Jonathan Miller, Alan Bennett, Dudley Moore and Peter Cook* (© BBC)

The filming of The Golden Age *restored the College briefly to Elizabethan times (right: courtesy of Colin Shepherd)*

the lengthy text being given in an abridged version in the Fellows' Garden. The Players seem to have struggled to establish themselves in the early 1950s, partly because the College lacked a suitable theatrical venue. May Week productions (usually middle-brow affairs – Rostand, Drinkwater, Dorothy L Sayers) usually risked the outdoors, whilst Milton's *Samson Agonistes* was deemed suitable for the Chapel. For many years they seem to have confined themselves to readings, with the occasional enterprising production such as Middleton and Rowley's Jacobean thriller *The Changeling*, given in Hall in 1963. All changed in the late 1960s, when the upper hall of the School of Pythagoras was converted into a 144-seat theatre, originally with a raised stage at the south end. In a pattern that continues to the present day, Johnians began to treat themselves and others to two or three major productions a year, beginning with a spate of major Elizabethan and Jacobean classics between 1969 and 1973: *Cymbeline, Troilus and Cressida, Romeo and Juliet, The Knight of the Burning Pestle, Women Beware Women, Bartholomew Fair.*

The College building and grounds have themselves from time to time been seen as a theatrical setting, most recently during filming for *The Golden Age*, the sequel to *Elizabeth*, starring Cate Blanchett.

show that Johnians were expected to be *au courant* with the literary culture of their time.

The formation of the Lady Margaret Players in 1949 was marked by the first and, in all probability, the only revival of the *Parnassus Plays* ever to have taken place,

A REMINISCENCE BY SIR DEREK JACOBI (1957)

I arrived at St John's fresh from a sixth-form grammar and, whereas many of my contemporaries had done National Service and were thereby further along the road to young manhood, I had escaped the rigours of the call-up due to its abolition and still felt very much the schoolboy. During my three years I never lived in College, preferring the freedom of 'digs' with surrogate parents/landlords. I had arrived with something of a reputation in the theatre world acquired at the Edinburgh Festival Fringe as a schoolboy Hamlet, a reputation severely dented by my first foray into Cambridge acting: a very mediocre and badly cast performance in an American play called *All the King's Men*. There followed nursery productions at the Amateur Dramatic Club.

After that, life at the University consisted mainly of playing parts in a series of acting companies – the ADC, the Mummers, the European Theatre Group and the Marlowe Society, touring both at home and abroad during the vacations and consigning my academic career into the small hours and even smaller corners of my consciousness. Lectures always gave place to rehearsals, essays to performances, and degrees to reviews. My eventual 2.2 was ever acknowledged as the typical 'actors' degree'.

We thespians possessed a veneer of professionalism; we were the blind being directed by the blind but always in front of a live and usually enthusiastic audience. Thanks to the likes of John Barton and Dadie Rylands at King's College, voice technique, fencing expertise and stage discipline became some of our acquired skills. Ex-students, now professional directors, would return and pass on their experience and knowledge. Some of us (not me) even had theatrical agents lined up before leaving College to enter the cut and thrust of the real world. It was my drama school rather than my university and my first professional job at the Birmingham Repertory Theatre held lesser terrors for me as I felt I had been in rep already most of my adult life. I am sorry to say that I never acted in St John's, but I well remember Harry Hinsley who rescued me from not one, but two, examination mishaps and ensured that my time at Cambridge was not over before it had almost begun!

Derek Jacobi in a Marlowe Society production of 1960 with Ian McKellen and Elizabeth Proud (© Cambridge Arts Theatre)

19 TIES WITH THE WIDER WORLD

Individual members of the College maintain contact with the worldwide academic communities to which they belong. The College as a community also greatly values its ties with the wider world, some of which date back many years, and is constantly seeking to expand these ties in mutually beneficial ways.

EUROPE

In Europe, well-established links exist with Uppsala, Heidelberg, Pavia and Utrecht Universities. Student exchanges with the first began well over fifty years ago and have continued annually without a break. In 1966 Mike Brearley was the Johnian nominee at Uppsala.

The Heidelberg programme began in 1979. Originally designed for linguists, exchanges now take place between disciplines as diverse as theology and chemistry. The exchange with Ghislieri College, Pavia, began in 1982 and brings students to St John's during the long vacation to study a wide range of subjects. Johnians going to Pavia tend to follow courses on Italian literature or the history of art.

The contact with Utrecht came about when Ray Jobling – then Senior Tutor – was invited to advise on the development of a tutorial system for Utrecht's new University College, which was to be established on Oxbridge college lines. A succession of able undergraduates have since come to St John's for two or three terms. One of these took a Tripos paper, achieved First Class marks, and was made a Scholar. A tutor from Utrecht who came to study tutorial method at the College later returned to supervise in Maths. In return, St John's has sent Maths and Physics students to Utrecht on summer courses.

The value of these exchanges can be seen from the fact that a number of students from the various 'linked' universities have subsequently applied and been accepted for graduate courses at St John's.

In the wake of the dramatic political events of 1989–90, the College instituted a programme of Visiting Fellowships from Eastern European and Russian universities, and this continues to this day.

NORTH AMERICA

Links with the Americas go back as far as the seventeenth century, when a number of Johnian Nonconformists left for New England. Rev. Peter Bulkley (1600) emigrated in 1635 – fifteen years after the Pilgrim Fathers – and led the party which founded Concord, Massachusetts, where he was pastor till his death in 1659. Two further 1635 emigrants, Rev. Nicholas Baker (1628) and Rev. Thomas Carter (1626), became Ministers at Scituate, Mass. and Woburn, Mass. Rev. Timothy Dalton (1610) emigrated in 1636, having been suspended by his bishop, and settled at Hampton, New Hampshire, where he too became Minister. Rev. William Worcester, Vicar of Olney, Bucks, till 1638, emigrated in the following year and was appointed first pastor of Salisbury, Mass. George Cook (1626) became Speaker of the General Court of Massachusetts in 1645 before returning to England as a Colonel in Cromwell's army.

Alexander Whitaker, who emigrated to Virginia in 1611 and is famous for having baptized Pocahontas and married her to John Rolfe, was the son of William Whitaker, Master of St John's from 1585 to 1595.

The first student from the New World to be entered in the admissions register was John Headley of New

England, admitted in 1674. Students also came from the West Indies. Drewry Ottley, admitted Fellow Commoner in 1774 from St Kitts, presented some fine silver candlesticks which now grace the Master's Lodge. William Penn, son of the last Governor of Pennsylvania, was admitted Fellow Commoner in 1795 and went on to show a celebrated weakness for the bottle. (King George IV quipped that he was a 'pen which had been cut once too often'.)

The distinguished Johnian mathematician J J Sylvester was Professor of Mathematics from 1876 to 1883 at the new Johns Hopkins University, whence he returned to take up an Oxford chair. A commemorative medal struck in his honour by Johns Hopkins is in the College Library. Ernest Benians (Master 1933–52) wrote a *Historical Sketch of the United States* in 1943. Frank Thistlethwaite (see Chapter 10, *History*) also wrote widely on American history. Hugh Brogan (1958) published a substantial *History of the United States* in 1985.

Over the years, the College has hosted many students and academics from North America. One of the most illustrious is the Pulitzer Prize-winning poet Richard Eberhart (1927: Hon Fellow 1986), who died in 2005 at the age of 101. Some have come under the aegis of the Marshall Scholarship programme. Others have benefited from special scholarship schemes, including Keasby Bursaries and Davies-Jackson Scholarships. The latter are specifically designed to afford experience of a Cambridge college education to an American student of similar background to that of the anonymous benefactor – from a US university or college not of the first rank, which does not usually envisage sending its graduates to a British university. They have achieved impressive results. One student won a Larmor Award as one of the outstanding all-rounders of her year.

The College has regular undergraduate exchange programmes with MIT and Caltech (the California Institute of Technology).

Many Fellows have at various times lived and worked in the United States. The previous Master, Peter Goddard, is currently Director of the Institute of Advanced Study at Princeton.

The Johnian Society of the USA (JS–USA) keeps in touch with nearly 700 alumni (see Chapter 27), and in recent years the College Choir has carried out a number of highly successful engagements in North America.

The College also has longstanding connections with Canada. One of its Honorary Fellows, Frank Iacobucci (see Chapter 14) is a distinguished Canadian lawyer. Alumni have included the late Lord (Ken) Thomson of Fleet (1945). A reunion of Canadian Johnians, attended by the Master, was held in Toronto in March 2006.

MIDDLE EAST, INDIA AND PAKISTAN

The story of the College's connections with the Middle East begins in the Library, which was one of the earliest in England to acquire a manuscript of the Koran – in 1637, a decade before the first English translation of the text. The Library also possesses several important Persian and other oriental manuscripts, including the valuable Nizami *Khamsah* text from 1540, and documents from 1770 containing evidence of the first educated Indian traveller to England. Edward Palmer (1863: Fellow 1867), Professor of Arabic in the 1870s, catalogued the University's Arabic, Persian and Hindustani manuscripts and went on to participate in expeditions to the Near East and Egypt, in one of which he was killed.

The latter part of the nineteenth century saw the arrival of increasing numbers of Indian students at the College. One of the first, Nurul Huda, gained an LLB in 1881 and went on to practise in the High Court, Calcutta. It was the custom in the early years of the last century to award two or three places to Indian undergraduate students, one of whom would be funded by the Government of India, and a strong connection developed at that time with the Indian Civil Service (ICS). Joseph Tanner (1882: Fellow 1886) lectured on Indian history to those at Cambridge studying for the ICS and also examined for the Service. Of Indian students, Mahadeo Bhide (1904) was awarded an

DR MANMOHAN SINGH (1955)

Dr Manmohan Singh, the first Sikh Prime Minister of India, was born in 1932 in a small Punjabi village, now in Pakistan. He came to St John's in 1955 and in 1957 achieved a First in economics. He was awarded the College's Wright Prize for distinguished achievement in both 1955 and 1957. Following a PhD at Nuffield College, Oxford, he returned initially to an academic career in India. Subsequently, following a short period at UNCTAD, he became Chief Economic Adviser to the Finance Ministry in Delhi and Secretary to that Ministry from 1976 to 1980. In 1982, the year he was appointed Governor of the Reserve Bank of India, he was made an Honorary Fellow of St John's. In 1985 he was appointed Deputy Chairman of the Indian Planning Commission, and from 1987 to 1990 he was Secretary-General and Commissioner of the South–South Commission chaired by Julius Nyerere. In 1991 he was elected to the Rajya Sabha, the Upper House of the Parliament of India, as a representative of the Indian National Congress. From 1991 to 1996, as Finance Minister in the administration of Prime Minister Narasimha Rao, he was responsible for the programme of liberalization and deregulation which created

the conditions for India's subsequent vigorous economic growth. From 1998 to 2004 he was leader of the opposition in the Rajya Sabha during the administration of the BJP. In 2004, when the Congress Party returned to power under the leadership of Sonia Gandhi, he was nominated by her as Prime Minister. He was awarded an Honorary Degree by the University of Cambridge in 2006.

Dr Manmohan Singh meets students in the Master's Lodge

exhibition and emerged as Twentieth Wrangler. Another – Byramji Cama – unhappily died in 1902 following a riding accident. His father commemorated him in a College prize for the student placed highest in the ICS exams. In 1901 the College appointed Raghunath Paranjpye as its first Indian Fellow.

Many Johnians served in the ICS and some wrote highly significant works on Indian affairs. Sir Denzil Ibbetson, Lieutenant-Governor of the Punjab, wrote on Punjab ethnography. Sir William Lee-Warner, who became Secretary of the Political and Secret Department of the India Office, wrote on the Native States. H L O Garrett founded the Punjab Records Office in Lahore, collecting together not only the official government records, but pre-existing state documents. Without his efforts, the historic record for the Punjab might well not exist. Another Johnian, Sir Thomas Gibson-Carmichael (later Baron Carmichael),

served successively as Governor of Madras and Bengal.

Amongst more recent Johnians who have achieved great distinction are Dr Manmohan Singh, Prime Minister of India (see panel) and Abdus Salam, Nobel Laureate (see Chapter 8). Both men were born in the same small district of the Punjab. Others include Dr Nagendra Singh (1936), President of the International Court of Justice 1985–8, and Vikram Sarabhai (1937), who became Chairman of India's Atomic Energy Commission and Space Research Organisation.

Currently, the College maintains a link with St Stephen's College, Delhi.

AUSTRALIA AND NEW ZEALAND

For over 150 years, the College has had continuing contacts with both Australia and New Zealand. George Selwyn (1826), Bishop of New Zealand 1841–67, played a determining role in Church development there.

142

Another Johnian, Alfred Domett (1829), served as Prime Minister of New Zealand in 1862–3, while Sir James Allen (1874) was Minister of Defence from 1912–20 and the country's effective leader for two years during the First World War. Sir Francis Bell (1869) served briefly as Prime Minister in 1925. The writer and artist Samuel Butler (see Chapter 15) spent some years in the South Island as a young man, farming and exploring. His memories of New Zealand landscapes set the scene in his novel *Erewhon*.

Many Australians and New Zealanders have studied, or held Fellowships, at the College. Sir Mark Oliphant (1901–2000) came to St John's as a Teaching Fellow in 1934. His outstanding achievement at Cambridge was the identification, with Rutherford, of tritium as an isotope of hydrogen. After the war he moved to Canberra, and in 1971 was appointed Governor of South Australia. Elected Honorary Fellow in 1951, he maintained close links with the College. The plant physiologist Sir Rutherford Robertson (1936), also an Honorary Fellow of the College, held many eminent academic posts in Australia, including that of Pro-Chancellor of the Australian National University.

Amongst Johnian bishops in Australia, James Moorhouse (1849), Bishop of Melbourne 1876–86, presided over the synod which framed the constitution of the Church in Australia, and was influential in the early history of Trinity College, Melbourne. Archbishop Peter Carnley, a Research Fellow at St John's in the early 1970s, recently retired as Anglican Primate of Australia after twenty-five years in the archdiocese of Perth. He is an Honorary Fellow of the College.

St John's has benefited from a number of generous bequests from, or in memory of, Australians. Amongst these are a studentship in memory of William Elgar Buck (1867) for research in medicine or surgery; and a bequest by Professor James Davidson (1938: Fellow 1944–51) for the augmentation of scholarship awards. The Harper-Wood Studentship in English literature also has a strong connection with Australia.

Left: The Caliph Al-Ma'mun and the surgeon, from Nizami's Khamsah

Below: Sir Mark Oliphant KBE FRS *1901–2000 (© Elliott & Fry)*

Kikuchi Dairoku at his desk (by kind permission of the Cambridge Antiquarian Society)

EAST ASIA

St John's can claim an interest in East Asia spanning four centuries. Samuel Purchas, the father of Johnian geography (see Chapter 10), included forty sources in his *Purchas His Pilgrimes* that treated of the region wholly or in part. The earliest work from East Asia in the College Library is an illustrated woodblock print dating from the late Ming period (1368–1644).

In the nineteenth century, the College's involvement with China followed that of national politics on the one hand and Victorian religiosity on the other. If a Johnian, Lord Palmerston, put in train the events that, following the Treaty of Nanking in 1842, established Hong Kong as a British colony, it was another Johnian, Sir Percy Cradock, who more than a hundred and fifty years later,

in 1997, played a prominent role in negotiating Hong Kong's return to Chinese sovereignty.

In the late nineteenth and early twentieth centuries, Johnian missionaries brought educational practice and a more liberal attitude to women to late Qing and Republican society. W W Cassels (1877) was one of the 'Cambridge Seven', Albert Schweitzers of their day, who gave up promising careers in government or business to leave for the mission field in China. He was the first Anglican Bishop of West China, and his pro-cathedral, dedicated in 1914 in Baoning, near Chengdu in Sichuan, is now classified as a Protected Historical Site.

Students from East Asia came to St John's from the late nineteenth century onward. The first Chinese came from Malaysia and Hong Kong, through the school system that the British had introduced. Perhaps the most famous to take this route was Tun Sir Hau Shik (Henry) Lee (1921), who held office as both Minister of Transport and Minister of Finance in the Government of Malaysia, as well as many other senior positions in Commonwealth and Malayan organizations.

The record for Japanese students at St John's is especially strong. Two of Japan's most illustrious statesmen and modernizers of the Meiji period (1868–1912) came to the College. One was Kikuchi Dairoku (1855–1917), the first Japanese student in the University and a Wrangler, who matriculated in 1873. He became President of the Imperial University of Tokyo (1898–1901), Minister of Education (1901–3), Principal of Gakushuin, the Peers' School (1904–5) and President of the Imperial University of Kyoto. A second was Suematsu Kencho (1855–1920) admitted as a pensioner in 1883, the third Japanese student to enter Cambridge. He became a prominent journalist, translator, statesman and historian. He was the first person to translate into English *The Tale of Genji*, a story of court love written by a woman, and the first full-length novel in world history.

Two students from Peking University, Chun Thorpe and Ching Sung Woo, are of special interest because the date of their admission to the College, 1906, followed soon after the abolition by the Qing government of traditional

143

LOUIS CHA

Chinese students at Cambridge meet Louis Cha

Among Visiting Scholars currently attached to the College, special mention may be made of the famous martial arts novelist Louis Cha (Jin Yong). He is an almost legendary figure in China, where he commands much affection and a vast readership – even an asteroid in the solar system bears his name! It is a signal indication of Cambridge's high standing in Chinese East Asia that he should wish, in his eighties, to come to St John's to read for a graduate degree. His effortless command of classical Chinese of all styles, his knowledge of Chinese history and lore and his diffidence of manner have delighted the graduate community in Chinese studies. He is currently undertaking research on the figure of the Crown Prince and the problem of imperial succession in Tang China (AD 618–907).

He was awarded an Honorary Degree by the University of Cambridge in 2005.

examinations for entry to Chinese government service dating back to the seventh century: their arrival may be seen as part of the efforts of Qing reformers to broaden the scope of education to include scientific subjects. Sadly, their funding ran out after one year.

Since the Second World War, the number of students coming to St John's from East Asia, including Korea, Singapore and Taiwan, has steadily increased. Many come on scholarships to read practical subjects such as economics, engineering, law and medicine. They go on to be leaders in government, scientific research, the professions, and the prospering business life of the region, where there is now a substantial community of Johnians, many of whom maintain connections with the College: in Hong Kong alone, nearly sixty.

Under the College's Visiting Scholars scheme, scientists and scholars have regularly come from East Asia. A Buddhist scholar from Tainan in Taiwan, a

Visiting Scholar in 1997, deserves mention as the first Buddhist nun ever to take part in College life and dine regularly at a Cambridge High Table. Many of the current Fellowship have developed connections with universities in China, Hong Kong, Japan, Korea, Singapore and Taiwan and frequently visit the East Asian region.

OVERSEAS VISITING SCHOLARS AND COLENSO SCHOLARS

The College has long sought to foster overseas contacts. The Dominion Fellowship (established in 1949 and renamed the Commonwealth Fellowship in 1959) brought to the College each year an overseas academic to pursue research and to make contacts here. Those who came were predominantly from Australia, New Zealand, Canada and South Africa and were already established scholars.

Above: Ven Dr Daw-yuh Shih, Overseas Visiting Scholar for the Lent and Easter terms 1999

Above right: Professor Emma Falque of the University of Seville, Overseas Visiting Scholar 2002/3

The foundations of the current arrangements were laid in 1969 with the objective, made possible by increased availability of funds, of extending invitations to three classes of visitor: distinguished non-Commonwealth academics, scholars from Europe (particularly Eastern Europe), and promising young scholars from developing countries. The arrangements envisaged the College playing host to several scholars at one time, each staying for one, two or three terms, and representing a wide range, geographically, academically and in terms of career stage. Subsequently some places were reserved for visitors from less advantaged countries and from the Far East. In 1993 the Commonwealth Fellowship was subsumed into the general arrangements. The current scheme allows for up to six visitors at any one time, except in the Michaelmas Term when only three can be accommodated. All are sponsored by individual Fellows. For many years the scheme was fully funded by the College but, following a recent review of the conflicting demands on the College's finite resources, its funding was greatly reduced. For prospective visitors from institutions in affluent countries who continue to receive a stipend while they are on leave this change has not been a serious discouragement but inevitably it has had an impact on the numbers coming from elsewhere. The funding will be reviewed again in due course. Since the 1969 scheme was inaugurated nearly 200 scholars have participated. There

have been historians of Chinese Court music and of medieval Spanish kingship, researchers on the depths of the Indian Ocean and on the structure of quasi-crystals, experts on the economy of Brazil and the archaeology of the Sudan. A list of endless variety.

The College has been increasingly aware of the needs of higher education in southern Africa, not least through information provided in 1994 by Professor D A Maughan-Brown, a member of the College and at the time Senior Deputy Vice-Chancellor of the University of Natal. Two related schemes have been set up, both named after Bishop John Colenso (see Chapter 5). The first scheme, which has run since 1995, annually pays for a Fellow to tour southern Africa, give lectures and make contacts. The second, initiated in 2000, is closely related to that for Overseas Visiting Scholars. It has the aim of bringing one academic each year to the College for a term. Initially both schemes were focused on the University of Natal (subsequently a part of the University of KwaZulu Natal). Recently it has been widened to include institutions throughout southern Africa. Given the importance attached to these schemes, the funding has been maintained.

Overseas visitors have invariably found their stay beneficial and productive, and they have certainly brought the College a remarkable and valuable range of contacts with the wider world.

20 WOMEN AT ST JOHN'S

Opposite:Women undergraduates by the Shrewsbury Tower, with its statue of Mary, Countess of Shrewsbury, 1557–1632

Right: Sarah, Duchess of Somerset 1632–92

While female graduate and undergraduate students were not admitted to St John's until 1981 and 1982 respectively, women have played a key role in its history. From its foundation by Lady Margaret Beaufort, benefactions by women have enriched the College in many different ways. To Mary, Countess of Shrewsbury, we owe Second Court. To Sarah, Duchess of Somerset, we owe scholarships which still today support undergraduates as they did in 1683. In the Library, books presented by Mildred Cecil, Lady Burghley, and by Margaret Cavendish stand as a monument to their desire to promote Johnian learning. In the Chapel, beautiful stained glass presented by Margaret Taylor serves as a memorial both to her husband and to her own generosity.

All-male Cambridge has been transformed to the point where the current Vice-Chancellor is a woman and where the presence of women, as undergraduates, graduate students, Lecturers, Fellows and Professors is entirely taken for granted. Following Girton (1869) and Newnham (1871), the 1950s and 1960s saw the foundation of New Hall, Darwin and Lucy Cavendish. But even so women remained no more than one in seven of junior members. With changing social attitudes, a process was set in train which in less than twenty years changed Cambridge to a university in which every college accepted women and the ratio of women to men students moved to near equality. Churchill and King's went mixed in 1972. The last all-male college, Magdalene, did so in 1987.

In St John's the issue of the admission of women was first formally debated in May 1969, when a paper was discussed by the College Council. From that point,

opinion in favour of a change began to grow within the College. By the early 1970s a sizeable majority of junior members were strongly supportive of the admission of women and impetus to the cause of change was provided in May 1973 when the President of the JCR presented a request to consider going co-residential. The College Council responded by asking the various Tutors to assemble evidence and report, which they did the following year. The report noted the success of the moves at Churchill and King's and concluded that there was no lack of able women candidates. But it also expressed reservations about difficulties which might result if all hitherto all-male

148

colleges simultaneously admitted women. In view of these reservations and a strong division of opinion in the Fellowship, ensuing moves in the direction of change were slow. In May 1974, and again in February 1975, the Governing Body passed motions urging the College to consider changing its Statutes to make possible the admission of women. But it was not until November 1975 (by which time Girton had changed its Statutes to admit men) that a proposal to change the Statutes first came to a formal vote in the Governing Body. Such a change requires a majority in favour of two-thirds of those present and voting on two separate occasions. At this first vote there were 36 in favour and 29 against and the proposal lapsed. A further attempt in November 1977 also failed, the votes being 50 in favour and 30 against. But in October 1980, a two-thirds majority was obtained by the narrowest of margins – 57 to 28. The decision was confirmed in a second vote of 59 to 29 in November 1980.

Against change it was argued that at least some men and some women flourish best intellectually in single-sex institutions; that if it was appropriate for there to be some all-female colleges it was equally appropriate for there to be some all-male ones; and that admitting women to St John's could damage the existing women's colleges by making it more difficult for them to recruit able students and Fellows. In favour of change, it was urged that women's educational opportunities remained unfairly limited and that the College would benefit both academically and socially from their inclusion. As the voting figures indicate, a body of nearly thirty Fellows remained unconvinced of the need for change. But once the decision had been taken, the Fellowship agreed on the importance of uniting behind it and implementing it in an effective and wholehearted way. Once the Privy Council had approved the statutory change in March 1981, the College moved decisively. In that year nine women graduate students joined the College and the first woman Fellow was elected. The first group of forty-three women undergraduates matriculated in the following October.

Oh, mister porter, what shall I do?

MR ROBERT FULLER, head porter at St John's, Cambridge, who is referred to as "The Beast" by undergraduates and who is well known for his antipathy towards women undergraduates, yesterday greeting the first woman undergraduate to "invade" the college, Marguerite Holdsworth, 18, from Liverpool, reading classics.

St John's, founded 1511, ironically, by a woman—Lady Margaret Beaufort, Henry VII's mother—has just admitted 45 women undergraduates.

The 210 new entrants sat down to their first college dinner last night and were addressed by the Master, Prof. Harry Hinsley, who is the university's Vice-Chancellor. He was followed by Mr Fuller, who is well known for his strict discipline.

"I'll explain the college rules to them—then tell 'em how to break 'em." Mr Fuller said with a grin. He has been college porter for 36 years.

Eaden Lilley   cambridge

Ned Burnett   Emma McLaren   Sarah Brewster   Nicola Richards   Sarah Currie   Gabrielle Hodgetts
H.R.
Sue Taylor   Nicki Shanks   Vicki Robertson   Celia Tait   Jacqui Chao

Opposite: Head Porter 'Big Bob' Fuller meets Marguerite Holdsworth, one of the first women admitted to St John's, October 1982 (© Daily Telegraph)

Right: The 'Robins' Dining Society 1985 (© Eaden Lilley)

What was it like to come into residence in the midst of a hitherto all-male community of over seven hundred? Recollections from some of the 1982 group of women undergraduates conjure up vividly the challenges and excitements of those days. Some of the clashes and gestures beloved of headline writers did occur. According to Sharon Chen Cooper, 'The most difficult time was the first week or so. The sheer number of male students in the College was overwhelming in comparison to the forty-three female students. My earliest impression was on my first evening, being "greeted" by the sight of the rugby team dropping their trousers to the new ladies!' Another of the new entrants, Gabrielle Howatson, recalls, 'The day we arrived the flag was at half-mast and the Head Porter, "Big Bob" Fuller, was wearing a black armband. "This is a sad day for the College," he said.'

But stories such as these provide only one element of the picture. Tami Biddle, one of the graduate students admitted in 1981, recalls a different 'Big Bob'. 'I shall never forget,' she says, 'a little hand-written note in my box in

mid-December, inviting me to Christmas dinner at the Fuller household. Bob made sure that all the foreign students in College had such an invitation since he could not bear to think of them spending the holiday alone.' 'Once we were there we were part of his College,' writes one undergraduate from 1982. 'A fearsome reputation preceded him, but he turned out to be a pussycat as far as we girls were concerned,' says another. 'I had anticipated there might be some negative feeling as I understood not all the dons (and students) had supported the decision to allow women into the College. In contrast, I found Johnians very supportive and inclusive,' comments Kay Jackson, another of the 1981 graduate intake.

Women rapidly found their feet and made themselves at home. 'In those days, John's was one of the top sporting colleges,' writes Gabriele Howatson, 'and a core of the newly arrived women decided that to integrate well, we should form teams in all possible sports. I was roped into the 2nd VIII and the 2nd netball team. Rowing was most enjoyable in the summer's evenings, making one's way alongside the grassy banks of the

Cam, passing the occasional swan's nest. The wintry mornings were more painful, particularly when one had to break the ice on the river outside the boathouse.' Though Roger Silk, the head boatman, welcomed women to LMBC, the head groundsman was not too keen at first about women's teams playing on the College pitches. 'But as the year went on acceptance grew,' remembers Alison Samuels. 'The women were invited to the Hockey Club curry evenings, and out of chivalry were allowed to eat Madras instead of the Vindaloo obligatory for junior men.'

And women took on and adapted the College traditions in their own way. 'There were many male societies at John's, mostly named after birds,' recalls Gabriele Howatson, 'and so a group of seven of us decided to form a women's dining society, called the Robins. We held dinners every term, usually in the Wordsworth Room, where we could each invite a male guest, and a garden party in the summer on Cripps Lawn or in the Scholars' Garden, where we used to serve "pink cocktails".' The Flamingos, the female equivalent of the Eagles, was also founded very soon after the arrival of women.

While some students arriving in Cambridge are full of intellectual confidence, others are fearful that they will find themselves the dunce in a class of geniuses. The early women were not immune to this worry but were soon reassured. 'The greatest relief for me arriving at St John's was to find that most people were friendly, down-to-earth and rather like me intellectually, i.e. bright but not geniuses,' writes Judith Slater who came up in 1983. There were Fellows who let their dislike of the admission of women be known, but for the most part Tutors and Directors of Studies were very supportive and women found that they were well on top of the academic work. And the old leisurely customs were still then in force and appreciated. 'We had chemistry supervisions in the first year with a delightful old Fellow, for whom every four weeks or so there seemed to be an occasion which merited a glass of sherry and a piece of fruitcake,' recalls Fiona McAnena.

The sheer practicalities of life presented some problems. Women students were not impressed at having, in their second and third years, to trek across the older courts in a dressing gown to distant loos and bathrooms. But the recently built Cripps Building, where most first year students had their rooms, was better equipped, so the 1982 women did not face this awkwardness in their first year. The first year clustering in Cripps had the further advantage of enabling the year group to form its own community, where the 1982 women did not at all feel themselves swamped by the men. 'The College was very sociable at the time,' recalls Alison Samuels, 'and there was a great deal of reciprocal coffee/tea drinking in each other's rooms. This cut across the gender barrier too – I was introduced to Pink Floyd's *Dark Side of the Moon* by a male Johnian friend, while drinking tea in his room. I had many such friendships, and remember the College with great nostalgia as a place where I could and did associate freely and as an equal with men.'

She adds, 'I was fascinated by the history and

Professor Jane Heal, the first woman President of St John's (© W Suschitzky)

*Above: Sarah Teather
MP (courtesy of Brent
Liberal Democrats)*

*Above right: Winners of
the Larmor Award 2001:
Helena Shore,
Nancy Priston,
Susha Parameswaran,
Delicia Reynolds*

tradition of the College. I enjoyed the old Lower Library, with the secret alcoves in the bookstacks and the window bay to the river and I liked the Hall and Chapel, but was too shy to be present there often. But I don't think the gowns and the surplices should be abolished to encourage people like me. Rather the opposite – I gradually learned not to be socially scared or overawed by grandness, and as a veteran of formal College dinners, if the Queen ever does invite me to dine, I shall be prepared.'

Henrietta Butler, another of the 1982 group, also evokes the history and tradition of the College, in quoting Wordsworth in her speech proposing the toast to the College at a 2006 Old Johnian dinner:

> I could not print
> Ground where the grass had yielded to the steps
> Of generations of illustrious men
> Unmoved. I could not lightly pass
> Through the same gateways, sleep where they had slept,
> Wake where they waked, range that enclosure old,
> That garden of great intellects, undisturbed.

Here we find a likely response of any intelligent, imaginative human being, whether man or woman, to the experience of living and working in a college such as St John's. And it is in identification with the traditions and values of the College that we find the clue to the rapid and successful integration of women into the community which is St John's. Once the women were there, and were themselves effectively embodying the College's commitment to scholarship, intellectual

integrity and excellence then – whatever the ups and downs and occasional tensions – their being Johnians could not be in doubt.

Within a few years of going mixed the number of women junior members in the College had grown to about two-fifths of the total, from where it has risen to nearly one half today. The proportion of women in the Fellowship of necessity changed more gradually and now stands at a quarter of the non-retired Fellowship and a third of those elected since the change of Statutes.

In the early years after the change, the women Fellows, then numbering considerably under twenty, found it helpful to meet informally from time to time, to exchange views and to reflect on how they could best help the women junior members. With more women in the Fellowship and the change of Statutes receding into history, the need for this fell away. But women Fellows continue to press, with their male colleagues, to ensure that the College addresses issues of work–life balance and family support. The College has recently joined with Trinity, Churchill and Girton to found the Wolfson Court Nursery, for the children of Fellows, staff and junior members.

The women Fellows teach a varied range of subjects, including engineering, law, economics, languages, mathematics, medicine, English, philosophy, psychology and history and now include five Professors. Women take on a wide range of roles in College, as Directors of Studies, as members of the Council and as Tutors. At the time of writing the Admissions Tutor and the Tutor with responsibility for Graduate Affairs are both women. The Fellowship elected its first woman President, Professor Jane Heal, in 1999.

'As a current undergraduate it is easy to forget, and there is almost no evidence in everyday life to show, how recently women came to St John's.' So wrote Anna Turk, President of the Flamingos, in *The Eagle* of 2001. The change of Statutes and the debates that went with it occurred before most of today's junior members were born. To them it is entirely taken for granted that the College is for both men and women.

Today's women Johnians are still struck by the things which struck their predecessors a quarter of a century ago. Madeleine Crisp, up at St John's in the early 2000s, expresses again the abiding attraction of the depth of history manifest in the College: 'The traditions and idiosyncrasies that are evident throughout College and Cambridge life were part of what made us want to be there. I'm sure it wasn't only me who enjoyed feeling like Harry Potter the first time I walked through college in my gown to Hall.' And the extent and richness of ongoing activity also continue to impress themselves on Johnians. 'I met all sorts of people – from very different backgrounds from my own – and I met them on conditions of equality. I also met and liked people with a whole range of interests different from my own because we were brought together by College life. I don't consider my life in the College untypical – St John's is too big for only one kind of life to be typical. There were sporting Johnians, arty Johnians, musical Johnians, political Johnians, "natscis", medics and so on – and the life of the College drew on all of them. But I don't think that as a woman I belonged to a separate group.' So writes Alison Samuels of her experiences in the years 1982–5. Kay Jackson, arriving in 1981, was very struck to find the then small community of post-graduate women at St John's far more international than she had expected. Exactly the same pleased surprise at the vast variety of Johnians, in origins and interests, is echoed by today's students. Nancy Priston (JCR President in 2001, an anthropologist currently in Indonesia, and one of four women Larmor Award winners in 2001) comments, 'One of the overwhelming qualities of St John's is the diversity – both amongst the undergrad and the postgrad student body. There is something for everyone at John's.' The others of that Larmor quartet illustrate her point – Susha Parameswaran, scientist and musician, Helena Shore, medic and sportswoman, and Delicia Reynolds, now working as a lawyer among low-resourced communities near Washington DC. St John's is a large and welcoming and liberating place.

There are now around 2,000 women Johnians. They have moved out from the College into the worlds of finance, law, education, medicine, the arts and politics, and are to be found investing millions, pleading the cases of their clients, lecturing and publishing, treating patients, directing films, making music, being politicians and diplomats. From time to time they come back to alumni events at the College, to reminisce, to exchange news of their growing families, to remark on the improvements in the plumbing and to hear the Choir sing again. Importantly, they also come to talk to current junior members about the wider world and their experience there.

21 MASTERS AND SOME MEMORABLE FELLOWS

MASTERS

Over the nearly five hundred years of its existence, the College has had some notable Masters, from Nicholas Metcalfe, Bishop Fisher's chaplain and Archdeacon of Rochester, who 'left such a company of fellows and scholars at St John's College as can scarce be found now in some whole university', to James Wood, Master 1815–39, who oversaw the construction of New Court and was a major benefactor of the College. The six distinguished Masters who served the College from 1952 to 2004 are featured here.

Sir James Wordie CBE, Master 1952–59, by Rodrigo Moynihan RA

Sir James Wordie CBE (1889–1962)

James Wordie came to St John's following a degree in geology at Glasgow. Subsequent research in petrology brought him in touch with geologists returning from Scott's second expedition to the South Pole; and in 1914 he joined Shackleton's Antarctic expedition as chief of scientific staff. He spent a year on *Endurance* trapped in ice in the Weddell Sea and a winter marooned on Elephant Island while Shackleton made his epic voyage to South Georgia for help. Tough and laconic, he played an important part in maintaining morale with his dry humour – and willingness to trade his tobacco for rock samples.

Following the First World War, during which he served in the artillery and was wounded in the leg at Armentières, he joined expeditions to Spitsbergen, returning to a Fellowship at St John's in 1921. There followed a long series of Arctic and Antarctic expeditions. From 1937–55 he chaired the Scott Polar Research Institute of which he was a founder member. He advised Sir Vivian Fuchs on his Trans-Antarctic expedition. As President of the Royal Geographical Society from 1951 to 1954, he welcomed back the expedition under Sir John Hunt which made the first ascent of Everest. He is commemorated by the Wordie Glacier in Graham Land and Wordie Crag in Spitsbergen.

At the College, he was successively Tutor, Senior Tutor and President, becoming Master in 1952. In all those roles he was known as a shrewd and accurate judge of people. He resigned as Master in 1959 owing to ill health.

Far left: The Rev. Dr J S Boys Smith, Master 1959–69 (© Eaden Lilley)

Left: Professor Nicholas Mansergh OBE FBA, Master 1969–79, by William Narroway

154

The Rev. Dr J S Boys Smith (1901–91)

Anyone who reads J S Boys Smith's *Memoirs of St John's College 1919–1969* will be struck by the quiet, underlying passion for orderly administration and development – of the College, of the University, of Cambridge itself. A key decision of his career illustrates this. A University Lecturer in Divinity and the Philosophy of Religion from 1931, he was elected Ely Professor of Divinity in 1940 and might have been expected to continue in that position. But the position of Senior Bursar of the College fell vacant in 1943 and, as a former Tutor and Junior Bursar, he was invited by the then Master, E A Benians, to apply. He took the highly unusual step of leaving the Chair for the Bursarship, in which he was to serve for fifteen years until his election as Master in 1959. 'The prospect of again devoting myself to the interests of the College was extremely attractive to me,' he wrote in his memoirs.

The College owes him much for his stewardship of its estate – above all, perhaps, for his negotiation of the purchase of land from Merton College, Oxford, which enabled the construction of the Cripps Building. The University and City are also in his debt for his role in the establishment of Darwin, New Hall and Lucy Cavendish Colleges, and for his sensitive and judicious approach to the use and development of the College's extensive land holdings in Cambridge. He was Master for ten years, and Vice-Chancellor from 1963 to 1965.

Professor Nicholas Mansergh OBE FBA (1910–91)

Nicholas Mansergh was elected to a Fellowship at St John's in 1953 following his appointment as the first Smuts Professor of the History of the British Commonwealth. Born in County Tipperary and educated at school in Ireland and at Pembroke, Oxford, he began his career as a Tutor in Politics at that college, producing three books on Irish affairs by the time he was thirty. He acted as a specialist on Irish affairs in the British Ministry of Information (1941–4) and as Director of its Empire division (1944–6), being awarded the OBE for his wartime service. After a short period at the Dominions Office, he was appointed Abe Bailey Professor of British Commonwealth Relations at the Royal Institute for International Affairs, where he began work on his major *Survey of British Commonwealth Affairs*. As Smuts Professor, he wrote prolifically, and embarked on a major task as editor-in-chief of the India Office's documents on the transfer of power in India. This resulted in the twelve volumes of *The Transfer of Power* which appeared between 1967 and 1982.

At St John's he won esteem for his largeness of mind, his courtesy, his diffidence and his charm. It was these qualities no less than his academic distinction which led the Fellows to elect him Master in 1969. For ten years he served the College with dignity and constant attention to its affairs, his resonant voice and occasional idiosyncratic pause (and intervening 'Ah!') an

Above: Professor Sir Harry Hinsley OBE FBA *Master 1979–89*

Above right: Professor Robert Hinde CBE FRS FBA*, Master 1989–94*

increasing source of affection to the Fellows. Though he spent his working life in England, he retained close personal connections with Ireland and was buried, as he wished, in Tipperary. The Taoiseach attended his memorial service.

Professor Sir Harry Hinsley OBE FBA (1918–98)

It seems unlikely that any Master will ever again stand as close to the country's destiny as did Harry Hinsley during his youthful wartime service with the Code and Cypher School at Bletchley Park, to which he was recruited in 1939 while still an undergraduate (he graduated BA in 1944) and where he was to meet his future wife, Hilary. For years his work there, for which he was awarded the OBE in 1946, remained highly classified, and it was only much later that details emerged of the role he had played in naval intelligence arising from Bletchley's code-breaking activities, which he himself came to estimate had shortened the Second World War by two years or more. His monument as a historian – the five massive volumes of *British Intelligence in the Second World War*, published between 1979 and 1990 – bears a close relationship to his wartime work.

Elected Fellow in 1944, he lectured in history from 1950, being promoted in 1965 to Reader and in 1969 to Professor in the History of International Relations, both personal appointments in a field which he did much to foster at Cambridge. Meanwhile, he served the College

as an inspirational teacher of History, and as President, and in 1979 was clearly the right person for the Mastership, which he held for ten years. During his term of office, in 1981, the decision was taken to admit women to the College. In 1981–3 he also served as Vice-Chancellor of the University. He was knighted in 1985. By turns witty, stoical and enigmatic, he is remembered as a truly remarkable figure.

Professor Robert Hinde CBE FRS FBA (1923–)

Robert Hinde is a biologist and psychologist whose long and distinguished career is marked by careful research and insights into animal and human behaviour, coupled with deep concern about the future of humanity. Starting with birdsong he probed questions of non-verbal communication, learning, territory and aggression, display and ritualization. More recently, he has explored the development of mother–infant behaviour. His intellectual and ethical trajectory can be judged from the titles of the many books which he has written, edited and co-authored. *Animal Behaviour* (1966) leads to *Biological Bases of Human Social Relations* (1974) and to *Individuals, Relationships and Culture* (1987). In 1999 he published *Why Gods Persist*, a challenging reflection on the social and psychological functions and development of religion and religious behaviour. He served in the RAF in the Second World War and his later long-standing interest and involvement in the aims and

Professor Peter Goddard
CBE FRS, Master
1994–2003, by Tom
Phillips CBE RA

objectives of the Pugwash movement can be seen in *War: A Necessary Evil?* (1994) and *War No More*, a joint work of 2003 with the Pugwash co-founder and Nobel Peace Prize winner Sir Joseph Rotblat, exploring factors that make war more likely, and factors that stop countries going to war, and emphasizing the global need for education in world citizenship. He had many a lively debate with his predecessor as Master, Sir Harry Hinsley, on the subject of nuclear deterrence.

Robert Hinde was a Royal Society Research Professor in Cambridge (1963–89) and, from 1970 to 1989, Honorary Director of the Medical Research Council's Unit on Development and the Integration of Behaviour. In 1988 he was appointed CBE. At St John's, he became a Fellow in 1951, was Steward (1956–8) and Tutor (1958–63). Elected Master in 1989, he served for five years. During this period, the major project for the College was the new Library, and he threw himself single-mindedly into the business of steering it through and raising funds for the Library Appeal. The success of the project was in no small measure due to his zeal and persistence. He has been described as having 'a great capacity for drawing people out'.

Professor Peter Goddard CBE FRS (1945–)

An undergraduate and later (1969–73) a Research Fellow at Trinity College, Cambridge, Peter Goddard spent two years at CERN, Geneva, where he began working with others on what became string theory, a central theme of his subsequent work. Following his return to Cambridge, he became a Fellow of St John's in 1975. The following year he began work with David Olive (a Johnian) and others on magnetic monopoles and extended objects in field theories. In 1989 his contributions to theoretical physics were recognized by election as FRS and promotion to Reader in Mathematical Physics: a Professorship of Theoretical Physics was established for him in 1992. He played a key role in the creation and establishment of the Isaac Newton Institute for Mathematical Sciences which opened in 1992, and served as its first Deputy Director. Thereafter he led the planning and fund-raising for the Centre for Mathematical Sciences – a complex of seven new buildings rehousing the Mathematical Departments alongside the Newton Institute on a seven-acre site. Together, these constitute one of the world's largest centres for research and teaching in the mathematical sciences.

He served both as Tutor and Senior Tutor at St John's in the 1980s and in 1994 became Master of the College, serving for nearly ten years before taking up his current appointment as Director of the Institute for Advanced Study at Princeton. In 1997 he was awarded the Dirac Prize, jointly with David Olive; and in 2002 was appointed CBE.

157

Above: Sir Joseph Larmor MP FRS 1857–1942 (© G E Briggs)

Above right: Professor Norman Jopson 1890–1969

SOME MEMORABLE FELLOWS

Space is limited and choice invidious, but certain names come up again and again. *Larmor* left a strong mark on the College, not least through the Larmor Awards. The diminutive *Jopson* was the kind of 'character' that students love to recall. *Sykes Davies* was elusive but extraordinarily well remembered. *Jackson* influenced reform of the British machinery of justice, and was a formidable sailor. As Dean, *Bezzant* crossed the path of many – sometimes ominously. *Daniel* was not only a great College man, but for a time a national figure through television.

Sir Joseph Larmor FRS (1857–1942)

Larmor was a man of great achievements – Senior Wrangler in 1880, Fellow from 1885, and Lucasian Professor of Mathematics 1903–32. A Fellow of the Royal Society in 1885, he was its Secretary from 1901 to 1912, and its Copley Medallist in 1921. Knighted in 1909, he sat as Unionist MP for Cambridge from 1911 to 1922. His *Aether and Matter*, published in 1900, was a forerunner of Einstein's Special Theory of Relativity of 1905. He was the principal creator of classical electron theory and the first to give the formula for the rate of radiation of energy from an accelerated electron. His work on precession of nuclei in a magnetic field is a major plank in the theoretical basis of nuclear magnetic resonance spectroscopy, now widely practised in

chemistry and biology research laboratories and in medical applications and hospital scanners.

But he is remembered in the College for two quite different things. First, for the Larmor Awards for all-round excellence. Secondly, for his opposition to the installation of baths on the grounds that 'we had done without them for 400 years, why begin now?' and that since undergraduates were only there for eight weeks at a time, 'what was the point?' His obituary in *The Eagle* stated that 'he dearly loved an argument and never forgot that he came from Northern Ireland'. Once the baths were built he became a regular user until, health failing, he retired to his native province, where he was Freeman of the City of Belfast.

Professor Norman Jopson (1890–1969)

'Joppy', as he was universally known, lived in College and seemed an integral part of it: scarcely a day passed when he was not seen walking through the Courts in animated conversation, often with a group of young people. Generations of undergraduates remember him as the diminutive figure who in summer would sit for hours under the old copper beech by the Kitchen Bridge, gradually turning the same colour as the tree; and who in winter, shrouded in a heavy black overcoat, made his way round town on a drop-handled bicycle.

A Johnian (1909), his career as a linguist took him into the War Office, Admiralty and Foreign Office

The Rev. Canon J S Bezzant 1897–1967 supervising in his rooms in New Court, 1959 (courtesy of the Rev. John Tarrant)

before his appointment as Reader in the School of Slavonic Studies in London, a post he held from 1923 to 1937. Professor of Comparative Philology at Cambridge from 1937, he headed the Department of Uncommon Languages at the Postal Censorship during the Second World War. He knew dozens of languages and would deploy them at the drop of a hat. He once made a plea for Pidgin at a dinner in Melbourne. Unlike English, he said, Pidgin is able to distinguish between 'we' meaning 'the two of us' and 'we' meaning 'our group' and illustrated this with an example from the Pidgin New Testament where the disciples say to Jesus sleeping in the boat amongst the storm: 'We feller all bugger up, you boss no care.' Paul Gottlieb (1964), whose father had known 'Joppy', recalls being invited as a freshman to take sherry with a host who said that he would talk that evening in Latvian, 'which he would find a very easy language to understand'.

The Rev. Canon J S Bezzant (1897–1967)

James Stanley Bezzant imprinted his personality on several generations of undergraduates. As Dean both of Chapel and of College discipline, he was considerably more visible than most other Fellows – sometimes uncomfortably so – though his bark was always worse than his bite. There are many stories. Of the thirty men sent down one day and reprieved the next. Of the miscreant unexpectedly discovered ('Oh God!' 'No, just

His earthly representative.') Of the day following the College fireworks display which woke Cambridge for ten miles round when, after an hour of telephonic complaints, he refused to take further calls with the order to the porters, 'Tell them the Dean is drunk!' Of his often sardonic mode of expression (see his response to the Bishop in Chapter 5). He enjoyed a wide reputation in the Church for sceptical acerbity and his (anonymous) Prefaces to *Crockford's Clerical Directory* were well known.

He was so much of the College that it was hard to believe he had been anywhere else. Yet his career had first been made in Oxford, where he was Vice-Principal of Ripon Hall in 1924 and Chaplain of Exeter College in 1927; and in Liverpool, where he was appointed Canon Residentiary and Chancellor of the Cathedral in 1933. During the Second World War, he had served as Chaplain on three different ships, and survived the sinking of HMS *Repulse*. His faith had been tested in fire and he knew the importance of courage.

Professor Meredith Jackson FBA JP (1902–86)

Meredith Jackson (1921) qualified as a solicitor after gaining a First in law but decided against practice and returned to Cambridge. He developed an interest in legal administration and published an outstandingly successful book, *The Machinery of Justice in England* (1940), which has gone through several editions. A Permanent Secretary to

Above: Professor Meredith Jackson FBA JP 1902–86

Above right: Hugh Sykes Davies 1909–84

the Lord Chancellor's Department ascribed to Jackson's influence many changes over the whole field of legal administration during the decades following its publication.

Elected Fellow in 1946, he was appointed Secretary to the Royal Commission on Justices of the Peace, and subsequently served on government committees on subjects ranging from mental health to town and country planning. Himself a JP, he became Chairman of the Legal Committee of the Magistrates' Association, and eventually its Vice-President. In 1966 he was elected to the Downing Chair of the Laws of England.

A great sportsman and climber in his youth, he was also a very considerable sailor. In 1927 he crewed in an attempt to cross the Atlantic in a small craft and later acquired a boat of his own – a 39ft converted fishing vessel reputed to have been at Dunkirk. Arthritis in the hip did not deter him from some remarkable voyages. A crew member on one of his Atlantic crossings recalls a man of great strength and self-reliance who, in a storm in the Bay of Biscay in 1965, edged along the boom over twenty-foot seas to shorten sail without turning a hair – a feat of courage at any age and astounding in a man of sixty-three with arthritis so severe that he needed a bicycle to get about on dry land.

Hugh Sykes Davies (1909–84)

Hugh Sykes Davies, Director of Studies in English on and off for almost forty years, was not, according to his *Eagle* obituary, 'an easy man to know at deeper levels'. A Surrealist poet in the Thirties, and reputedly a member of the Cambridge Apostles, he was for many years a member of the Communist Party. There were erroneous rumours in the media at the time of Anthony Blunt's exposure that he had been the mysterious 'fourth man'. All this was a far cry from his major interests – Wordsworth, fishing, the use of English, and riding his motorbike. Of these, it is probably the second and fourth which left the strongest impression on his students. He would fish for roach below the Bridge of Sighs to use as live bait, keeping the roach in the bath in his rooms in Chapel Court. Michael Haughton (1944) recalls: 'On several freezing winter days we would catch the train out to fish the Forty Foot Drain in the Fens. Sometimes we would have to break the ice. Hugh claimed that a pike gave as good a fight as a salmon. I think he championed the pike as being a working-class fish.' George Watson (Fellow 1959–) has noted that he was always 'into' something, but then lost interest and moved on. For Professor John Beer (1948), Sykes Davies was 'one of the most *memorable* people I have ever known' who 'much enjoyed opportunities for plotting and intrigue' and was 'constantly revealing new sides to his personality'. A son of the Methodist manse, he was married six times, twice to the same lady, and once to Kathleen Raine, the poet.

Professor Glyn Daniel FBA (1914–86)

Imaginative, enterprising and scholarly, Glyn Daniel came to national attention in the early 1950s as one of the first 'television dons', starring in the *Animal, Vegetable, Mineral* quiz programme watched by millions. Later he became a director of Anglia TV and of the Cambridge Arts Theatre. He wrote one of the earliest Cambridge detective stories, inventing 'Fisher College' between Trinity and St John's. He was a *bon viveur* who wrote on French cuisine – his *The Hungry Archaeologist in France* combined gastronomy with the great sites of Lascaux and Carnac. As Steward of the College from 1946 to 1955 he proved fully equal to the post-war task of replenishing its wine cellar.

But behind the Welsh élan and showmanship was a dedicated and meticulous scholar who, in the course of a career stretching back to before the Second World War (during which he served with distinction in RAF photographic reconnaissance in India), established himself as one of the founding fathers of modern archaeology, publishing a number of highly influential works, not least on megaliths (of which he liked to call himself an *aficionado*). He was Disney Professor of

Archaeology 1974–81 and, with his wife Ruth, edited *Antiquity* from 1958 to the year of his death. A passionate believer in the value of friendship, he, together with Ruth, established the 'Johnian Connection' – a periodic meeting for discussion and good fellowship which brought together archaeology students of all vintages, and has recently been revived. Lord (Colin) Renfrew (1958) recalls how 'all of us found our interest in the past quickened and our horizons enlarged by his curiosity and sense of fun and infectious enthusiasm.'

Left: Professor Glyn Daniel FBA 1914–86

Opposite: The Great Gate of St John's

22 COLLEGE STAFF

For its day-to-day operation, the College depends on a considerable number of administrative and domestic staff, under the overall charge of the Domestic Bursar. Some of these have very visible roles and are frequently encountered by members of the College during residence. Others toil in the background and yet are essential to College life.

One staff member, Ralph Thoday, gained national recognition for his work. Head Gardener from 1928 to 1960, he was appointed MVO for his contributions to horticulture – this at a time when the College Kitchen Garden and Orchard in Madingley Road (on the present site of Churchill College) supplied the College with vegetables and fruit. Vaughan Crook (Head Gardener 1978–2005) maintained the high standard set by predecessors with the help of his dog, who chased the Canada geese off the Backs. His successor, Adam Magee, and his dog, continue in the same tradition.

The staff most frequently encountered by students have always been the Porters. Many will remember Cecil Butler, eventually Head Porter from 1967 to 1969. Another with a long earlier service to the College, 'Big Bob' Fuller, was Head Porter 1969–85. A big man, he was also larger-than-life in character, making himself strongly felt both in College and on the cricket pitch as umpire, but always fiercely loyal. Initially against the admission of women, he became their keen supporter.

The College is unique in having its own large sports field close by and at the Grange Road end lives the Head Groundsman. For many years (1963–99) the post was held by Jim Williams, a kindly man, helpful to all. Likewise, generations of 'boaties' came to know and appreciate Roger Silk, the College Boatman and coach,

Head Porter Dennis Hay keeps the rain off his colleague John Soley

who gave outstanding service to LMBC for over forty years, and still coaches and takes crews to Henley.

The College Kitchens in the 1950s and 1960s were in the charge of Sidney Dring – although to question their kitchen accounts members may more often have met Fred Lloyd. Service in Hall establishes characters, a present familiar face since 1986 being Franco Elia. Conference organizers come to value the efficiency of

Staff outing by charabanc, 1945

the Catering and Conference Department under Sarah Bridges.

The first Lady Superintendent bringing room service under central control was Miss Alice Price, who was appointed in the late 1930s. The present incumbent is Penny Herbert.

The staff of the College Library give important guidance to users. Before internet databases, such guidance rested weightily on people like Norman Buck who joined as a boy in 1929, finally retiring in 1982 as Sub-Librarian.

Though they may remain largely unrecognized by junior members, all of the staff in the College Offices and the Bursary are essential to the life of the place. Prominent amongst these was Bill Thurbon who began working in the College in 1920, was Bursar's Clerk 1955–70, and subsequently assisted the Archivist, Malcolm Underwood, for a further twenty years. Arthur Martin spent the whole of his working life (1926–68) in the service of the College, rising to the post of Chief Clerk. He always took a keen interest in every aspect of College life and had a wide influence, so much so that to many he was known as 'St John'. Long service is

widespread. A mainstay of the Tutorial Office is Sheila Smith, Senior Tutor's Assistant, who joined in 1960 and is still going strong.

Care of the buildings has lain in the hands of successive Superintendents of Buildings. Some may remember Mr Austin from the 1930s, and later Mr Richmond and Mr Bailey through the great restoration of the Second and Third Courts in the late 1950s and beyond. A more recent holder of the post, Stan Moorhouse, came to be widely known by students because of his great love of rugby. The work of the stonemason S E R Vigar will survive for many years to come.

Wally Reynolds had been apprenticed as a cabinet maker at Eaden Lilley; after war service he joined the College staff in 1955. His legendary craftsmanship is to be seen in the magnificent Combination Room table with its many mahogany sections that together run the length of the room.

St John's has been, and is, extremely fortunate in its staff and was delighted when it recently became the first Oxford or Cambridge college to receive the prized 'Investor in People' Award.

Left to right:

Sidney Dring

Bill Thurbon
© Cambridge
Evening News)

Norman Buck

23 War and Post-War

Wartime

Johnians were involved in the Second World War from the enlisted ranks to the upper echelons of government – Sir James Grigg (1909) was Permanent Secretary at the War Office from 1939 and Secretary of State for War from 1942 to 1945. They were to be found on all fronts, in the Navy, Army and RAF, in government ministries, and in research and intelligence establishments. Members of College might also, in the words of wartime Master E A Benians, 'hear a familiar Johnian voice nightly upon the news' in the person of Stuart Hibberd (1912), broadcaster for the BBC.

As many as thirty Fellows were absent on war service at one time. One hundred and twenty members of the College, one chorister and one member of College staff lost their lives, and many more were injured. Of those who died, about one-half served in the Army, one-third in the RAF and the remainder in the Navy. Amongst those commemorated on the War Memorial in the Antechapel are David Haig Thomas (1928) and Sir Roderic and Sir Iain MacRobert (1933 and 1936). Haig Thomas rowed in the 1932 Los Angeles Olympics and discovered a new island off the Canadian coast. He joined the Parachute Regiment at the outbreak of war and died on the first day of the Normandy landings. The MacRobert brothers served in the RAF, and died in action in 1941 within a month of each other. Their mother purchased a Stirling Bomber, named *The MacRoberts' Reply*, in memory of her sons, and an RAF aircraft has continued to bear this name ever since.

Of those who saw action in the Army, Vladimir Péniakoff (1915) formed his own elite fighting force in the North African desert. Known as 'Popski's Private Army', this operated behind enemy lines and landed in Italy with the first Allied troops. 'Popski' became a Lieutenant Colonel and was awarded the Croix de Guerre, MC and DSO. Freddy Chapman (1925) spent three years operating behind Japanese lines, organizing and leading reconnaissance and operational parties with legendary endurance and resourcefulness. Promoted Lieutenant Colonel, he won a DSO and bar. Michael Calvert (1933) set up and trained the Chindits in Burma with Orde Wingate. Promoted Brigadier at thirty-one, Calvert led the Chindits to several brilliant successes, and later commanded the Special Air Service. Described as 'the bravest of the brave', he won many British and foreign military honours and was recommended for the VC.

Johnians also made their mark in the Air Force and the Navy. Wing Commander, later Air Commodore, Gerard Paul (1926) served in Bomber Command, winning the DFC and various foreign honours. Dr Roland Winfield DFC (1928: Fellow 1946–54; see panel) served as Wing Commander in the RAF Volunteer Reserve. Reginald Foster (1946) and Ronald Curtis (1940) both won the DFC and bar as wartime Squadron Leaders. Stuart Bateson (1920) served as Captain aboard three ships, and rose to the rank of Rear Admiral. John Barnes (1936: Fellow) was mentioned in despatches and won the DSC, while Peter Danckwerts (1948) served in the RNVR and was awarded the GC in 1940 for disarming landmines.

Others showed great courage as Resistance fighters. A former POW in Italy, George Reid Millar (1928) served with the Special Operations Executive (SOE).

BLETCHLEY PARK

The German Enigma machine, encoding wartime messages of the highest sensitivity, allowed its operators 159 million million million possible settings daily. A gifted group of Johnians made a major contribution to cracking this and other codes, with some fifteen members of the College working at 'Station X', the code-breaking operation at Bletchley Park in Buckinghamshire, at some stage of the war.

Harry Hinsley (see Chapter 21) went to Bletchley Park as an undergraduate late in 1939. In April 1940 his detailed analysis of an unusual build-up of enemy shipping in the Baltic led him to alert the Operational Intelligence Centre (OIC) at the Admiralty, but his warning was ignored – and Britain was caught unawares by the German occupation of Norway. Two months later Hinsley reported that a group of German warships was about to leave the Baltic: 'For about a fortnight I pretty well rang the OIC once or twice a day and said: "Look, you ought surely to pass a signal out on this. Can you possibly pass a signal out?" They showed some interest, but were not sufficiently convinced to send a warning to the Home Fleet.' Tragically, HMS *Glorious* and her two escort destroyers were sunk, with the loss of 1,500 lives. Harry Hinsley remembered how the OIC 'resisted Bletchley's suggestion that such a warning should be sent to ships at sea. It was not prepared to accept inferences drawn from an untried technique by civilians as yet unknown to its staff.' Thereafter the OIC began to take reports from Bletchley more seriously, and Hinsley himself became a key member of the code-breaking operation, the leading naval intelligence analyst in Bletchley's famous Hut 4.

Max Newman (see *Electronics and computing* in Chapter 8) went to Bletchley in 1942, by which time he had been a Fellow for nearly twenty years. His special contribution to the code-breaking operation was designing the Colossus machine, the world's first programmable electronic computer (and forerunner of the post-war digital computer), which played a key part in deciphering the Lorenz code used by Hitler and his high command. The special section set up to design the new machine was known as 'The Newmanry', and the first version of Colossus was installed at Bletchley Park in May 1943.

But it was not only German codes which were broken at Bletchley Park, and an important member of the team unlocking Japanese codes was Peter Laslett (1935: Research Fellow 1948–51), who joined the Royal Navy in 1940. In 1942 he was sent to the School of

Bletchley Park (© Nick Jarvis Image Supplies, courtesy of Images of England)

Oriental and African Studies to learn Japanese, and from there to Bletchley Park in 1943. He recalled: 'We had to look for repeated messages, and tried to figure out the sentence structure to work out what the code groups meant … My great asset, I suppose, was that I was one of the very few people there who had actually served at sea, so I knew the type of terminology that might come up in any given situation. This, of course, was extremely useful in predicting what code groups might be expected to come next.'

Harry Hinsley – whose tutor Hugh Gatty (1925: Fellow 1931–48; Librarian 1937–48) was another notable Johnian at Station X – estimated that without the code-breaking activities at Bletchley Park, the war would have lasted two, or even three years longer.

Peter Hennessy (1966), a pupil of Harry Hinsley and a leading contemporary historian, declares: 'The contribution of this most super-secretive set of Johnians to licking Hitler and his Axis allies was kept under wraps for nearly thirty years – though the incomparable Harry Hinsley used to practise retrospective signals intelligence when teaching medieval history: "Imagine Charlemagne. He's on the blower to the Pope. What's he saying?" They were the stuff of legend, and Newman's extraordinary achievements are still spoken of with awe inside the British intelligence community.'

Parachuted into France in 1944, he worked with the French Resistance under the code-name Emile. His exploits earned him the MC, DSO, Légion d'Honneur and Croix de Guerre. He later wrote three books about his wartime experiences. Harry Alfred Rée (1933) began the war as a conscientious objector, but in 1942 joined the SOE and worked with the Maquis. His exploits, including near capture, numerous acts of sabotage and hand-to-hand combat, earned him the DSO, Croix de Guerre and an OBE.

Many Johnians put their intellect to the service of their country in scientific research. Max Newman (1915: Fellow) joined Bletchley Park in 1942, where Sir Harry Hinsley (Master 1979–89 – see Chapter 21) also played a distinguished part. Computer pioneer Sir Maurice Wilkes (1931: Fellow 1950–; see Chapter 8) helped develop coastal radar defences. The work of Sir Fred Hoyle (Fellow 1939–72: see Chapter 8) on naval defensive radar enabled operators to determine the altitude of an enemy plane. Sir Frederic Bartlett and Kenneth Craik carried out distinguished work in applied psychology, and Sir Frank Engledow advised the Government on food supply (see Chapter 8: *Biological sciences*).

Over thirty members of the College were taken prisoner. Professor Sir Jack Goody (1938: Fellow 1961–), captured at Tobruk in 1942, became a POW in Italy and Germany. His account of his escape from captivity and subsequent recapture, *Beyond the Walls*, has been published in several languages. Ralph Ince (1924) was taken prisoner by the Japanese at the fall of Singapore. He spent the next three-and-a-half years in captivity, and worked on the infamous Burma-Siam railway. His typescript *Reminiscences of a POW in Siam*, held in the College Library, gives a harrowing account of his experiences.

Several members of College were conscientious objectors. P J Hume (1936) joined the Friends' Ambulance Unit, and by 1940 had become its Secretary, organizing its operations in Finland and in London during the Blitz. He later became the Unit's recruiting

ROBERT HINDE REMEMBERS A COLOURFUL CHARACTER

When I think about my colleagues individually, each one of them is a pretty colourful character. But when I think of them as a bunch, there are some who stand out. The most important one for me was Roland Winfield, son of the austere lawyer, Sir Percy Winfield.

After release from the RAF, I came up in January 1946. Roland taught me physiology. That was a piece of luck for me, because at first I hated Cambridge and without him I would almost certainly have packed it in and become an airline pilot at twenty times what I was getting as an undergraduate. Roland was a breath of fresh air. A medic, his ambulance had been machine-gunned at Dunkirk. He trained as a pilot, and flew virtually every type of operational aircraft on ops to find how to ameliorate the stress of the crew. He understood my problems and I felt a bond with him.

But the hazards he seemed to have escaped in the war had taken their toll. Before he left the RAF he won a race down the up-staircase in Piccadilly Circus in the rush hour. When I asked him about a small stuffed crocodile which appeared in his College room, he replied, 'Oh my grandfather came home with it one night and could not remember where he got it from.' (What the very proper Sir Percy would have thought, I cannot imagine: perhaps it was a maternal grandfather.) With his encouragement, I got through Prelims and began to enjoy Cambridge.

Roland might have made the perfect Cambridge don. He loved old silver, and had a good collection of his own. He loved painting: one story in his autobiography tells how, after the war, he locked himself in the Scott Polar Research Institute and sat through the night marvelling at Wilson's paintings of Antarctica. But apparently post-war Cambridge was too much for him. I heard (but cannot verify) that he was accused of putting benzedrine (amphetamine) in students' drinks, and arranging supervisions at 03.00 hours. He departed. From my perspective it was a very great loss. The College thrives on a little bit of colour: perhaps the Council felt that his colour was the wrong shade.

Left: Professor Sir Jack Goody in Moosburg POW camp, Germany, 1944 (courtesy of Sir Jack Goody)

Below: M P Charlesworth addressing Canadian Servicemen in First Court c.1940

established on the Chapel Tower, and specially painted boards designed to indicate the presence of mustard gas were placed in the Courts.

The College mercifully suffered no damage from enemy action, although Michael Haughton (1944) recalls a near miss: 'One evening, sitting in a room in Second Court listening to a record of Beethoven's Ninth, the music was drowned by the pulsating sound of a V1 flying bomb which narrowly missed the tower of the Chapel. We continued listening to Beethoven's affirmation of peace on earth.'

The Combination Room played a historic part. In March 1944 a model of Normandy beaches was laid out for a briefing of commanders and staff of 30th Corps in preparation for the D-Day invasion. E A Benians recalled 'a vast plan of cliff and down constructed on the floor of the Combination Room – we were never officially told what it was.' The College Council were asked to approve the use of the Combination Room for a highly secret and unspecified purpose. Approval was granted: no minute was made.

officer and lost his life in 1942 aboard a torpedoed ship.

From December 1941 to December 1948, *The Eagle* published a Roll of Honour reporting the death or capture of members of the College. A memorial service for the fallen was held in December 1946, and in November 1954 two side panels, designed by Sir Edward Maufe, were added to the 1914–19 Memorial in the Antechapel.

Most of New Court was occupied throughout the war by a training wing of the RAF. An armed sentry was posted on the Bridge of Sighs and a 'civilian pass' required to move from the Old Courts to the New. The Rev. J S Boys Smith recalled that there were no lights showing from windows or staircases and that on approaching the Bridge it was prudent to stamp one's feet to make the sentry aware of the approach. Other rooms were used for Army courses, and the College also accommodated Dominion and American soldiers. About two-thirds of the normal number of junior members remained in residence, adapting to rationing and fuel shortages, and as necessary to military duty and roof-top fire-watching. Windows were blacked out, the Paddock fence was surrendered in a national collection of iron railings, crops of onions and potatoes replaced the lawns in Chapel Court, an observation post was

POPPY DAY

While other universities had Rag Weeks, for two decades after the Second World War students in Cambridge were given the run of the city on only one day in the year – Poppy Day, the Saturday before Remembrance Sunday. Organized on a college-by-college basis, with competition to raise the greatest sum for the work of the Earl Haig Fund in aid of disabled ex-Servicemen and Servicewomen, this involved a very considerable effort by individual college organizers and their helpers. The main attraction for many was the procession of floats through the city streets. In 1959 the undergraduate Johnian organisers – Robert Jordan (1958) and John Garner (1958) – secured the loan of five lorries from local firms for floats (out of a total of nearly forty) with themes such as 'We've never had it so good' (an echo of Harold Macmillan's 1957 slogan), 'St John's College Bird Sanctuary', and 'Lunatik III' (an echo of the Russian Sputnik). There was an LMBC Cycle Marathon from the Earl Haig pub at Hounslow to Cambridge Guildhall where it was met by the Mayor. A St John's Revue in the Forecourt staged six showings during the day. In the afternoon a well-known escapologist defied death in New Court, and in the evening a Jazz Dance took place in New Court Cellars. Throughout the day there was a 'Sale of

Degrees' at the Great Gate. St John's raised over £850 from a Cambridge total of £12,000.

Poppy Day continues in Cambridge, but without the Rag. The divorce seems to have begun in the 1960s, with a shift in focus away from the Earl Haig Fund as the designated charity.

St John's Poppy Day float 1959 – David (now Lord) Hope is second from the left playing the oboe (courtesy of Lord Hope)

169

POST-WAR

At the end of the war, considerable numbers of ex-Servicemen returned to the College to resume courses which military service had interrupted and were enabled to complete 'short' degree courses. In consequence of National Service, which continued for fourteen years after the war, freshers often arrived with considerable experience of life. Up until the late 1950s, there were still undergraduate ex-National Servicemen who had seen military action before embarking on their degree courses.

Ted Crisp (1939) recalls his return after war service: 'Some of us returned to complete our studies in 1946 when the average student age rose overnight from eighteen to twenty-seven. The returning warriors from

active service and POW camps [were] a hard-drinking, hard-swearing, cynical bunch.' Robert Hinde (1946) expresses surprise, looking back, at 'how little we talked about the war. We tended to mix with other ex-Servicemen, but not to discuss our experiences. For my part, the long and mostly uneventful trips over the sea that I had been making as a flying-boat pilot did not give me much to talk about, but that sort of reason did not apply to others. Probably there were a number of reasons. Reticence and fear of being seen to be shooting a line was certainly one, but what else? Wanting to forget? Survivors' guilt? Probably, but also wishing that they had not had to kill. Such reticence is a pity. The horrors should be talked about, so that people will be less willing to go to war in the future.'

POST-WAR RATIONING

Post-war shortages of almost everything made for spartan living in the College for several years. A Notice from the Steward dated 18 July 1946 sets the scene:

> With the introduction of Bread Rationing it is regretted that it will no longer be possible to serve bread with lunches or dinners in hall. All Members of the College over 18 are entitled to 9 Bread Units per week, and it is proposed that 3 of these should be retained by the kitchen to cover flour and bread used in cooking, the remaining six being used for the purchase of bread from the kitchens on Mondays, Wednesdays and Saturdays, at the scale of 2 Bread Units for a 1lb 14 oz [850g] loaf.

Things remained bleak. On 8 November 1947, the Steward advised that the Ministry of Food were reducing the sugar ration by 2oz [60g], and alterations in the fat ration had been made such that the fortnightly allowance of bacon would be 2oz, and the cheese allowance would be 2oz per week 'if lunch was not taken'. Jam allowance was set at 1lb [450g] per month. On 12 November Fellows and MAs with dining rights at High Table were asked to note that the weekly ration of 3lbs [1.36 kilos] of potatoes per head permitted only one potato at each main meal.

Against this background, the attraction of the Pig Club (see panel) needs little emphasis.

Opposite: This view from the Chapel Tower over the Great Gate leads the eye up Trinity Street in the direction of King's Parade

THE PIG CLUB

In the austerity which followed the Second World War, many items of food were rationed, including meat. However, in 1946 the Ministry of Food sanctioned the creation of 'Canteen Pig Clubs' for the purpose of 'encouraging pig keeping as a means of saving waste; keeping pigs by means of the cooperation of members; and the provision of meat for the users of a canteen or dining hall'. (It will be noted that actual nutrition was only a tertiary objective.) The College took the opportunity, and for the following eight years, until the end of rationing, St John's College Pig Club pigs were kept at the College's Kitchen Garden and fed, as was statutorily required, on College swill. The College members dining in the 'local canteen' benefited accordingly. It was intended that half of the pigs reared should find their way to the Ministry, but sometimes that failed to happen.

After the end of rationing, there was considerable reluctance to disband a society which had been to the great mutual benefit of Fellows and College staff, and had nourished robust links between them; and it was determined, in the words of Benny Farmer and of John Crook (Secretary of the Club 1959–84) that it should continue 'for social and unspecified purposes as a glorious anomaly'. And so it did. In 1996 it celebrated its Golden Jubilee and to this day continues to bring its members together (membership is by election and is highly prized) for periodic conviviality – it even has an anthem set to music by Robin Orr (see Chapter 17) – and the consumption of maupygernons (gaily coloured meatballs: a medieval dish).

24 A Great Sporting Tradition

St John's has long enjoyed a reputation for outstanding sporting achievement. Pride of place is taken by the Lady Margaret Boat Club, founded in 1825, and the chapter begins with a review of LMBC's prowess over the years, including a look at the evergreen Fellows' Boat. It goes on to detail the distinguished Johnian record in field sports: rugby, soccer, hockey, cricket, athletics.

LADY MARGARET BOAT CLUB
– THE GOLDEN AGE

LMBC, founded only ten years after the Battle of Waterloo, is the oldest boat club in Cambridge. It was instrumental in founding the Boat Race in 1829, and it is a matter of quiet satisfaction that the first Cambridge crew rowed in Lady Margaret colours. And what colours! The scarlet jacket which forms the most vivid part of the LMBC uniform gave the word 'blazer' to the language.

For over 180 years, the history of LMBC has been deeply interwoven with that of the College. Though founded forty years too late for the poet Wordsworth (who, to judge from Book I of *The Prelude,* would have made an excellent stroke), it was in good time for Samuel Butler, author of *Erewhon*, who coxed the Head of the River May Boat in 1857. Nineteen years later, the engineer Charles Parsons rowed bow in the May Boat, learning something, one supposes, about hydrodynamics. Stars from the past include P Colquhoun, founder in 1837 of the Colquhoun Sculls and President of Leander 1882–91; C J D Goldie, the great Cambridge stroke of 1870–2, after whom the Goldie Boat House is named; and A C Dicker, who won the Diamond Sculls at Henley three times.

In 1854–7, the Club won the Visitors' Cup at Henley three years running. Amongst later successes, LMBC won the Ladies' Plate at Henley in 1925, 1930 and 1933. In 1926, LMBC went Head of the Mays, and the sons of no less than three members of that genetically gifted crew repeated the experience of being in LMBC Head boats.

After the Second World War the College Chaplain, Canon Noel Duckworth – who had coxed Cambridge to wins in 1934–6 – was inspirational in revitalizing the Club on his return from prisoner-of-war camp in Singapore.

LMBC winning the Grand at Henley 1951 (© Eaden Lilley Photography, Cambridge)

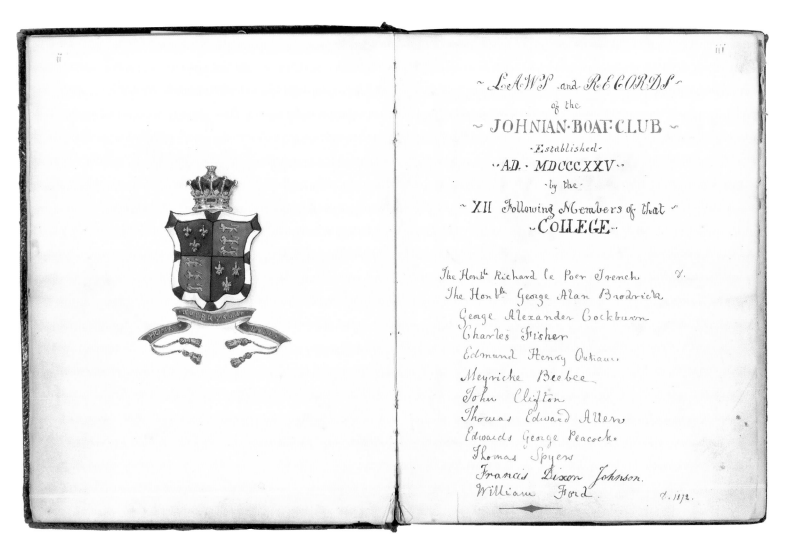

The original LMBC
'Laws' of 1825

In the vintage years of the late 1940s and early 1950s the Club notched up a remarkable series of triumphs. In the 1948 London Olympics, it furnished two members of the British VIII which won a silver medal. In 1949 LMBC won the Ladies' Plate in record time. The following year, LMBC had six members of the Blue Boat and won the Visitors' Cup. This was followed in 1951 by the blue riband of British rowing – winning the Grand at Henley – and LMBC had five members in the Goldie VIII which won the Gold Medal at the European Championships. In 1952 the Club won the Ladies' Plate again with what was virtually the 2nd VIII. In that year, LMBC had nine members in the British team at the Helsinki Olympics, and six of these won the Grand at Henley, rowing as Leander. As if that were not enough, Lady Margaret was Head of the Mays for five consecutive years, from 1950 to 1954.

THE FELLOWS' BOAT

Scene: the Long Reach, an early morning in May 2006. Enter, slowly, a rowing VIII full of exhausted men of mature years, some of them middle-aged and grey-haired, wearing faded red T-shirts and miscellaneous shorts, some alarmingly baggy. Another ageing figure, riding a bicycle, is shouting at them. What is this apparition, this Dad's Army of the River Cam?

The LMBC Fellows' Boat has featured in the May Bumps no fewer than twenty-four times since 1970, when a group of Fellows first occupied a vacant slot in the Bumps. They included Richard Perham (now Master), Peter Linehan (now Dean), David McMullen (now Professor of Chinese) and, as cox, John Durack, one of Richard Perham's tutorial pupils. In 1973 the Boat made four bumps and Messrs Perham and McMullen, together with George Reid (later Senior Bursar), Andrew Macintosh (later Dean) and the cox Mervyn King (now Governor of the Bank of England), gained their oars, with *The Times* noting that 'their collective IQ must have been the greatest of any crew ever seen on the Cam'.

Further success followed in 1989, with oars going to Dick McConnel, Nick McCave and David McMullen – Perham and Macintosh coaching from the towpath. On day two, the Fellows hit

the bank, knocking Peter Clarke (later Master of Trinity Hall) off his seat, but recovered amazingly to over-bump Girton's 3rd VIII near the finish. The 1991 boat, stroked by Andy Woods, also gained its oars, a feat repeated in 2000 with (by now Professor) Woods again at stroke. The Fellows continue to seek glory and relive happy memories of a lost youth.

The Fellows' Boat which over-bumped Girton's 3rd VIII, Mays 1989

LMBC triumphant at Henley Women's Regatta in 1991 (courtesy of John Shore)

Roger Silk, Boat Club Manager 1961–2002, with 1st May Boat 2003, chasing Trinity Hall

Since then, there have been many further successes, with the men Head of the Mays on ten further occasions and the women Head of the Mays in both 1991 and 1992. There have also been stars such as Mike Sweeney, President of the CUBC in 1965–6, stroke of the LMBC boat which won both the Ladies' Plate and Visitors' Cup in 1966, and, from 1993, Chairman of Henley Regatta; and Anne-Marie Stapleton who won a Gold Medal in the 1993 World Championships as member of the Great Britain Light IV. But there has not yet been anything to match the brilliance of the Golden Age of LMBC in the early 1950s when Lady Margaret was synonymous with Cambridge, and indeed British, rowing.

LMBC TODAY

LMBC continues in extremely good shape not only in terms of sporting prowess but as a powerful contributor to the social life of the College. Year after year it attracts a healthy cohort of keen oarsmen and oarswomen, many or most of whom will never have rowed before. Each year more than 150 students are active members of the Club; upwards of six men's and four women's Eights regularly turn out for the May Bumps.

With its new Boathouse and Fours shed, completed in 2002 and 2003 respectively, the College has rowing facilities which are second to none among Cambridge colleges. The Boathouse also accommodates the Robinson College Boat Club under a mutually beneficial arrangement which was renewed in 2005 for a further five years.

The LMBC Association's support of the Club continues to be of great importance through its purchase of boats and blades, and assistance with the funding of training camps and racing at Henley. LMBCA members provide invaluable assistance with coaching. Roger Silk, who officially retired as Boat Club Manager in 2002 after some forty years of service to the Club, also continues to lend a most welcome hand with coaching.

The Bumps Suppers continue as major events in the College calendar, and have lost little of their exub-

THE 'CROSS-CHANNEL BOAT RACE'

One of the most unusual events in College boating came about in June 2005, when seven crews lined up in Dover to race across the Channel. Not only did an LMBC team win the three-and-a-half hour race by three minutes, but the event had also been initiated and organized by Johnians. Four Cambridge crews, two from Oxford and one from sponsor Deloittes braved the choppy waters of the Channel to raise £10,000 for Cancer Research UK. One of the LMBC crew, Frank Scheibe, recalled that 'getting the blade out of the water was easier said than done. With increasing wind speed, waves started to leap over the side. Soon the self-bailers couldn't cope any more and it became important to use any slipstream the pilot boat provided. At one stage, a mountainous supertanker barred our way and we were tossed about by the waves of Channel ferries.'

The 'Cross-Channel Boat Race' of 2005

erance, though they are perhaps not quite the same as they were in the 1950s. The story is often told of a Bumps Supper when J S Boys Smith was Master (the Master traditionally is President of LMBC) at which Dean Bezzant (always to be found at Bumps Suppers – and for good reason) was moved to declare that the next man to throw an apple at the Master would be sent down, whereupon from the deep recesses of the Hall a pear sailed in the direction of the Head of House, who maintained his perfect wintry smile throughout. Those who wish to hear the sequel to this story should turn to Chapter 25.

A REMINISCENCE BY GARDNER CADWALADER, US OLYMPIC OARSMAN AND MEMBER OF THE CAMBRIDGE BLUE BOAT OF 1972

Rowing for LMBC was wonderful. I had rowed in the States and we worked and worked; twenty-four-mile practices. We rowed all winter, covered with ice; all summer, baked by the sun; had to win, had to win. We never had the sense of fun, nor the spirit of rowing for its own sake. So the delight of messing about on a crooked little river with coaches imparting poetic wisdom while teetering atop bicycles was splendid and thoroughly pleasant for me.

I had competed internationally before I found myself, almost by accident, at Cambridge. Coxes with tiny brimmed hats, bow ties, clinker-built tubs, swans, beer and everyone in peals of laughter about Monty Python. Alice in Wonderland, or rather Gardner in Wonderland! It was all so magical and amusing. And having the

fellow who fixed the boats coach us was another surprise – our esteemed Roger Silk.

And the Bumps! What a composition of orderly pandemonium, smashing blades, a cow or two and troops of tweedy men clomping about in wellie boots. And holding a chain at the start of the race and being pushed out by a pole! Are you kidding? I had competed in a race with twenty VIIIs abreast for three miles on a colossal lake in college back home.

The attitude was spirited, competitive and the very best of amateur athletics; for the pure pleasure of doing the sport – and the greatest fellowship that changed my life.

176

THE FIELD SPORTS

'… we feel that all who join in the College games will feel the benefit of such a healthy and inexpensive amusement.' So concludes the account of activities of the Football Club in *The Eagle* for 1869. This sentiment clearly did not fall on deaf ears, for the subsequent record of the College in both winning major competitions and breadth of participation is second to none. If there were a 'Baxter' (academic achievement) table for sport, it is a fair bet that St John's would head it. There is a vigorous spirit about the place created by widespread participation. Of course there are stars in abundance, but also the 4th men's football XI, 3rd badminton team, 2nd women's rugby XV; much breaking of sweat. There are not only Eagles and Flamingos, but also Budgies (rugby), Sparrows (football) and Tits (hockey) whose main function seems to be to promote enjoyment, sometimes of sport. The college system actively promotes vigorous participation across the whole university. Where else among a population of some 12,000 will you find around a hundred football, fifty hockey, fifty rugby and thirty cricket teams, including both men and women, not to mention numerous other sports? Cambridge undergraduates (and some graduate students and Fellows) must be among the healthiest in the world (except when injured).

A recurring theme of all the accounts of sports from the earliest days is injury. Notes commonly occur in early *Eagles* that the College could only field twelve men to the opposition thirteen because X was 'hurt'. Our Victorian forebears may have worn silly caps but it is very clear they got stuck in very firmly indeed. All the annual reports of modern times include numerous mentions of injury, not least in water polo. The 'gentler' sex, having established Football, Hockey and Rugby Clubs by 1990 also report significant levels of injury in the pursuit of victory. It is not a luxury to have the Sports Injury Clinic at Fenners or a very busy College Nurse.

In 1874 the single Football Club resolved that games should be '… played six days a week, three days

according to the Association rules and three days according to the rules of the Rugby Union.' The separation of the Football Club into separate clubs following Rugby Union and Association rules occurred in 1875. Cricket has been played much longer, from at least the mid-1800s, and accounts of matches feature in *The Eagle* of 1865. In Lent 1899 *The Eagle*'s chronicle notes, 'A Hockey Club has been started in the college this term.' So by the turn of the century, College clubs had been established in all four major field sports.

RUGBY UNION FOOTBALL

The Rugby Club has long been a major force in the Cambridge game. With old rivals Magdalene, Downing and Jesus, it dominated up to a few years ago. It still does, but has been joined by two graduate colleges, St Edmunds and Hughes Hall, who from time to time are able to put out teams dense with Blues, often of international standing. Nevertheless St John's has won Cuppers four times in the last eleven years and a dozen times since the war. The last eleven years have also seen seven League championships, with the 'double' on three occasions. As recently as 1993 the College fielded a 3rd XV but nowadays it is difficult to field two full sides. The decline of coaching in schools and the demanding nature of the game make it less accessible to the novice than football.

On the other hand, there is the success of the women's rugby team. Most of the Red Girls learn the game from scratch and have proved highly successful, winning Cuppers six times and the League on seven occasions since 1995. Alumni prior to 1982 should not imagine a cadre of female behemoths. Though tough and fleet of foot, they bear no resemblance to the traditional notion of the 'muddied oaf'.

The Club has had Blues almost too numerous to mention by name, though the College's Senior Bursar, Chris Ewbank, must be excepted, as must Rob Andrew, who was also a cricket Blue. Rob Andrew's academic career was nearly derailed by the demands of playing international rugby, and it was only a wise tutorial

177

intervention (on academic grounds) that prevented him from joining what turned out to be a disastrous British Lions tour. This meant that he could go on, unsullied by Antipodean mauling, to the feats as England fly-half (seventy-one caps) for which he is renowned, notably the last-minute dropped goal to secure defeat of Australia in the final of the 1995 World Cup.

ASSOCIATION FOOTBALL
Football is the most popular game played in College, with four men's and two or three women's teams in the Leagues. It is fiercely competitive across the University: St John's has won Cuppers only seven times and the League five times since the war. Internationals and professionals do not tend to emerge from universities, and the College's most distinguished footballer was in fact the great cricketer Trevor Bailey who won an FA Amateur Cup-winners medal for Walthamstow Avenue

HOCKEY
Hockey is possibly the most successful of all the field clubs in university competitions. Since the war the Club has won Cuppers nineteen times and the League nine, and between 1987 and 1997 only failed to win the Cup twice. The trophy cabinet contains a delightfully arrogant little shield from the hockey Cuppers 'golden age', which lists '1988: St John's; 1990–1993: St John's; 1989: A N Other'. A major talking point is the lack of an all-weather astroturf pitch. Few games at the top level are now played on grass.

Above: The 'Red Boys' (1st XV) battle against Jesus 2003 (courtesy of Claude Schneider/ CantabPhotos)

Left: Lydia Tong in action in the Mixed Hockey Cuppers Final against Magdalene May 2005 (courtesy of Claude Schneider/ CantabPhotos)

Above: College League football match against Churchill October 2005 (courtesy of Claude Schneider/ CantabPhotos)

Right: Mike Brearley batting for Middlesex against Hampshire 1980 (© Adrian Mitchell/ Getty Images)

Far right: Trevor Bailey batting for England against Australia at the Oval 1953 (© Hulton Archive/Getty Images)

CRICKET

Cricket suffers from being played in a short term dominated by examinations, when a League is impossible, and Cuppers is often affected by the weather or deficiencies in organization. So winning seven times in the last forty years is an excellent record. And dull would he be of soul who, visiting the playing field, failed to recognise the beauty of the setting for this most cerebral of field games, where both physical and psychological warfare is carried on. It is no accident that one of the most distinguished Johnian cricketers, Mike Brearley (Middlesex 1961–82, Captain of England 1977–81) should have been a philosophy lecturer and a psychoanalyst. Winning the Ashes was not his only skill. The College's other great cricketer, Trevor Bailey – Essex and England – also had plenty of time to think while holding Australia at bay for four-and-a half hours in 1953, earning the nicknames 'Stonewall' and 'Barnacle'.

ATHLETICS

The early College went in for 'real tennis'. A court was built against the wall of the Master's orchard in 1574, and the Loggan print of 1690 suggests that the sport was still going strong over a hundred years later on a court across the river. Later still, Howard Angus (1963) was world real tennis champion from 1976 to 1981.

From the early days of organized sport there have been athletic competitions in College, initially in the form of a sports day. The report of that held at Fenner's in February 1867, began 'Walking Race. All disqualified. No prizes given.' Later intercollegiate competitions and a cross-country running team spawned many champions and Blues, but none greater than Chris Brasher (see panel).

Robert Howland in the 1930s (© Sports and General)

CHRIS BRASHER CBE (1928–2003)

Winner of the Gold Medal in the 3,000 metre steeplechase at the 1956 Olympics, Chris Brasher (1947) was the College's outstanding athlete of the twentieth century.

Chris Brasher in action during the steeplechase final at the Melbourne Olympics 1956, where he won the Gold in record time (© Getty Images)

While at Cambridge he was President of both the CU Athletics and Mountaineering Clubs, and in 1951 won the World Student Games 5,000 metres and came second in the 1,500 metres. Dr Peter Roe (1949) ran second-string to him in the 1952 Athletics Cuppers three-mile event. He recalls that Brasher was 'by far the strongest runner in the field but for the first mile ran with me, showing me how to take maximum wind protection from runners just in front and prompting me at intervals to overtake one or other of them. At one mile, the race leaders now being some distance ahead, he said he would have to leave me, and proceeded to go on and win – but then came back and ran alongside the track, encouraging me over the last lap or so. A true sportsman!'

In 1954 he was part of the team (Brasher, Chataway, Bannister) which achieved the four-minute mile. Thereafter, he became a leading sports journalist and for a time Head of General Features at BBC/TV, and was a long-time athletics columnist with *The Observer*. In 1977 he established a successful leisure clothing company. His great achievement in later life was to see the potential for, and actually establish in 1981, the London Marathon, of which he became Chairman and President.

Right: Jim Williams, Head Groundsman 1963–99 (courtesy of Mrs Rita Williams)

Below right: The Eagles 1984, with Rob Andrew, Chris Ewbank (now Senior Bursar) and others (© Eaden Lilley Photography, Cambridge)

Bottom right: Some Flamingos of 2006: Antonia Da-Silva Teixeira, Kosnatu Abdulai, Rebecca Fisher, Fiona Danks

The canard that sporting achievement is inversely correlated with academic ability and achievement is given the lie by a host of Firsts among Johnian Blues. The classic case is that of R L 'Bede' Howland (1924), a Double First in Classics, a Triple Blue (cricket, hockey and athletics), Captain of the British Athletics team 1934–5, and British record-holder for putting the shot 1930–48, who also became Fellow, Senior Tutor and President of St John's.

There are many other sports where team prowess has been displayed in recent years, including badminton, basketball, netball, croquet, tennis, swimming and water polo. And individual skill is seen in the martial arts of fencing, kendo and boxing. All in all, Johnian sportsmen and women are a vigorous lot.

This account would not be complete without mention of the playing fields across Queens' Road, used as such since 1858. They have been superbly maintained as top quality playing surfaces by a succession of Groundsmen, notably Jim Williams, who looked after them for no fewer than thirty-six years until his retirement in 1999.

EAGLES AND FLAMINGOS

The sporting elite of the College are to be found in the ranks of the Eagles and Flamingos Clubs, to which outstanding sportsmen and sportswomen from all fields are admitted in limited numbers, by election. The Eagles started as a tennis club some time around 1870, but fairly soon spread its wings to include not just lawn tennis players, but University Blues or College Colours in a variety of sports. There is a tradition that the Cambridge University Hawks' Club was formed in 1872 when a proposal to allow members of other colleges into the Eagles was rejected.

The chief junior Eagle, known as the Secretary and, informally for some years now, as Big Bird, wears a fine cap of ancient vintage as his badge of office on official occasions. (It is a well-travelled headpiece, having been whisked off to Canada by one holder some decades ago, and only returned on deathbed repentance.) 'Bede' Howland, mentioned above, Secretary of the Eagles in the 1930s, wrote that 'it is a club whose chief function is to exist', a tradition honourably continued when the parallel Flamingos Club was established, following the admission of women to the College in 1982. The programme of both clubs is essentially social, with a joint dinner and a joint dessert each year which Fellows who are also Eagles and Flamingos cheerfully attend.

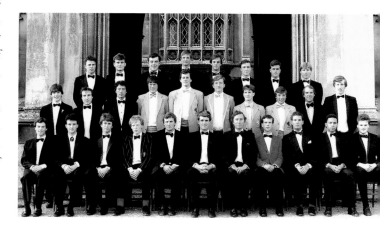

25 'DEANING'

Peter Linehan, Dean

Though the concept remains unacknowledged by the *OED*, for undergraduates of a certain disposition the reality of being 'deaned' retains an importance which goes beyond the entitlement it provides to membership of the Horticultural Society (established by the then Captain of Rugby on being assigned gardening fatigues after planting an orphan sapling in the New Court lawn; aka the Snatch Club and by other aliases) and even to the dubious distinction of an invitation to 'Dean's Desserts' (since, as the *OED* does disclose, discipline, the maintenance of which under Statute XXXVII falls mainly on the Dean, does not just mean punishment).

In the reign of Dean Bezzant, who ruled the roost in my own undergraduate days and combined the reputation of a liberal theologian with the social attitudes of Attila the Hun, 'deaning' could mean sudden death. For Bezzant, the last of hanging and flogging deans, sending down was not so much the final solution as an opening bid. I was myself sent down only once, as one of thirty-odd so treated at a Bumps Supper, after Bezz had advised our coach against throwing an apple at the Master and said coach had instead sent a pear in that direction. 'Mr XXX, I send you down.' Murmurs of 'unfair, unfair'. 'Mr XXX, I send you down. *I send the whole table down*,' adding, as we trooped out, 'And I mean it.' Which of course meant that he didn't but that we were all in for a morning of contrition and forgiveness in the Deanery while the Great Man ('It would give me no pleasure to blight a young man's career at its very outset…') quenched his considerable thirst. What Bezz would have made of a demand recently made under the Freedom of Information Act requiring all college deans to provide details of collegiate crime and punishment over the past two years must be left to the imagination.

Bezz was both deans, Dean of Souls and Dean of Bodies, and, when on his retirement the College decided that God deserved the undivided attention of a dean of his own, the affairs of Mammon were entrusted to a layman, the first of whom was Renford Bambrough. Renford, who had the trick of presenting his left profile to the errant visitor and slowly turning his head to fix him with his penetrating, philosophical gaze, was Dean during the Troubles, *c*.1970, when the insufferable righteousness of the malcontents must have robbed the office of what little fun it ordinarily afforded.

Having two deans indistinguishable by title provides the porters with the problem of deciding whose post is whose (I advise sniffing for the odour of sanctity), but is probably in better accord with the canonical prohibition on clerical shedding of blood. Not that much blood is shed in an average decanal week, even in the month of February, which regularly proves to be the cruellest month for the Dean, presumably on account of the interaction between sap rising and clouds descending.

Perhaps because the stakes are now lower, undergraduate mischief these days tends to be less imaginative than it once was, with in recent years nothing to match the minicar suspended from the Bridge of Sighs or the larger-than-life-sized photograph of Dean Bambrough's penetrating, philosophical gaze fixed to the clock-face on New Court and scanning the entire Backs like that of an Albanian Dear Leader.

One major change since Bezz's time, of course, is Women, and one of the pleasant consequences of Women is Parties. Some idea of the Way We Live Now is

Johnian Proctor and 'bulldogs' from a different era

provided by the following exchange between the Dean and the '69 Bridge Street Twelve' after an unlicensed and riotous gathering early one Michaelmas Term:

Dean: Very bad business, this. Lets the College down badly, shocking, lets yourselves down too. Very bad example to the new boys and girls. (etc. etc.) … *However*, I am informed that the College has twelve other rooms not yet disposed of. Admittedly, not amongst our best addresses. Broom cupboards in graduate hostels, places out towards Royston and Ely, that sort of thing. Nevertheless, *twelve* rooms … Twelve … So you must *go* …

[Dean counts silently to ten while twelve big lads clutch at one another, tear hair and faint in coils]

… *go back* to 69 Bridge Street…and never let anything like this happen again. I fine you £1,000.

The 12 (as one): God bless you, Mr Dean; you're a Brick, Sir, etc. etc.

Their Spokesman (hesitantly): Dean, we are most grateful. Would you be so good as to come to number 69 for a little party (with your permission of course, Mr Dean), at 6 on Tuesday?

And there it was, 'Whisky or champagne, Sir?'

Bezz would at least have felt comfortable with that.

26 THE LIGHTER SIDE OF LIFE

Opposite: The 2006 May Ball – time off in a punt

Right: The 2006 May Ball – a 'Crystal Palace' in Second Court

The College has highly developed skills in organizing entertainments. Each year it hosts fine indoor occasions – the Dinner for members of the Foundation (the Master, Fellows and Scholars), held in the Hall, is one. It also lends itself to such agreeable outdoor functions as tutorial barbecues in the Fellows' Garden. But it is the St John's May Ball, widely famed as one of the best parties in the world, where the magnificence of the College, indoors and outdoors, is employed to best, and most memorable, effect. At the other end of the scale of elegance comes the subterranean Clarkson, or 'Boiler', Room, of which more anon. More surreptitious events are also retailed in this chapter – escapades, climbings-in, and a mystery.

THE MAY BALL

Held in the week following the May Bumps, the Ball has grown in scale and variety over more than a century. Originally it was the preserve of the Lady Margaret Boat Club. The first record of a summer ball at St John's is a dance card for the 'Lady Margaret Ball' of 1888. By the early twentieth century it had become a College-wide event and, war-time apart, a ball has been held every year, ensuring continuity of experience amongst the largely undergraduate organising committee. Now a major event, it requires the agreement of a code of practice on matters such as noise and safety with two Councils, College and City.

Ticket prices including dinner have soared from one guinea (£1.05) in 1892 to £10.50 for a double ticket in 1971 and an arresting £335 in 2006 (albeit with a reduction for those who forego formal dinner in the Combination Room). The three hundred participants

of 1920 had risen to two thousand by 1970, and that is still the number today. Tickets, sold online with a priority period for members of the College, sell out within hours of the website being launched. Turnover has grown from £220 in 1907 to £9,000 in 1971 and now to a staggering £250,000. The Ball is entirely self-financing.

The advent of VAT in 1973 posed a challenge both to the Senior Treasurer and to the Customs & Excise computer. The former had to learn how to deal with the requisite quarterly returns. The latter had to be trained to understand how it was that a business with negligible turnover in three of the quarters could have such a large turnover in the fourth. Happily the local inspector proved sympathetic!

186

The Ball's main programme of events has changed over time in response to changes in taste. Ballroom dancing was once the only entertainment, but now dancing of any sort plays a rather minor role. Other forms of entertainment are lavishly provided at various sites: perhaps cabaret in a marquee in First Court; swing-boats on the Backs; a variety of musical programmes in the Hall and in Third, New and River Courts; a fortune teller; a masseur; a casino; to say nothing of a range of bars serving every possible type of food and drink, with ice sculptures.

The traditional firework display is memorable. In former days there were no restrictions on when fireworks could be let off; one year during a difficult period of the Cold War a spectacular firework display in the early hours of the morning caused many inhabitants of the city to fear that the Russians had invaded – or so they claimed. Today, the display has to finish by 11 pm but is hugely impressive visually and auditorily, with a choreographed musical accompaniment.

Unsurprisingly, security requirements have become more stringent over the years. There was a time when a few members of the Rugby Club patrolling the boundaries of the Ball provided a sufficient deterrent to prospective gate-crashers. Nowadays, that function has passed to stewards accredited by the Security Industry Authority, with a couple of police constables on hand, just in case. With increased concerns about security, the custom (fondly remembered by participants in balls three or four decades ago) of emerging from the College shortly after pipers had welcomed dawn from the New Court battlements and following a steel band around the town, is no more. In its place, the custom has revived of a photograph of 'survivors' at 6 am.

There are numerous stories of crises on the night. On one occasion, the present Master and President of the College (both then senior members of the May Ball committee) arrived in College shortly before the Ball was due to start to find a music group demanding to know where their piano was. The fact that no piano had been specified in the contract did nothing to diminish the tension. Eventually, and with considerable effort and trepidation, a concert piano was moved by a posse of stalwarts all the way from the School of Pythagoras to the relevant marquee, where somehow it survived the night.

When well over an inch of rain fell during the 1973 Ball, a good many participants appeared to conclude that this was entirely the fault of the committee and clamoured for a refund. In fact, only one was made. This was where an over-assiduous committee member,

Left: The May Ball Committee 1969 with Derrick Lyon, Richard Aikens, Peter Hennessy, Paul Batchelor, Richard Perham, Roger Morgan, Michael Williams, John Browne and their partners

Below: Discotheque in the 'Boiler Room'

CAR ON THE CAM

Mark Rushbrooke (1960)

Did the idea come over a pint at The Mitre or munching bread and cheese at a 'War on Want' lunch? Could a few Johnian engineers and friends do something to match the car on the Senate House roof before we all went down? How about a car suspended below the Bridge of Sighs? OK, let's do it!

First we had to get a car. With a little persuasion the owner of a breaker's yard near the Kinema let me have a decaying 1928 Austin 7 provided it was stripped of everything saleable. After many hours' work all that was left was a body, four wheels and some steering. No seat, brakes, lights, engine or gearbox.

In the early hours of 8 June 1963, Chris Parker (1960) towed the shell towards Chesterton Bridge where Richard West (1960) and others had lashed two punts together. Loading was nearly disastrous – only rapid adjustment to narrow supporting planks stopped the car plunging into the river. Guided by flashing torches – and hiding under Magdalene Bridge while a policeman passed above – the punts proceeded upstream. Adrian Padfield (1960), waiting in his rooms by the

Bridge, dropped the ropes to the team below. The moment of truth. Would the ropes hold? Would the car roof take the strain? The car rolled off the front of the punts and came to rest with wheels just touching the water. Perfection!

Car on the Cam 1963 (courtesy of Mark Rushbrooke)

187

seeing an awning sagging with rain and about to collapse, managed to empty the entire contents over an unsuspecting couple. Soaking wet, and with the lady's bouffant hair-do reduced to a soggy haystack, they demonstrated a formidable rage which the refund did little to pacify. The committee member made no further attempts to empty awnings that night.

THE CLARKSON ROOM (AKA 'THE BOILER ROOM')
Hidden away under the Cripps Building, with basic facilities and a capacity of one hundred, the Clarkson Room is available for parties and discos put on by College organizations and individual members. It is a place for beginning-of-year 'squashes' recruiting members for clubs and societies and is arguably a place of choice for devoted drum and bass music fans. Ask people what they remember about it and you will be told of hot, claustrophobic evenings, bumps on the head from low-hanging pipework, and a floor sticky with spilt drinks.

The 'Boiler Room' is also notorious for the black paint with which it is decorated. This comes off on anything that touches it. At a toga party some years ago, party-goers predictably used their bed-sheets for their costume (some with more success than others when it came to creating a toga that stayed on for more than three minutes). Down in the half-light, it was difficult to see what was happening but many bedders were severely puzzled the following morning to find blackened sheets in many student rooms. Reflecting on the rooms named in honour of the College's two great anti-slavery campaigners (see Chapter 7), a current Fellow sums up the position thus: 'I did always think it was a bit hard on Clarkson to get that black hole named after him when Wilberforce has a much nicer room in College – but that pretty much reflects their relative standing when they were working on the slavery issue. Clarkson did the donkey work while Wilberforce did much of the elegant talking.'

NIGHT CLIMBERS

St John's, with its rich variety of buildings, has provided a happy hunting ground for 'night climbers' since this daring – or foolhardy – pursuit first came into vogue in the mid-nineteenth century. According to the classic text on the subject, *The Night-Climbers of Cambridge* by the pseudonymous 'Whipplesnaith' (1937), the Drain-Pipe Chimney in New Court was one of the classic climbs, fit to rank alongside the Trinity Kitchen Plateau and the notoriously severe Chetwynd Crack in King's as one of the stiffest challenges in the 'sport'. John Steegman, author of *Cambridge* (1940), considered such ascents to be 'romantic, hazardous climbs, where the reward of success was a circumscribed and private glory and the penalty of failure was being either crippled or sent down'. For Johnian climbers, scarcely less popular than the Drain-Pipe Chimney was the Chapel Tower, usually attempted from Chapel Court (on one occasion, LMBC-inspired, accompanied by scarlet oars which were lowered into the arms of the saintly statues near the top, causing mirth or dismay, according to viewpoint, the following morning). The attraction of risking life and limb by climbing Cambridge buildings has understandably declined in recent decades.

The Rev. David Wills (1955) recalls being woken one night during Tripos by bodies climbing over him in his bedroom close to the Bridge of Sighs. It was a hot night and the window stood wide open. The 'bodies' had monkey-hopped across the outside of the Bridge, using the grilles, and the fastest route to safety lay across his bed. Years later, a man sitting next to him at a College reunion dinner thought he might have been one of the visitors 'for whom I was none too grateful'.

An uncommon pursuit

ESCAPADES AND CLIMBING-IN

Several letters from alumni of a certain age show that climbing into College and decorating its architecture with exotic objects still count as (literally) high points in their lives. For many, even fairly routine climbing-in caused a rush of adrenalin which has never been forgotten. As Adrian Parker (1965) recalls:

'One of our group was very law-abiding, and in his third year we determined to make sure he had this experience – up and over, in a dinner suit. Under some pretext we went out late and he just had to follow – quite exciting when your head is five metres in the air and the clearance to your trouser crotch is of great interest.'

David Chillingworth (1961) remembers how, while he was in New Court, late-night returners would climb the Virginia creeper, on occasion knocking on the bedroom window to be let in. Others recall that certain windows in Third Court rooms were expected to be left ajar.

The most unusual climbing-in story relates to a man with no legs, told by Michael Brander (1941) of Peter Black (1945), a Johnian ex-Royal Navy Lieutenant gravely injured in the war. Four members of the College were hauling him by rope over the railings into North Court when a policemen appeared, and had to be persuaded to turn a blind eye. Next came a Porter, who also turned a blind eye. The feat was successful.

Another story is told of the discovery of loosened bars to a ground-floor window. The advice of the Head Porter of the time was to let well alone, because 'they're like rats. Stop one hole up and they'll just find another.' One of the leading escapades is that of the car suspended below the Bridge of Sighs (see panel), but there are many others. Tony Greeves (1946) writes graphically of the appropriation of a Magdalene canoe by six Johnians on the eve of finally going down:

'And so it was that the College awoke one bright June morning to find the skyline of New Court dramatically altered. Not only was there a chamber-pot gleaming like a jewel atop the central spire, but a Magdalene canoe was proudly hanging between the pinnacles over the south gate.'

It seems that the culprits did not stay to watch further, but 'folded their tents and stole away.' Another confession comes from Ted Crisp (1939) who admits to placing a 'V' sign on the rose surmounting the Chapel chancel roof under the stimulus to roof-climbing given by his duty as wartime fire-watcher. 'Today's students,' he laments, 'don't know the pleasure of breaking the rules and getting away with it.' The attitude to such escapades by the College authorities seems to have been one of gloomy resignation. One Dean was heard to comment: 'Oh, not again! Why don't they think of something new?'

Tony Croft (1959) recalls a live duck being smuggled into dinner in Hall, with the Steward tunnelling under the tables in hot pursuit and receiving a great cheer when it was recaptured and safely returned to the Backs. He also tells of an occasion when *Varsity* was short of news and he was challenged to a hoax duel over an imaginary slight to a mythical lady. This got into the national press and resulted in his being dragged from bed at seven o'clock in the morning and reprimanded by the redoubtable Dean Bezzant for his 'dangerous exploit'.

189

GHOSTS AND MYSTERIES

Peter Linehan, Dean

I have written more than enough already on the subject of knocks on the ceiling at twenty to one in the morning and bloody chamber-pots. (On the site of a condemned hospital what else would one expect?) Instead, let me pass on the story told me by Michael Gilchrist (1957) about his uncle Ronald (1923):

'Ronald's tutor told him of three dreams that he had had on consecutive nights. In the first dream he was in a street in Cambridge which he had never previously visited; next day, he found himself in the actual street. In the second dream he was looking at a beautiful bridge; he came across it in a book next day. In the third dream he was in the room of a colleague who had recently died. There was a trap-door in the floor, with a ring in it for lifting. The Tutor told Ronald that he did not wish to take this any further. This instantly spurred Ronald to investigate. With several friends, he went to the room. There was a carpet on the floor, underneath which was a trap-door with a ring. They opened the trap, and found the colleague's will, in which he had bequeathed a sum of money to the tutor.'

Consultation of the published College records reveals that the tutor in question was B W F Armitage (Fellow 1919–25), a figure whose departure from the College remains shrouded in a certain sort of mystery; the deceased colleague G D Liveing FRS, who died on Boxing Day 1924 at the age of ninety-seven; and the room I1 New. 'That he has left no direct descendant is a matter for regret,' wrote Liveing's obituarist, W E Heitland. (But, according to the new *DNB* he did leave, to someone, an estate valued at £19,908 12s. 2d (£580,000 in today's money). A combination of the editor's tight schedule and I1's recent wall-to-wall carpeting, which the Domestic Bursar is unwilling to have unglued, prevents further enquiries, at least for the time being. But meanwhile it may be noted that Liveing's set remained vacant for the remainder of the year 1924–5.

27 THE JOHNIAN SOCIETY AND JOHNIAN SOCIETY OF THE USA

The Johnian Society was founded in 1923 to promote contact with and between former members of the College. It has a wide membership of former Johnians and its affairs are managed by a representative Committee. In addition to the key annual event – the Society's Dinner held in College on a Saturday in December – there is a bi-annual Lecture, of which the most recent was given by David Pountney CBE. The Society also holds an Annual Golf Competition for the Sir Edward Marshall Hall Cup.

In recent years, the Society has given various forms of financial support to junior members, notably through travel exhibitions and access bursaries. Up to six travel exhibitions are awarded annually, usually to under-graduates embarking on academic study or socially useful projects outside Europe. Recent exhibitions have

Sir Philip Thomas, Marc Feigen, Nick Corfield and Professor Richard Perham at Cambridge's 800th Anniversary launch in New York November 2005

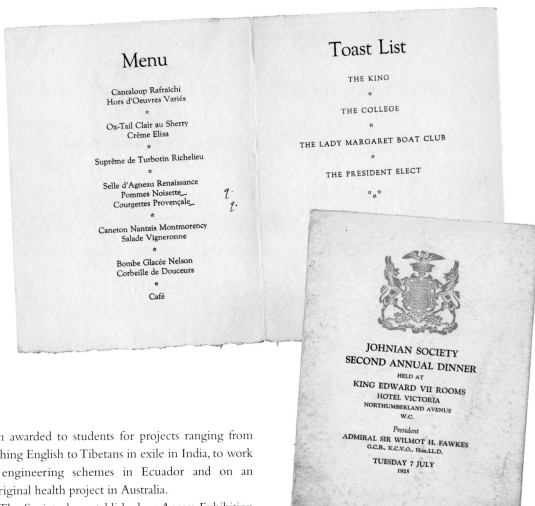

Menu

Cantaloup Rafraîchi
Hors d'Oeuvres Variés

✻

Ox-Tail Clair au Sherry
Crème Elisa

✻

Suprême de Turbotin Richelieu

✻

Selle d'Agneau Renaissance
Pommes Noisette
Courgettes Provençale

✻

Caneton Nantais Montmorency
Salade Vigneronne

✻

Bombe Glacée Nelson
Corbeille de Douceurs

✻

Café

Toast List

THE KING

✻

THE COLLEGE

✻

THE LADY MARGARET BOAT CLUB

✻

THE PRESIDENT ELECT

✻✻✻

JOHNIAN SOCIETY
SECOND ANNUAL DINNER
HELD AT
KING EDWARD VII ROOMS
HOTEL VICTORIA
NORTHUMBERLAND AVENUE
W.C.

President
ADMIRAL SIR WILMOT H. FAWKES
G.C.B., K.C.V.O., Hon.LL.D.

TUESDAY 7 JULY
1925

Menu from the Johnian Society annual dinner 1925

been awarded to students for projects ranging from teaching English to Tibetans in exile in India, to work on engineering schemes in Ecuador and on an aboriginal health project in Australia.

The Society has established an Access Exhibition Fund in support of the College's commitment to widening access for students, and in particular its bursary scheme which is designed to ensure that no capable student is deterred by financial considerations.

The Society enjoys a warm relationship with the College. The Master attends the Annual Dinner of the Society, and both the Master and a Fellow of the College are ex officio members of its Committee, ably chaired for a number of years by Colin Greenhalgh (1960). Distinguished Johnians are invited year by year to serve as President. On behalf of all Johnians, the Society aims to support the College in its quincentenary celebrations in 2011 and in its future academic mission.

The Johnian Society of the USA (JS–USA) was established in 2002 on the initiative of Marc Feigen, who read history at St John's on a Thouron Scholarship. Its aim is to strengthen the bonds of friendship and support between the College and its members who are resident in the USA, of whom there are nearly 700. Marc helped organize 'Cambridge in America', and wished to help the College advance its work in the United States as well. Addressing the first meeting of JS–USA, he said he 'learned to think at Cambridge –

that happened in supervisions, in the Library, but it happened mostly in the informal social environment of the College. In a place of almost perfect cloister, we set out to discover the world.' JS–USA was fully supported by the then Master, Peter Goddard, who was keen for Johnians in the USA to remain engaged with the College. The Johnian Society of the USA has now become an integral part of the St John's network. Peter Goddard and the present Master, Richard Perham, have made regular visits to the United States over the years, attending events in New York, San Francisco, Los Angeles, Boston, Washington DC, Seattle and Philadelphia. Over 500 Johnians and their guests have attended; many come back to events in Cambridge from time to time.

The College has greatly welcomed the generous financial support of US donors – something over $14 million has now been raised, including a munificent donation from Nick Corfield (the founder of Frame Technologies which pioneered Adobe software) who is a member of JS–USA.

28 TODAY'S COLLEGE

UNDERGRADUATES: THE ADMISSIONS PROCESS

St John's is proud of its admissions process, which is based entirely on academic merit and aims at admitting applicants who would benefit most from becoming junior members of the College. Each year the College interviews around 700 candidates competing for some 170 undergraduate places, and organizes well over 1,500 interviews – more than 700 hours' worth – within a ten-day period in December. Applications at St John's are well balanced across all subjects; usually about half of the annual intake turn out to be in arts and half in science subjects, and generally roughly equal in male and female numbers. Encouragingly, financial pressures have thus far not changed this balance.

Successful applicants are enthusiastic about and excited by their subjects. To test their potential, interviewers may introduce a 'mini-supervision' as part of the interview. It is often said that students from certain schools will have an edge at interview because their schools are able to prepare them better. But an experienced interviewer will quickly spot whether a student has been coached for the interview, and will look beyond this.

The Senior Tutor, Matthias Dörrzapf, writes:

'The College is not primarily interested in a candidate's existing knowledge; we want to expose them to something new at the interview and observe how they respond to it. We want to see them arguing logically and addressing unseen problems analytically. They need to demonstrate that they are comfortable working in an unfamiliar environment and generally show a "spark" for their subjects. At some other universities drop-out rates in the first years of an undergraduate course can be as high as fifty per cent – clear signs of a poor admissions process. At St John's the interviews give feedback about the applicants' suitability for a Cambridge course and whether, based on our experience, we believe that the applicant stands a chance in the high level and demanding pace of the Cambridge Tripos. Modular A-levels and an increasing number of course-work elements in school assessment are encouraging school-children to memorize rather than strengthen the understanding of their school material. It is therefore an increasing challenge for our admissions process to test the potential of candidates for understanding rather than just ability to memorize. Students at St John's have the enormous privilege of being in an outstanding support system – one which starts at the point of admission.'

POSTGRADUATES AT ST JOHN'S

Postgraduates play an important role in today's College, of which they form a significant part.

The status of graduate student is of relatively recent origin by Cambridge standards. The PhD (Doctorate of Philosophy) appears to have begun life in Germany in the later nineteenth century as part of a rigorous scientific training. It spread to the United States and then gradually, after the First World War, to the UK. The first Johnian to be awarded a PhD, in 1924, was a New Zealander, L J Comrie, whose supervisor was the famous astronomer and physicist, Sir Arthur Eddington. Comrie went on to a distinguished scientific career himself, in astronomy and punch-card computation, being elected FRS in 1950.

The numbers grew through the 1930s, chiefly in the sciences. Fifty years ago, there were some seventy

Above: Graduation Day: students leave the College for the ceremony at the Senate House

Right: Postgraduate students in the Samuel Butler Room

graduate students in St John's, compared with 500 undergraduates. Today, there are still roughly 500 undergraduates but postgraduates number just over 300. Admission, like that of undergraduates, is based on academic merit and potential, but with the added dimension of requiring acceptance by one of the University's departments. St John's is one of the most sought-after colleges for postgraduate work, and hard choices have to be made as to whom to admit. The Tutor for Graduate Affairs, Sue Colwell, has overall responsibility for graduate admissions and the graduate students as a body. Once admitted, they make a significant and valued contribution to the supervision of undergraduates, in addition to acquiring the high-level skills that their courses are designed to impart.

In recent years there has been a substantial growth in students on one-year M Phil (Master of Philosophy) courses, for various reasons. Arts and humanities graduates are now commonly expected to do an M Phil course before attempting a PhD, and many like to see if they enjoy research before committing themselves to the three years required for a PhD. Some M Phil courses are geared to professional preparation: for example, a student will do a year in development studies or

international relations before taking up employment with political organizations, or in diplomacy. Some are serving officers in the military. In a few cases, a one-year course may be taken to defer a decision on employment, especially if prospects are currently poor in the desired field, or indeed as a way of changing field. From the perspective of the University and the College,

one-year courses can be effective in attracting high-quality students in what is an increasingly competitive international market for postgraduate education.

About one-third of the annual postgraduate intake is from St John's itself. (The College's clinical medical students and veterinary students form part of the graduate community.) Overall, about half the graduate students come from overseas, from the US and continental Europe, East Asia, South Africa, Australia and New Zealand and a wide range of other countries. About half will stay for more than one year. Many of the PhD students go on to academic careers. Some will

Left: The Samuel Butler Room marathon team in Berlin May 2005

Opposite: Frisbee on the lawns in front of New Court

secure Research Fellowships, at St John's or another college; others will go elsewhere, in the UK, in their country of origin, or further afield. Some take up different employment: in business, for instance, or the financial sector.

Funding for postgraduates comes from a variety of sources. In the case of UK students, research councils and charities are most often the funding body. EU students can receive the fee element from research councils, but have to find their maintenance grant elsewhere. The Cambridge Trusts (European Trust, Overseas Trust, Commonwealth Trust) are traditional funders of foreign students: a more recent but important arrival is the Gates Trust. From its own resources, St John's offers about six fully funded Benefactors' Scholarships each year to external students of the highest quality, and in addition funds some three of its own students. Nonetheless, many end up self-funding or piecing together funding from a mixture of sources.

A big difference between Johnian postgraduates and undergraduates is that the former live mostly in hostels and are in residence throughout the year. They have their own common room in College – the Samuel Butler Room – and for many years (on an initiative introduced by a young Dr Perham, now Master) have been invited to dine occasionally with the Fellows at High Table. There is also a special Graduate Students Dinner each January. A Fellow, Professor Boyde, working with the Tutor for Graduate Affairs, has the happy task of promoting a range of postgraduate social activities, from country walks (including stops at appropriate hostelries) to candlelit readings of ghost stories in the Combination Room in December. The graduate students have some societies of their own but are also welcome participants in the general College societies, in many of which they have made their mark – not least in the College sports teams. It has all come a long way since 1924.

195

LOOKING TO THE FUTURE

Professor Richard Perham, Master

As I believe this book will have amply demonstrated, St John's College has much to be proud of in the lasting contributions its members have made to life in many different spheres of activity: intellectual, the arts and sciences, engineering, medicine, politics, the law, government and business, sport, entertainment, the list is endless. As it reaches towards its 500th anniversary, its standing has probably never been higher, but the College, like Cambridge as a whole, faces two major, growing challenges: the erosion of public sector funding at home, and the globalization of higher education everywhere.

For the past 50 years or so, higher education in the UK has become increasingly reliant on the funding provided by the Government. That funding is now spread much more thinly over a vastly increased number of universities, reflecting the rise in numbers attending university, from around five per cent of each UK year group in the 1950s to closer to fifty per cent today. At the same time, and this is bound to intensify in the future, we find ourselves competing for talented students and Fellows in an ever-widening international market. The world is not standing still; neither are we. Over fifty per cent of our graduate students now come from overseas, as do more than ten per cent of the undergraduates and an increasing number of the Fellows. This is not something to lament; it has brought us a vibrant intellectual and social mix, in which it is a joy to live and work.

The Fellows and I have no doubt that St John's can continue as an outstanding home of creative scholarship, teaching and innovative thinking, and play its full part in ensuring that Cambridge retains its position as one of the world's leading universities. We are dedicated to making that happen. But, the College must have a plan that is carefully thought through and the resources to enable it to compete with the best elsewhere. Our key objectives can now be stated:

- continuing the College's enviable tradition of open access, which allows undergraduates and graduate students of outstanding ability and promise, regardless of financial means or background, to benefit from the education we offer;
- maintaining the small-group teaching system, which contributes immeasurably to the educational experience of our students;
- fostering the exciting and innovative research of international distinction we believe in;
- building upon the College's traditional outward-looking philosophy by promoting collaborations in scholarship, research and teaching across the world, not least in some of its poorer regions;
- providing an experience for our students that goes beyond the purely academic and encompasses artistic, cultural, sporting and social opportunities; and
- ensuring that the breathtakingly beautiful buildings and environment of the College are not just properly maintained but are continually upgraded to provide for the demands of the twenty-first century.

A tall order and it won't come cheaply. A big increase in our endowment will be key to its success. We have benefited from the outstanding generosity of benefactors over five centuries. We will strive to manage and grow our existing resources, but we are very clear that much more will be necessary. St John's is actively participating in the University's 800th Anniversary Campaign for Collegiate Cambridge, launched in 2005 with a target of £1 billion. The University accepts that a gift to the College, though it remains with the College as the donor intends, is recognized as contributing to this overall target. The St John's College Campaign now in its formative stages is therefore timely, and the celebration of our 500th Anniversary in 2011 will feature prominently in it. We look forward keenly to its success.

The history of the College is one of teaching and research of high international distinction and of creating opportunities for the gifted and talented in the UK and worldwide, yet also that of a great community of teachers and taught. As the College prayer has it: a place where love of the brethren and all sound learning shall ever grow and prosper. In these pages we have documented something of the recent past of St John's and the deep affection (all the stronger because we don't always take ourselves too seriously) in which the College is held by those privileged enough to have been educated here or to have been associated with it in many other ways. We are now looking ahead and planning for a future as bright as the past. A great College deserves no less. On 1 December 2006 the Fellows pre-elected Professor Christopher Dobson to succeed me as Master from 1 October 2007 and he, I know, will be fully committed to its success. *Vive laeta Margareta!*

The Master and Dr Manmohan Singh in conversation with students in the Master's Lodge, October 2006

SUBSCRIBERS

Professor Chris Abell	1976
Rev. Dr M J Absolon	1951
Steve Acklam	1965
Aubrey Adams	1967
Alan M Afif	1963
Sir Richard Aikens	1967
Ronnie Aked	1980
David Aldous	1970
Sir Charles G Alexander	1941
James L Alexander	2003
John L F Allan	1954
Dr Robert Russell Allan	1951
M G Allderidge	1954
Lois Allison	2001
Tim Allison	1984
P J Allitt	1943
George Ames	1938
Michael Alford Andrews	1957
Anonymous	1986
Lisa Anson (née Whewell)	1986
Barry Appleton	1986
Aaron Armstrong	1992
Dr Nicole Francesca Armstrong	1994
Dr Ray Armstrong	1968
Tim Arnold	1978
Dr Pieter Arriens	1960
Roger Ashburner	1964
Michael Louis Ashby	1945
Andrew Ashcroft	2003
John V Ashforth	1949
Alex Ashworth	1995
Julian Astbury	1958
Alison Margaret Anne Atherton (née Russell)	1992
Justin P Atkinson	1996
P D Atkinson	1941
Vladimijr Attard	1988
Dr Daniel Aubrey	1955
Kate Aubury	1992
Dr Charles Avery	1959
J A Aveyard	1962
David Norman Axford	1953
Philip K Ayton	1967
Shlomi Azar	2001
Pascale Baboulet-Flourens	1988
David Backhouse	1951
Michael Bacon	1968
Dr David Bailey	1969
Clare Bailey	
Dr John Bailey	1966
Steven Bailey	2003
Peter Baird	1962
Alan Baird	1950
Ian S Baker	1973
Jonathan Baker QC	1974
Richard Balasubramaniam	2001
Jeremy Ball	1962
Tom Ball	1993
John Bamber	1949
John M Barber	1961
Neil C Barber	1953
Rupert Barclay	1975
Sonny Bardhan	1996
Stuart Barker	1949
Mr Daryl John Barker MBE	1973
D S Barley	2003
Richard P G Barlow	1971
William S Barnard	1962
Anita Barnes	2001
Francis Baron OBE	1964
David Barrère	1966
Dr Leonard M Barrett	1944
J C Barringer	1950
Dr J W Barrington	1980
Alick Bartholomew	1949
Dr D J Bartlett	1943
Hugh Frederic Bartlett	1940
George Paterson Barton	1948
Major J H Barton	1934
Eric Bassett	1933
Mr D A Batchelor	1974
Nigel Bates	1975
A J Bates	1991
Jim Bausor	1979
Richard Baynham Siddall	1966
John E P Beale	1986
David Beare	
C H Beaumont	1954
Henry F Beaumont	1947
John R Beaumont	1949
Jonathan Beels	1962
Dr Alan Begg	1973
David Belfall	1966
Jonathan Bell	1991
Stuart Bell	1971
Mark C Bellamy	1978
Dr James Bellini	1963
David Beamish	1970
H Michael Benians	1943
Benedict T L Bennett	1988
Phillippa M Bennett	2001
Dr M J R Bentall	1988
Alan Bentley	1975
K W Berentzen	1954
Donald Berry	1948
Dr Gerard Berry	1948
Mark Bertram	1961
William Bertram	1968
David Betts	1957
Theresa Biberauer	1996
Rosie Bichard	1986
David Biddulph	1969
Dr Nicola Bignell	1986
Guy Billington	1965
Karen Birch (née Thomas)	1992
D R J Bird	1957
G D Birtles	1943
Roger S Bivand	1969
Sandy Black	1982
Dr J A Black	1989
David M Blackburn	1956
Duncan Blackburn	1980
Anthony Blaiklock	1974
J M Caroline Blakeney (née Robinson)	1999
Dr Neil Bliss	1953
W Blyth	1965
Eleanor M Boag	1998
M G C Boatman	1959
Major W M G Bompas	1939
Stephen Bond	1991
Christopher J Bonsall	1970
David Bonsall	1974
Graham Booth	1954
Charles Booth-Jones	1947
David Stuart Boothman	1989
Ian S Borthwick	1956
Andrew Bostock	1997
Clare Bostock (née Palmer)	1998
R J B Bosworth	1966
Ian C Boulton	1971
John Boumphrey MA	1948
John Blow	1946
A J Bowen	1958
Dr Kenneth Bowen	1953
William O Boyes	1967
Rev. M L H Boyns	1945
John Wynn Boys Smith	1961
Stephen Boys Smith	1964
John A Bracewell	1979
P M C Bradshaw	1948
Karen Braganza	1998
H C Bramley	1960
Dr R A C Bramley	1959
Dr B P Brand FRPS	1943
Simon Bransfield-Garth	1979
Stephanie Bransfield-Garth	1982
C H Braybrook	1936
Michael Brearley	1960
Anthony Bridgewater	1979
D Brierley	1955
A H Brind	1944
John Broadbent	1963
Benoit Broch	1999
Ivor W Broomhead	1942
The Venerable J Michael Brotherton	1956
Georgina Browes	2002
A H Brown	1960
Alistair Brown	1980
Nicholas Brown	1977
Nigel Brown	1959
R A L Brown	1975
Steve Brumpton	1995
Patrick Joseph Bryan	1960
Stephen Buck	1977
Derek E Bucknall	1958
David Buckton	1954
Peter Budgen	1954
Damon Buffini	1981
David Budenberg	1980
J A Burdon-Cooper	1958
Julian Burling	1971
Dr C Paul Burnham	1952

Name	Year
Mr N D Burns	1963
Tim Burrage	1980
John Burren	1953
Simon Burrows	2000
Claude Bursill	1943
Dan Burt	1964
Lisa V Burton	1987
Mr Trevor Burton	1979
Warwick Burton	1973
G L Butcher	1948
Phillip M Butler	2006
R F C Butler	1944
Jo Butt	1958
John A H Butters	1957
Dr John Buttrey	1958
Oliver Buxton	2003
Henri M Bybelezer	1972
Douglas Byrne	1942
Dr A W Cairns	1974
Alex Callander	1979
Dr A J P Campbell	1952
Colin Campbell	1960
Dr David Campbell	1976
Harold C Cannon	1950
Rudolf Cardinal	1993
Rev. Canon G G Carnell	1937
Mr Robin J Carr	1962
Andrew Carrier	1980
Ian Andrew Carstairs	1969
Martin J Carter	1969
Bryan Cartledge	1951
Harry Cartwright	1937
R J Cashmore	1962
Anthony R Catterall	1972
John C Caygill	1956
Mr Chadwick	1977
John P Chambers	1963
Ben Chan	2003
Christina C K Chan	1999
Bryan Chapman	1944
Dr E J C Chapman	1980
J C B H Chapman	1984
Peter Charlton	1964
R I H Charlton	1956
David Charters	1950
J Bryan Chaumeton	1948
Eu-Gene Cheah	1984
Philip M Cheetham	1959
Dr Tim Chilcott	1961
David Chillingworth	1961
Clive Chivers	1964
Dr Oliver W Choroba	1996
N B M Clack	1949
Dr Michael Clark	1957
G P M Clark	1965
David J Clarke	1984
Jonathan G Clarke	1957
Mr P H Clarke	1949
Peter J Clarke CBE	1957
Roger Clarke	1957
Tim Clarke	1968
J E Clay	2002
John Clegg FRCS	1957
B Cleghorn	1965
Brigadier John Clemow	1930
Mr Dan J Cliffe	2003
Henry T Clifton	1946
Richard Clifton-Hadley	1973
Peter Cobb	1945
Alan Cockayne	1943
Paul Cockerham	1976
Neil Cockroft	1980
Gilbert Cockton	1977
Tom Cogan	1966
Dr Jeremy Cogswell	1956
Mr James R Colgate	2005
Dr Peter Collecott	1969
Andrew J Collier CBE	1959
Neville Collins	1947
Peter Collins	1962
Bernard C Collyer	1961
Rev. Alec Colson	1939
Vince Colvin	1978
Q M Compton-Bishop	1977
Julian Kitto Comrie	1956
Rev. Paul C N Conder	1953
Dr Richard Connaughton	1989
Simon Connell	1989
Stephen Connell	1965
George F Connelly	1940
Hugh Constable	
Mark Constable	1980
Dr F B Cookson	1955
D R Cooling	1957
John Coombs	1959
B A Cooper	1966
Brig J S Cooper OBE	1945
Jeremy Cooper	1970
Michael Cooper	1950
Mr M E Coops	1950
Christopher Cope	1986
C Cope	1962
Sir Brian Corby	1949
Hugh Corner	1961
Alan M Coulson	1973
David Coulton	1964
Mr John P Covington	1961
Andrew M Cowan	1977
Professor Russell Cowburn	1990
Jefferey W Cox	1962
Dean T Cox	1995
Richard Crack	1959
The Rt Hon. Sir Percy Cradock	1946
Richard E Craig	1979
Alastair Crawford	1978
Dr A F Crick	1941
Edmund Crisp	1939
Madeleine Crisp	2001
The Rt Hon. Lord Nigel Crisp	1970
John Critchley	1950
A D Croft	1959
J A Crook	1939
John Cross	1947
H Crosthwaite	1941
Rob Crow	1961
Roger Crowther	1951
Charles Cruden	1993
Durward Cruickshank	1947
John Cruickshank	1978
Donald Crump	1957
Martin Cruttenden	1958
Peter Cullinane	1962
David Curnock	1964
Geoffrey Currey	1955
T Curtis	1952
Dr W D Cussins	1944
R N Dailey	1952
Francis D'Alquen	1961
Andrew Darke	1970
Mrs S C Darling	
W H Darling	1948
Lisa Davey (née Caulton)	1990
Dr Graham Mark Davies	1995
Glyn Davies	1960
Dr J Huw Davies	1980
Neil Davies	1976
Dr Neil Davies	1966
P T Davies	1948
Timothy Davies	1963
Trevor R Davies	1956
M G Davis	1970
Tom S Davis	1968
Khaled I Dawas	1988
Anthony Dawson	1971
Neville J Day	1948
Mr N J T de Fonseka	1971
V C de R Malan	1969
Samantha De Silva	1997
Christopher Dean	1969
Robert J Dee	1949
James Dee	1999
Benjamin P Deery	2003
The Lord Deramore	1929
Mike Derbyshire	1962
Dr Frederic Devas	2001
Robin Devenish	1961
Dr Arthur Dewar	1964
Adrian C Dewey	1979
Caoimhe Ni Dhálaigh	2001
Lorenzo Di Biagio	2004
Susanna Di Feliciantonio	1997
Robert Dick	1958
Dr John Peter Dickinson	1957
Allan W Dickinson	1944
Jonathan Dickman	1989
Mark Dimmick	1958
Rodney Dingle	1949
Robert Dingwall	1968
Martin T Dinter	2000
Stephen P Diver	1975
Laura E Dix	2001
Roger Dix	1974
Rev. Canon Peter Dodd	1954
Nigel Dodds OBE MP	1977
Dr Martin Dodson	1950
Chris Dolby	1980
Anna Rachel Dover	1991
Peter Dowben	1977
Vicky Downes	1999
Dr H R Dowson	1961
Dr Laurence Drake	1982
A J Drew	1952
Mr Paul A Droar	1965
Thomas Brian Duff	1953
Robert Duncan	1957
Jonathan Dunley	1988
Gilbert Dunlop	1979
Geoffrey D Dunn	1953
Ian W H Dunn	1964
Patricia Dunnett	1988
John Durack	1967
Richard Durbin	1979
Dr P N Durman	1989
A S Durward	1955
H A Duxbury	1954
Amy Dymock	2000
Dr R J Eaglen	1956
Dr D A (Tony) Earnshaw	1949
B C D Eastick	1935
R F Eberlie	1953
Hugh Eddowes	1954
Elaine Eggington	1983
Charles F Elias	1944
Georg Ell	2000
Dr Kenneth Elliott	1951
Sally Elliott (née Holt)	1992
Dr J S Ellis	1954
Mr K Ellis	1952
David Ensor	1975
Dr G C Evans	1931
Sir Anthony Evans	1954
Arwel O Evans	1981
J Wynford Evans	1952
John M Evans	1962
Dr M C Evans	1963
Commander Vincent Evans	1942
Canon Owen Everson	1953
Chris Ewbank	1980
Stefan Fafinski	1986
Mr Paul Jonathan Fairchild	1987
Dr R W Fairhead	1944
David Fairweather	1992

200

Name	Year	Name	Year	Name	Year	Name	Year
Paul Farrington	1960	Matthew Garnett	2000	Dr Mark Gurnell	1996	Rob Heap	1964
M N Farwell	1979	Chiara Garofoli LLM	2004	P M Gurowich	1974	H R Hearn	1949
Professor John Faulkner	1956	John F Garrood	1944	David Gutman	1977	Nick Hedges	1979
Dr Graeme Feggetter	1964	Helen C Gartland	1987	Dr Jan B Gutowski	1996	Dr Sue Heenan	1982
M A Feigen	1983	Martyn Gaudie	1947	Dr Yvonne W M Ha	1987	Jonathan Hellyer Jones	1970
Brian Fenwick-Smith	1956	John A Gent	1975	Dr J B Hacker	1961	P J Hennessy	1966
P Fenwick-Smith	1941	Raymond F George	1959	Peter Hacking	1947	Mrs E M Hennessy	
Clare Fidler	2000	Dr Emad George	1982	Peter Elliot Hadley	1986	Andrew James Herbert	1975
Patrick Field	1947	F C German	1954	Gary Haigh	1983	Paul T Hercus	1962
James Filer	1955	Santosh Ghosh	1987	Mr Matthew D Hall	1997	Emmanuelle Heriard Dubreuil	2001
Peter W L Filtness		T J Gibbons	1930	George G Hall	1947	Donald Hewlett	1939
MA DIPTP MRTPI IHBC	1970	Simon Gibbs	1967	Ian Hall	1982	H W Higginson	1929
Duncan Finnie	1981	Jessica Gibbs	1995	Jonathan Hall	1987	Dr Roger Higson	1965
Kenneth John Fisher	1948	Christopher W K Gibson	2005	Mr L G Hall	1935	Mr H M Hill	1972
David M Flacks	1972	Colm M H Gibson	1987	Peter Hall	1971	Margaret Caroline Hill	1983
Dr S G Fleet	1955	Michael Gibson	1974	J F Hall-Craggs	1953	Michael Hill	1968
Roger G Fleming	1954	Dr William Thomas Gibson	2001	Richard K B Halsey	1962	Stephen Hill	1979
Graham Fletcher	1971	Charles Gill	1980	Lesley Hamill (née Reid)	1991	K A Hills	1945
Rosemary C Fletcher	2001	B J Gillespie	1951	Alexander Hamilton	1951	John Graham Firth Hind	1958
Michael J Fogg	1967	Jonathan D Gilmour	2005	Myles Hammett	1969	Robert A Hinde	1945
Gen Lin Foo	2002	Prof John Gittins	1956	Christopher Hammond	1961	David Hines	1961
D B Forbes	1982	Dr Peter Gittins	1943	Dr Allen W Hancock III	1966	Christopher J Hirst	1977
Alexander Ford	2002	Mr Michael Glasspool	1956	Heather Hancock (née Wilkinson)	1984	Professor J B Hall	1956
Austin Forey	1981	Ian Gledhill	1978	Rev. N J Hancock	1998	Peter Hobbs	1962
The Rev. Dr Kenneth Forster	1944	Professor Martin Goalen	1964	William J H Harbage QC	1979	John Hobson QC	1990
Andrew Foster	1978	Maurice Godfrey	1965	Mr Charles Harding	1971	James Hodge	1938
B S Foster	1945	Robin Godfrey	1974	Sir William Harding	1945	Gabrielle Hodgetts	1982
Charles Foster	1981	D H Golby	1958	David W G Hardy	1952	Phil Hodkinson	1977
Rev. E J G Foster	1931	Mel Goldberg	1957	Paul G Hare	1964	David C Hogg	1954
Garth Foster	1963	Victor Gomersall	1963	Mr Dhruvkumar		Dr Neil L Holden	1972
Stephen Foster	1981	Henry Goodman	1952	Deepakkumar Haria	2003	Richard C T Holden	1976
Timothy Foster	1977	Christopher W H Goodwins	1955	Dr N A Harker	1951	D John Holding	1945
Jake Fowler	1978	Sir J R Goody	1938	Dr Roger H Harper	1958	M Holdsworth	1982
John A Fowler	1938	A P Goudy	1944	P A R Harrall	1996	Dr J M Holford	1986
Basil Fox	1947	J R Gough	1944	John Harries	1964	Rev. John Hollins	1955
Simon France	1951	Dr Andrew Gould	1978	D J Harris	1948	A H B Holmes	1970
Benedikt Franke	2005	Julian Gould	1995	Nigel Harris	1967	Bobby Holmes	1944
Andy Franklin	1977	Mark Gould	1980	John N Harrison	1951	John Holroyd	1952
P D Fraser	1983	Tony Gould	1964	Tony Harrison	2000	Andrew S B Holt	1985
Dr L B Fraser	1957	Leonard John Govier	1943	Mr S M Harrold	1987	Derek Holtham	1969
Guy Freeman	1983	Andrew Grace	1990	John Harry	1947	Martin Holtham	2002
Bernard Freudenthal	2003	Peter J Scott Graham	1956	Peter Hartnell	1972	Andrew Honeybone	1962
Mr John Frith	1951	Robert B Gray	1968	Brian W Harvey	1954	C M Hood	1966
T J Froydenlund	2001	Dr Ivor Grayson-Smith	1961	Professor Jonathan Harvey	1957	Emma Louise Hooper	
P J M Fry OBE	1941	Dr J E Green	1956	Rowan Harwood	1979	(née Howard)	1984
David Richard Fryatt	1969	James R Greene	2002	Dr M T Haslam	1952	Lord Hope of Craighead	1959
Peter Fuchs	1959	Peter A Greenwood	1975	Dr Dimitrios Hatzis	1983	Bryan Hopkin	1933
Jonathan Furness QC	1975	Tony Greeves	1946	Michael F Haughton	1944	Dr Mariette Wilhelmina Hopman	1988
His Honour Judge Mark Furness	1967	Alan Gregory	1946	Milan L Hauner	1968	Richard Hopwood	1975
Dr Richard Furze	1967	Geoffrey Gregory	1949	Oliver Hawkins	1963	Sir John Horlock	1946
Simon Patrick Fynn	1985	Paul David Griffin	1967	Michael Hawkins	1948	Perran Horrell	1990
David Michael Gainford	1978	R F Griffin	1954	Mr T Hawkins	1981	W Roger Horrell	1953
Fabio Galantini	1988	Dr Jo Griffiths	1996	Edward Haws	1944	J P Horrocks-Taylor	1955
Professor Thomas P Gallanis	1992	P M Griffiths MA DIP ARCH	1969	Michael Hawtin	1960	Tim Horsler	1964
Dr Albert Galy	2005	David Griggs	1959	John Hayman	1937	A J Hosking	1949
G J Garbett	1951	Hugh Grootenhuis	1977	D W Hayter	1955	Ivan Houghton	1960
Peter Garbett	1948	Gus Guest	1964	Martin Hayton	1973	Guy Houghton	1965
John Garner	1958	Rev. Robin Gordon Guinness	1957	K H Head	1945	D Howard Davies	1952

Geoffrey Howe	1967	Peter J Jones	1959	David Lewis	1975	John Man	1990
J T Howe	1944	Tim Jones	1974	Gilbert Lewis	1972	Dr Pamela Manners	1983
Jeremy Howe	1950	Trevor Jones	1969	Iolo Wyn Lewis	1963	Martin Manning	1965
Geoffrey Howell	1951	Victor F J Jordan	1956	John Scott Lewis	1946	Paul R Manning	1973
Roger S P Howell	1977	Dr R R Jordan	1958	John H Lewis	1952	Professor Nicholas Manton FRS	1971
R I L Howland	1956	Christopher A Joseph	1958	Paul Lewis	1959	Trevor Marchington	1949
Dr H J Hoyland	1950	Andrew Joyce	1972	Tim Lewis	1972	Sir John Margetson	1945
Neil Hufton	1967	J C Judson	1970	Jeremy Yuen Lim Li	2003	Donald Mark	1975
I E M Hughes	1951	Chris Kay	1978	John Libson	1956	Martin J Marriott	1973
Manon Hughes	2005	Giles Keeble	1968	Lim, Boon Wee	1982	Chris Marshall	1965
Tony Huish	1985	David Keeling	1960	Paul Lindon	1981	R C Marshall	1952
Dr Richard Hull	1996	Gareth Keene	1962	Garth Lindrup	1977	Rev. John Martin	1960
Dr Timothy Hunt	1973	M E Kingsley Kefford	1958	Timothy C Line	1948	John Martin	1950
Bryan Hunt	1943	Sir David Kelly	1956	P A Linehan	1961	Richard Martin	1980
Mrs Fiona Hunt		H Clifton Kelynack	1934	J C R E Ling	1957	Ian Marvin	1964
Sam Hutt/Hank Wangford	1959	Alan Kent	1942	Roger H Linstead	1954	Nigel Masding	1990
Patrick Hutton	1949	Paul B Kent CBE	1956	Mr John S Liquorish	1969	Julian Mash	1980
Frank Iacobucci	1962	Dr Norman Kenyon	1960	Tom Lissauer	1966	Richard Mash	1985
Natalie Iceton (née Bunting)	1991	Paul G Kenyon	1963	P M S Litton	1982	Hugh Mason	1960
John Imlach	1959	James Keough	2004	L M B Livingstone-Learmonth	1997	Alexander Massey	1995
Professor Colin Ingram	1982	Dr Eric Kerrigan	1997	John Lloyd	1945	J S Massey (née Hurst)	1985
David V Ingram FRCS	1958	G Kerslake	1953	Steven John Lo	1995	Dr Peter Matanle	1983
Rachel Ip	1995	Adam Kilgour	1992	Timothy W Lockwood	1969	Caroline Joyce Mather	2002
Rev. Graeme Jackson	1949	Brian F King	1953	Ruth Emma Logan (née Hardy)	1996	Harold Gordon Mather	1939
R F Jackson	1939	J Murray King	1951	Joanne Loizel (née Thomas)	1983	William Mather	1969
Andrew J Jacovides	1955	Professor M A King	1972	Michael Long	1965	Benjamin Frederick	
Nick Jacques	1993	Dr M S King	1956	Michael J Longman	1974	George Mathers	1998
Nick James	1972	Rev. A E R Knopp	1929	T R W Longmore	1943	P C Matthews	1974
Miss Claire Jarvis	2003	Dr Geoffrey Knowles	1964	Barry Ian Lord	1974	Anthony May	1983
David Jeffery	1946	Ryuzo Kodama	1973	Dickon R Love	1988	Sholto Mayne Hanvey	2002
Robert Jeffery	1974	Dr Dinah R Kohner	1992	Richard Lovell	1965	Mark McAllister	1976
Bryan Jeffrey	1954	Danis Koukoularides	1993	The Rev. Emma Loveridge	1984	Peter McBrien	1983
Mark Jeffries	1975	Nota (formerly Nigel) Kreiman	1978	Sir John Loveridge	1942	Duncan W J McCallien	1989
D P Jenkins	1944	John Krumins	1983	Edward David Low	1942	Desmond McCann	1967
H John Jenkins	1949	John C Lackington	1966	Simon Lowe	1976	Rev. Andrew McClellan	1989
N S Jenkins	1979	Clare Laight		John Luke	1959	John F McCollin	1974
Trevor D Jenkins	1971	Nicholas Laird	1962	Brian Ming Yan Lum	2002	John McCulloch	1978
Ian F Jenkinson	1961	Bryan Highfield Laister	1950	C N Lumb	2004	John McCutcheon	1959
Timothy Jenness	1989	Roger Lambert	1961	Michael Lumley	1957	Roger B McDaniel	1954
Philip Jeynes	1969	Christel Lane	1990	Dr John Morgan Lunn	1953	Kirsty McDonald	1997
Guy Jillings	1957	Adrian Langford	1978	David E Lyall	1948	Dr Rich McDowell	1996
Nabila Jiwaji	1997	Miss B C Lanham	1997	Dr Anthony Lynch	1954	Vernon McElroy	1974
D A Johnson	1953	Dr Jonathan Lawley	1959	The Rev. Dr P A Lynn	1962	K M McFadyean	1944
J A Johnson	1939	Roderick J Lawrence	1974	D W Lyon	1966	David M P McGlade	2002
Michael F Johnson	1954	Dr John A Leake	1958	Malcolm MacInnes	1960	Iain McGlashan	1950
Colin G Johnston	1972	Robert Leaper	1940	Patrick John Macintosh	1981	Neil McIntyre	1977
Dr Keith Johnstone	2004	E H Leaton	1948	Mrs B B Mackay		Hugh McKeag	1958
Adam Jollans	1977	D C Ledger	1954	D K Mackay	1940	Robert Wallace McLaren	1972
Mr W M Jollans	1942	David Lee	1957	Richard J Mackenney	2003	Sir Robin McLaren KCMG	1955
Christopher Ian Jones	1976	Lennard Lee	2002	R K MacKenzie Ross	1954	A J W McNulty	1976
Dr David Jones	1961	Stacey C Lee	1991	Ian Brine Mackintosh	1944	Murray Clyde Meikle	1971
David Pritchard Jones	1944	Jack Leeming	1945	D D Macklin	1947	Simon C Melen	1979
Donald W Jones	1952	Julian Legg	1984	Dr Jamie Macleod	1972	Jeremy Mercer	1980
His Honour Graham Jones	1954	Don Lennard	1961	Malcolm Maddock	1967	R L Merson	1937
Hywel F Jones	1946	Yves Leservoisier	1952	Donald Hindley Makinson	1938	Leon Mestel	1957
Nigel Jones	1984	C W Leung	1999	Phil Makinson	1994	A A B Metcalfe	1961
Nicholas W Jones	1975	Peter J Le Voir	1973	Dr Neil Law Malcolm	1968	W D Millar	1944
Professor Peter G Jones	1970	Dr Alun Lewis	1974	R E Malins	1938	Alastair Miller	1971

202

Name	Year	Name	Year	Name	Year	Name	Year
James L Miller	1952	Donald A Nield	1957	James H Peachey	1963	Gerald Ratzer	1963
Anthony Milton	1990	Dr Pete Nienow	1984	J D C Peacock	1952	C C Rawlinson	1987
Peter Milton	1961	Phillip Nightingale	1975	John R Peberdy	1949	Dr Sandra A Rayner	1983
Catherine Milward	1994	Richard L Nobbs	1960	Professor Brian Peeling	1951	E J Read	2001
Dr Neda Minakaran BA BM BCH	2001	Basil Noble	1939	Chris Pennock	1978	James J Read	1947
Claire Mitchell	1998	Peter S Noble	1960	Professor Sir Denis		Philip Redfern	1940
Neil Mitchell	1973	Tim Norfolk	1972	Pereira Gray OBE	1954	Paul Redhead	1970
R M Mitchell	1980	William J Norman	1955	Richard N Perham	1958	P M Redmond	1955
Christopher John Mockler	1970	Barry North	1954	D J Perry	1951	Dr Kylie D Reed	1995
Michael Moeckel	2002	David Norwood	1945	Michael Perryman	1973	C R Reese	1949
Thomas Moisley	1974	Ash Notaney	1994	David Peters	1949	Professor Kenneth Reid CBE	1972
Ralph Molland	1945	John E B Notley	1973	Richard C Petersen	1941	R W H Reid	1942
Julian Molyneux	1980	John Nutt	1969	Dimitrios Petousis	2001	Roger Reissner	1960
Chris Montagnon	1962	G H Nuttall	1950	Philip Pettifor	1965	Roger Remington	1956
Nigel Montagu	1977	Andrew Nutter	1998	Philip Reynold Pfaff	1932	Jonathan Rennert	1971
Michael Monteiro	2005	Michael A Oakley	1956	Annamarie Phelps (née Stapleton)	1984	J Revill	1956
B J Moody	1945	Alan Oates	1952	Ian Phillips	1955	Geoff Reynolds	1953
Mark Moody-Stuart	1960	Jennifer Oates	2002	Dr Jonathan Phillips	1970	Jonathan Rhodes	1967
Andy Moore	1979	Leonard Ogden	1943	Alan W Phipps	1979	Dr W J St E-G Rhys	1950
Greg Moore	1974	John O'Keeffe	1967	Russell Picot	1976	Don Riach	1945
Penny Moore	2001	J L O'Kill	1956	Fionn Pilbrow	1998	M W Rich	1965
R V More	1962	James Oldroyd	1931	Antony Pinchin	1976	Claire Richards	
Glyn J Morgan	1938	Steven Ollerearnshaw	1967	Ursel Pintschovius	1993	(née Carter) MA FCA	1984
David Morley	1976	Mr Carl Olsson	1973	Leon Piotrowski	1979	David A Richards	1978
Julian M B Morrell	1980	Mr A C Orchard	1940	Christopher Platt	1927	W Eric Richardson	1946
Desmond Morris	1945	Keith Orrell-Jones	1958	David Pollard	1974	Andrew Ridgway	1989
John R Morris	1952	M Orrell-Jones	1952	Ian Pong	2005	Justin Ripman	1980
Peter L Morris	1955	Paul Outridge	1972	Miss Sonia Ponnusamy	1997	David W Ripper	1946
Paul Howard Morris	1973	David N H Owen	1943	Geoffrey Poole	1962	Dr Donald James Roberts	1948
Dr R Denis T Morris	1973	Dr J R Owen	1957	Dr Guy R Pooley	1987	E Theo Roberts	1942
Prof R Hugh Morton PHD	1970	Alan Oyston	1951	Professor Andrew N Porter	1964	Hugh T Roberts	1960
David Moss	1965	Captain Peter Pacey RN	1969	Robert Portsmouth	1989	Ian Michael Roberts	1975
Matthew Moss	1990	Adrian Padfield	1960	Sir Richard Posnett	1938	Keith Roberts	1964
Malcolm D Moss	1962	Stephen Page	1974	B P Pothecary	1942	Roy Stewart Roberts	1959
Richard E Moss	1960	Lawrence Paine	1957	Andrew R Potter MBE	1969	Thomas A H Roberts	2003
Dr Stephen Moss	1960	B K H Palmer	2000	Ernest Joseph Powdrill	1937	Trevor Roberts	1962
Paul Moxon	1991	Caroline Palmer	1989	Katherine Powlesland	1987	Charles Robertson	1980
R K Muir	1953	Mr M T Palmer	2003	Alan Joseph Pownall	1944	Major Colin Robins OBE FRHISTS	1955
Hans-Harald Müller	1998	Stephen Palmström	1966	David Price	1955	Tim Robinson	1989
Andrew Mummery	1967	Robert Palmström	1968	Dr David Clive Price	1967	Brian H B Robinson	1948
Necati Munir Ertekun	1943	Professor Theodore D Papanghelis	1981	Geoffrey A Price	1936	John William Robinson	2002
Osman Munir Ertekun	1970	Peter Parham	1969	Peter H M Price	1956	P F Robinson	1971
Kieran Murphy	1976	Andrew Paris	1978	Richard Price	1988	Paul Roderick	1976
Michael G Murray	1941	M N Park	1963	Dr Nancy Emma Claire Priston	1998	Dr Peter F Roe	1949
Saul Nathan	1984	Adrian G Parker	1965	Jeffrey Prowse Smith	1938	Brian Rofe	1954
Amir Nathoo	1998	Hugh Parker	1969	George Pullan	1946	P D C Rogers	1956
Ed Naylor	1982	John Parker	1957	Dr Malcolm C Pullan	1992	David A Rogerson	1981
John Naylor	1966	Roger Parker	1999	Gordon Pullin	1956	Humphry Rolleston	1974
Frank Neale	1968	Douglas Parkes	1951	John Purkiss	1980	Eric S Room	1947
Richard Nelmes	1962	Joelle K Parkinson	2001	Professor Kenneth Pye	1977	Dan Rootham	1965
Mike Nelson	1972	Neil Parkyn	1962	Sir John Quinton	1950	F D Rose	1989
Peter J Neville	1974	F D Parsons	1976	Alan C Radford	1971	Alexis Rose	1996
Edward I Newman	1954	Roger Parsons	1960	Professor Sheena E Radford	1984	Grahame Rosolen	1989
John A Newman	1964	Michael Parton	1984	John Rahtz	1966	N Rosser	1945
David Nicholls	1951	Jim Paton	1986	Theodore Rakintzis	1999	Charlotte E Rosser	1989
Mark Nicholls	1999	Milija N Pavlovic	1974	Gary Ralfe	1963	Sandy J Ross-Macdonald	1955
David H Nicholson	1945	Dr Jeremy K Payne	1975	David N L Ralphs	1959	Mark Rothera	1981
J A S Nickson	1968	Mr M F Peachey	1960	Dr Anneli Randla	1996	Lizzie Rogers	2004

John Rounce	1958	Deep Shah	1997	Michael Spindler	1966	Christopher Tholstrup	1993
John H A Rowland	1977	D A Shakespeare	1986	Peter M Spinney	1950	Gp Capt Michael I Thom	1954
Mark Rowntree	1963	William Shand	1955	G M Spooner	1971	David Thomas	1967
Christopher Royall	1970	David Sharman	1958	Dr R K Sprigg	1940	Jeremy W Thompson	1960
Stephen A Royle	1968	Brian Sharpe	1957	Professor Matthew Spriggs	1973	Robert William Thompson	1987
John Rucklidge	1956	Douglas William David Shaw	1945	Peter John Stacey	1967	A R Thomson	1952
Mark Runacres	1978	Dr J H W Shaw	1950	W B Stallard	1958	David G Thomson	1987
Christopher Rundle	1959	Jonathan R Sheldon	1974	Professor C T Stannage	1967	Jane Thomson	1996
Mark 'Harry' Rushbrooke	1960	Nicholas Sherwin	1979	Dr A C Starling	1996	Derek R W Thornbery	1948
D F H Rushton	1942	Anthony L Shiret	1974	Nick Starling	1974	Alan C R Thornton	1960
P L Rushton	1941	Howard P Shore	1979	Stephen Francis Stavrou	2002	Ralph Roland Thorp	1944
Stanley John Rushton	1949	Alan Shrimpton	1957	Ron L Steele	1952	Ben Thorpe	1991
Ian Russell	1963	Dr David Side	1948	Christopher Stephens	1950	S M Thorpe	1991
Michael W Russell	1963	Andy Sidwell	1974	J A Stevens	1967	Philip Tidswell	1978
J F Russell-Smith	1939	Professor Aubrey Silberston	1958	John Stevens	1970	Geoffrey Tierney	1973
John Frederick Rust	1947	Reggie Simeone	1944	Richard A Stevens	1962	Keith Tilson	1973
A B Ruth	1946	Mrs Celia Lacey Simm		Maylin Stevenson	1952	Nick Timmins	1960
C I Rutherford	1937	Frank Simm	1943	Dr Davina Stevenson	2001	Michelle Timoney	1991
David W B Sainsbury	1959	Alan Simmons	1960	D J Steventon	1967	Tancredi E Tincani	2000
John E L Sales	1955	Alan Simpson	1976	Charles Stewart	1974	Robert M Tindall	1961
Nigel Salisbury	1977	Paul Simpson	1964	Graham Stewart	1992	John S Titford	1964
Dr Amanda Salter	2000	Roger Simpson	1949	Hugh Martin Stewart	'947	Dr Roger B Titman	1964
The Rev. F B Salter	1963	Dr Devinderjit Singh Sivia	1981	T D Stirk	1960	Sylvana Tomaselli	2004
Theresa Salter	1988	G N S Slater	1950	Fred Stoddard	1981	Andrew Tomlinson	1977
Sam Samuels	1967	David Bryan Slingsby	1949	Robert Ian Stokes	1944	Prof Rolfe Tomlinson	1943
Julian Samuelson	1981	Mr Michael Smart	1982	Peter Stokes	1960	T B Tomlinson	1957
James Samworth	1994	A N Smith	1944	W G Stokoe	1942	Brian Tong	1956
Robin Sanders	1974	Colin D F Smith	1959	David Stonor	1962	David Bryan Topliffe	1979
Ian Aelwin Sanders	1976	David Hilbre Smith	1949	Mr C W Storr	1949	Malcolm Torry	1973
Jeremy Sargent	1974	Donald J Smith	1954	Adam Stronach	1987	Michael Tosdevin	1976
Yoshiaki Sasamura	1977	Duncan Smith	1969	Rupert Strudwick	1989	Ken Totton CENG FIEE	1977
Amanda Saville	1988	Glyn Smith	1971	I C Stuart	1940	C R B Townend	1938
Peter Scandrett	1971	J Harvey Smith	1952	Roger Stubbs	1969	Martin Towns	1995
John Scarborough	1957	J M B Smith	1964	Brig Nigel R Sturt	1950	Eugene P Trani	1998
Frank Scheibe	2003	M J S Smith	1954	Richard Suart	1971	Peter Treacy	1948
David Schickner	1980	N J Smith	1965	Stephen Sugden	1968	Mr T O Trotman	1979
C A Schmitt	1997	N M Smith	1987	David B Sutcliffe	1953	John Michael Trott	1949
Ernest Schofield DFC	1934	Peter Smith	1976	Dr Rachel Sutcliffe	1987	T Trott	
Rex Schothorst	1983	Raymond Smith	1950	Russell Sutcliffe	1974	M G Trotter	1956
Michael Schraer	1973	Rodney A M Smith	1963	Paul Sweeney	1991	Siu Kee Tsang	2001
A G Schroeder	1956	T P Smith	1971	Alan Swinburne	1966	John Tudhope	1969
Susan L Schwartz	1988	Isobel Anne Smyth	2002	The Rev. Prebendary		Dave Turnbull	1968
Simon Scott	1977	Paul Smyth	1970	J H Swingler	1938	A H B Turner	1958
Jock H Scott-Park	1949	J J Snewin	1972	John Sykes	1986	Dr Danielle Turner	2000
Alan Seal	1967	Julia Snoddy	1966	S W Sykes	1958	David Turner	1975
John Seale	1942	Geoffrey Soar	1951	Dirk Kaars Sypesteyn	1956	Martin Guy Turner	1976
Dr David G F Seaton	1967	Peter Soar	1949	R Taggesell	1975	Doug Twigg	1963
Julian Seeley	1995	Professor J A Soggin	1978	Arthur G Tait	1954	Catherine Twilley	1989
John T Clark Sellick	1950	John C Somerville-Large	1975	Robin T Tait	1951	Jim Tyerman	1979
Anna Sembos	1996	David Soulsby	1979	Andrew K S Tan	2005	Dr G J Tyler	1945
Stephen Senior	1989	Stuart M Southall	1977	D M Tanton	1971	Maurice S Tyler	1954
James Sergeant	1985	John Barnes Spargo	1945	John Tarrant	1956	B C Unwin	1952
Costas Z Severis	1968	Bernard Spatz	1960	Sarah Alexandra Tasker	1982	Graham Urquhart	1973
Nicolas Severis	1962	Michael J Spelman	1959	Dr Henry Dennis Taylor	1944	John Vallance-Owen	1939
Tony Seward	1962	Miss L A Spence	2001	Peter W Taylor	1965	Frans S P Van Buchem	1987
Emma Sewell	1991	Dr M P Spence	1941	J F Tearle	1947	John van de Poll	1993
M W Sewell	1940	P F Spence	1959	Lord Templeman	1938	Annemarie van Geel	2002
Dr Lachlan Shackleton-Fergus	1970	Dr Roger C Spencer	1964	Rosalind Tendler	2000	Mr P J Van Went	1966

203

Mike Vaughan	1958	Roy Waters	1949	Fred W Williams	1958	Teck Lee Wong	1989
Ian Veltman	1969	Stephen Waters	1959	Dr George Williams CBE	1936	John Wood	1981
John A Vincent	1956	William Watkins	1981	Dr J T N Williams	1948	John M A Wood	1962
Fred Vine	1959	Dr Anthony Watson	1950	Jeremy Huw Williams	1987	Dr P M Wood	1978
John Vinnicombe	1949	David Watson	1969	John Meyler Williams	1953	W Michael Wood	1960
John M Virgoe	1957	Dr Des Watson	1971	John Melville Williams	1951	B Woodcock	1942
Dr Z Volanthen		Jon Watson	1983	Liz Williams (née Hughes)	1988	J C Woodhouse	1970
G N von Tunzelmann	1970	Philip Watson	1995	P D Williams	1952	Mark Woodhouse	1986
Badri Nath Wadawadigi	2002	Charles Watts-Jones	1959	Dr Peredur Williams	1967	Peter B Woodhouse	1960
David C M Waddell	1951	Camilla Waugh	2000	Peter Williams	1949	David J A Woodland	1961
J St C Wade	1981	Edward J Wawrzynczak	1980	Peter Williams	1972	Professor Geoffrey Woodroffe	1956
Robert M Wager	1958	Derek Way	1947	T W Williams	1952	P A Woodsford	1960
Dr Barrie Walker	1965	Dr D B Webb	1966	Stephen Willis	1990	H D Woodward	1958
Howard Scott Walker	1973	Peter Webster	1986	A J Willson	1950	Joanna K Woolley	2001
Nathalie Walker	1998	B R Webster	1958	M R Wilmot-Dear	1980	Anne Worden	1984
Revd Richard George Walker	1936	G A C Weeden	1951	Henry D Wilsdon	1957	Ian S Wordsworth	1957
Nicholas Walkinshaw	1959	Dr Paul W H Weightman	1961	Allan C Wilson	1947	E J Worlidge	1948
Dugald Wallace	1942	Colin West	1973	Andrew J Wilson	1986	Dr Philip Wraight	1958
John Wallace	1963	John Weston Smith	1951	Major General Dare Wilson	1938	David M Wright	1953
Robert M Wallace	1976	Emma Victoria Whicher	1991	Sir David M Wilson	1950	James R G Wright	1961
S K Wallace	1950	David Whitaker	1951	Derek J Wilson	1977	John Wright	1970
Mr J A N Wallis	1950	Richard M White	1972	Gillian Wilson	1985	Linus Wright	1988
Mrs J A N Wallis		David Whitmore	1948	James E Wilson	1968	Peter Wright	1975
Nick Wallum	1994	Ben Whitmore	1991	Michael Wilson	1972	Pei-Shih Wu	1999
David E Wallwork	1958	Alan Whitney	1948	Paul Wilson	1967	John Wyatt	1951
E R Walmsley	1948	Roy Whittaker	1944	Robin Wilson	1982	D G Wynn-Wilson	1950
Julian Walsh	1975	Dr Peter J Whyte	1959	T Michael A Wilson	1973	Martin B Yallop	1986
Professor Rory Walsh	1969	Dr Frederick D P Wicker	1964	John G Windsor	1963	David J D Yarwood	1950
Sudhir Vyankatesh Wanmali	1975	R P Wickham	1955	Diego Winkelried Q	2004	Yeoh, Cheng Chuan	1978
Paula-Jane Warburton		N S Wide MC MA	1941	Dr Nitinant Wisaweisuan	1996	George Yeomans	1957
(now Parker)	1996	Philip A Wild	1976	Bernard W Wolfe	1935	Sonia R Zakrzewski	1993
Dr C R M Ward	1966	Peter Wilding	1974	Michael Wolff	1945	Paolo Alessandro Zanna	1992
Rev. D C Ward	1951	David Wilkinson	1975	Choon Wah Wong	1996	Cartsen Zatschler	1993
Mr Peter Ward	1962	Steve R Wilkinson	1973	C C V Wong	2003	M D Zimman	1998
R H Ward	1956	Adrian Tudor Williams	1971	Mr Felix Chun Ming Wong	2004	Denis Zuev	2000
Anthony John Waring	1956	D R H Williams	1963	Mr Jason Chun Hong Wong	2002		
The Rev. Nigel Warner	1969	David Williams	1982	Dr Man Pun Wong	1978		
Hugh G Waterfield	1954	David A R Williams	1955	R K Wong	1979		

INDEX OF NAMES

Bold text denotes authorial contributions. Italics denote illustrations

Abdulai, Kosnatu *181*
Adams, Aubrey 93
Adams, Douglas *126*
Adams, John Couch 61, *71*, 72
Adams, Robert 61
Aikens, Sir Richard 113, *186*
Airy, Sir George Biddell 73
Alexander, Dr John 95
Allen, Sir James 105, 141
Alston, Sir Edward 17, 115
Alvey, Henry 17
Andrew, Rob 98, 177, *181*
Andrews, Mike 41
Angus, Howard 180
Antonello, Dr Pierpaolo 99
Appleton, Sir Edward 84, *85*, 85–6
Armitage, B W F 189
Arnold, Dr Neil 98
Arthur, Thomas 136
Ascham, Roger 14, 97, 121
Ashton, Hugh, 17, 25
Atkinson, Sir Anthony 100–1, 107
Austin, Mr 163

Babington, Thomas 68
Babington, Charles ('Beetles') 73
Babington, Churchill 94
Bailey, Professor S J ('Dennis') 113
Bailey, Mr 163
Bailey, Trevor 178, *179*
Baker, Professor H F 84
Baker, Rev. Nicholas 139
Baker, Thomas 17
Baldwin, Professor Ernest 76
Ball, Jeremy 45
Balon, Adam 93
Bambrough, Renford 128, 182
Barker, Professor Graeme 95–6
Barnes, Professor John 101, 165
Barnes, William 1275
Barrère, Professor 61
Bartlett, Sir Frederic *76*, *100*, 167

Bateson, Rev. William 30, 55, 73–4
Bateson, Professor Gregory 94
Bateson, Stuart 165
Batsaki, Dr Yota 97
Bayliss-Smith, Dr Tim 98
Beadle, Dr Richard 97
Beamish, David 114
Beaton, Sir Cecil 61, *62*, 135
Beatson, Sir Jack 113
Beaufort, Lady Margaret 10, *11*, 13, 16, 17, 25, 35, 43, 60, 61, 64–5, 101, 129, 147
Becher, Professor Tony 128
Beer, Professor John *123*, 159
Behar, Sasha 97, 135
Belle, Alexis Simon 122
Benians, E A 61, 98, 140, 154, 165, 168
Benlowes, Edward 122
Benney, Gerald 66
Bentley, Richard 96, 122, 124
Beresford, Marcus 93
Bernstein, Lord 93
Bertram, Dr Colin 81
Bess of Hardwick 16
Best, Dr Victoria 100
Bezzant, Rev. J S 52, 157, *158*, 176, 182, 183, 189
Bhagwati, Jagdish 107
Bhide, Mahadeo 140
Biddle, Tami 149
Black, Peter 188
Blackman, Frederick 73
Blanchett, Cate 137
Bleehen, Professor Norman 117
Blumberg, Baruch 118
Booth, Robert 17
Boston, Peter 16
Boyde, Professor Patrick **18–24**, 99, 195
Boyle, Charles 128
Boys Smith, Rev. Dr J S 24, 37, 67, 98, 100, *154*, 168, 176
Boys Smith, Stephen **41**
Brander, Michael 188
Brasher, Chris *180*
Brearley, Mike 97, 139, *179*
Brenner, Sydney 118

Brewster, Sarah *149*
Bridges, Sarah *163*
Briggs, Professor George 73
Brightman, Rt Hon. Lord 115, *116*
Brogan, Professor Hugh 140
Brontë, Rev. Patrick 124
Brookes, Alexis 110
Brophy, Michael 66
Brown, 'Capability' 28
Browne of Madingley, Lord (John) 81, *92*, *186*
Bruford, Professor W H 99
Buck, Norman 64, *163*
Buck, William Elgar 142
Budden, Dr Kenneth 71, 73
Buffini, Damon 92, 114
Bulkley, Rev. Peter 139
Burnett, Ned *149*
Burr, Clive 67
Burren, John 41
Burton, Professor Graham 77
Butler, Cecil 162
Butler, Henrietta 151
Butler, Samuel 59, 61, 121, 124, *125*, 129, 130, 141, 172
Butterworth, Jez 128
Byron, Lord 83

Cadwalader, Gardner **176**
Cafe, William 66
Calabresi, Hon Guido 114
Calvert, Michael 165
Cama, Byramji 141
Cameron, Julia 71
Campbell, Dr A J P 44
Campbell, Dr Fergus 117, 118
Cannadine, Professor David 99
Cantrell, Henry 61
Caradon, Rt Hon. Lord 106–7
Carnley, Archbishop Peter 49, 142
Carrighan, John 61
Carter, Professor Sir Charles 108
Carter, Rev. Thomas 139
Cartledge, Sir Bryan 106
Cassels, Bishop W W 143
Casson, Sir Hugh 131

Casson, Conder and Partners 131
Castlereagh, Viscount 61, 104, *105*, 129
Catford, Sir Robin 105
Catherine of Aragon 13
Cavendish, Margaret 147
Cavendish, Sir William 17
Caxton, William 59
Cecil, Mildred, Lady Burghley 147
Cecil, Robert, Earl of Salisbury 10, 17, 21, *102*, 103
Cecil, William, First Baron Burghley 10, 17, 21, 59, 61, *102*, 103
Cha, Louis (Jin Yong) *144*
Chalmers, Sir Neil 106
Chao, Jacqui *149*
Chapman, Freddy 165
Charles I 12, 13, 58, 103–4
Charles II 58, 60, 104
Charlesworth, Rev. M P 97, 170
Chaudhuri, Amit 128
Chawner, Thomas 66
Cheke, Sir John 97, 121
Cheng, G len 127
Chillingworth, Dr David 41, 188
Churchill, Charles 122
Clarke, Professor Malcolm 114–15, *116*
Clarke, Professor Peter 99, 174
Clarkson, Thomas 61, 68–9, *69*, 187
Clasper, Mike 93
Clayton, Alan *134*
Cleveland, John 122
Cockcroft, Sir John 84, *86*
Coggan, Archbishop Lord 49, *50*
Coleman, Simon 94
Colenso, Bishop John 49, 61, 145
Coleridge, Samuel Taylor 68
Collins, John 59
Collis, Jeremy 43
Colquhoun, P 172
Colwell, Dr Sue 193
Comrie, L J 192
Conway Morris, Professor Simon 81
Cook, George 139
Cookson, William 123
Coombs, Mark 93
Cooper, Sharon Chen 149

206

Corby, Sir Brian 92
Corfield, Nicholas 17, *190*, 191
Cormack, Allan 84, *88*, 88–9
Coutts, Marian 130
Covington, Howard 93
Cowburn, Professor Russell 78
Cox, Professor Sir David 84
Cradock, Archbishop John 49
Cradock, Rt Hon. Sir Percy 106, 143
Craik, Dr Kenneth 76, 167
Crashaw, William 58
Crick, Francis 87–8
Cripps, Sir Cyril 17, 129
Cripps, Sir Humphrey 15, *16*, 17
Crisp, Madeleine 43, 152
Crisp, Lord (Nigel) 105
Crisp, Ted 169, 189
Croft, Tony 189
Crook, Alec 24
Crook, Professor John 42, 96, 97, 170
Crook, Vaughan 162
Cullinan, Edward 16, 24, 101
Cunliffe, Professor Barry 95
Currie, Sarah *149*
Curtis, Ronald 165
Curtis, Tom 43
Cussins, Dr Denys 41

Dairoku, Kikuchi *143*
Dalton, Rev. Timothy 139
Danckwerts, Peter 165
Daniel, Professor Glyn 61, 95, 96, 98, 157, *160*
Daniel, Ruth 160
Danks, Fiona *181*
Dante 18, 19
Darwin, Charles 59, 73, 74, 80
Darwin, Erasmus *74*, 115, 129
Dasgupta, Professor Sir Partha **108**
Da-Silva Teixeira, Antonia *181*
Davidson, Professor James 142
Davies, Gavyn 92, 109
Davies-Jackson scholarships 140
Dawkins, Professor Richard 74
Dawson, James 104
de Lanerie, Paul 66
de Quin, Rebecca 67
Dee, Dr John 59, 83, 136
Deer, Professor Alec 81
Denman, Joseph 69
Denman, Sir Roy 105
Denman, Lord Chief Justice Thomas 68, *69*, 113
d'Ewes, Sir Simonds 44, 124
Dicker, A C 172
Dick-Read, Dr Grantly 117
Dirac, Professor Paul 59, 62, 72, 78, 84, 85, *86*, 86–7, 129, 130

Dobson, Professor Christopher 77, 78, 197
Domett, Alfred 105, 142
Dormor, Rev. Duncan 53
Dörrzapf, Dr Matthias 84, 192
Douglass, Frederick 69
Dring, Sidney *162*
Duckworth, Noel 172
Dunn, Dr David 118
Dunning family 24
Durack, John 174
Durkin, Elizabeth *77*

Eberhart, Richard *127*, 140
Eddington, Sir Arthur *81*, 192
Ede, Jim 44, 130
Edgley, Dr Steve 77
Edinburgh, Duke of 133
Edward II 36
Edward VI 121
Edwards, James Keith O'Neill ('Professor' Jimmy) 126
Edwards, Dr Kenneth 77
Egan, Jennifer 128
Einstein, Albert 86, 87, 157
Elia, Franco 162
Elizabeth I 102, 121, 129
Engledow, Sir Frank 75, 167
Erasmus 13, 121
Essex, James, the Younger 22
Evans, Dr Clifford 73
Evelyn, John 58
Ewbank, Chris **34**, 114, 177, *183*
Ewin, William 104

Fairfax, Sir Thomas 59, 104, *105*
Fallows, Fearon 72
Falque, Professor Emma 145
Farmer, Dr Ben 98, 170
Fenn, Howard 67
Feigen, Marc *191*, 191
Fisher, Bishop John 10, 13, 17, 25, 35, 58, 121, 129
Fisher, Sir Ronald 74
Fisher, Rebecca *181*
Fleming, Sir Ambrose *81*, 82
Fleming, Sir Alexander 119
Foden, Giles 128
Foster, Reginald 165
Fox, Dr David 114
Franklin, Professor John Hope 69
Franklin, Rosalind 87–8
Friend, Professor Sir Richard 85
Frost, Sir Terry 130, 132
Fuchs, Sir Vivian *80*, 81, 153
Fuller, Robert ('Big Bob') *148*, 149, 162

Galy, Dr Albert 81
Gandhi, Sonia 141

Garner, John 169
Garrett, George Muswell 54
Garrett, H O 141
Garrison, William Lloyd 69
Gatty, Hugh 64, 166
George III 74, 115, 117
George IV 102, 140
Gibson-Carmichael, Sir Thomas 141
Gilbert, William 59, 78, 79, 130
Gilchrist, Michael 189
Gilchrist, Ronald 189
Gill, Eric 25
Gilligan, Andrew 109
Gilmour, Jonathan 40
Gisborne, Thomas 59, 68, 117
Glasscock, Dr Robin 98
Glover, T R 61, 96
Goddard, Professor Peter 78, 85, 140, *156*, 191
Goldie, C J D 172
Goodall, Jane 96
Goodrich, Bishop Philip 49
Goody, Professor Sir Jack 94, 101, *168*
Gore Lloyd, David 128
Goswami, Professor Usha 77
Gottlieb, Paul 158
Gray, Professor Christine 114
Gray, Thomas 124
Greene, Robert 121, 136
Greeves, Tony 189
Gregson-Williams, Harry 134
Grey, Lady Jane 14
Grice, Bill 44
Griffin, Professor Roger 41, 73
Griffith, Jamie (Jamie Bamber) 135
Griffiths, Rt Hon. Lord 115
Grigg, Sir James 165
Guest, Dr George 56
Guillebaud, C W 107
Gull, Professor Steve 73
Gunn, Thom 127
Gunning, Bishop 54
Gurney, Mrs Johanna 36

Habakkuk, Professor Sir John 98
Hackman, James 104
Haig-Thomas, David 165
Hall, John 113, 114
Hamilton, Professor W D (Bill) 94–5
Hamilton-Gordon, George, Fourth Earl of Aberdeen 102–3
Hardy, G H 84
Harker, Alfred 80
Harris, Professor Stephen 110, 118
Harrison, Jonathan 9
Hart, Keith 94
Hartree, Douglas 85
Harvey, Professor David 98

Harvey, Professor Jonathan 134
Haughton, Michael 41, 42, 159, 168
Hawking, Professor Stephen 85
Hay, Ian (John Hay Beith) 135
Hay, Dennis *162*
Haydon, Benjamin 62
Headley, John 139–40
Heal, Professor Jane 100, *150*, 152
Heath, Sir Robert 58, 113
Heatley, Dr Norman 76, *119*
Heberden, William 62, 115–16, 117
Heberden, William, the Younger 117
Heenan, Dr Sue **118**
Heitland, W E 189
Hennessy, Professor Peter 99, 166, *186*
Henrietta Maria, Queen *12*, 13
Henry VII 10
Henry VIII 10, 13, 14, 35, 121
Henslow, J S 73, 80
Herbert, Penny 163
Herrick, Robert 121, 122
Herriot, Walter 90
Herschel, Sir John *71*, *72*, 129
Herschel, Sir William 72
Hibberd, Stuart 165
Hill, Dr David *54*, 57
Hill, Sir John 92
Hill, Stephen 93, 114
Hillary, Sir Edmund *80*
Hiller, Alan 61
Hillman, Rev. Clive 53
Hinde, Professor Robert 76, 94, 101, 155, 155–6, **167**, 169
Hinsley, Professor Sir Harry 67, 98, 138, 155, 156, 166, 167
Hodge, Professor Sir William 84
Hofmann, Michael 128
Holbein, Hans, the Younger 13, 121
Holdsworth, Marguerite *148*
Hollick, Dr Frank 76
Holmes, W Richard 92
Holthouse, C L 83
Hooper, Steven 94
Hope of Craighead, Rt Hon. Lord (David) **115**, *169*
Hope, Adrian 67
Hopkin, Sir Bryan 40, 105, 109
Hopkins, Sir Frederick Gowland 76
Horlock, Professor Sir John 110
Horne, Professor Michael 110
Houghton Walker, Dr Sarah 9
Hounsfield, Godfrey 89
Howard, Professor Deborah 130
Howard, Thomas, Earl of Suffolk 103
Howatson, Gabrielle (née Hodgetts) 44, *149*, 150
Howells, Dorothy (née Dawe) 57
Howells, Dr Herbert 57